What Cartooning Really Is

The Major Interviews with Charles M. Schulz

What Carto Really Is—

THE MAJOR INTERVIEWS
with CHARLES M. SCHULZ

FANTAGRAPHICS BOOKS • SEATTLE

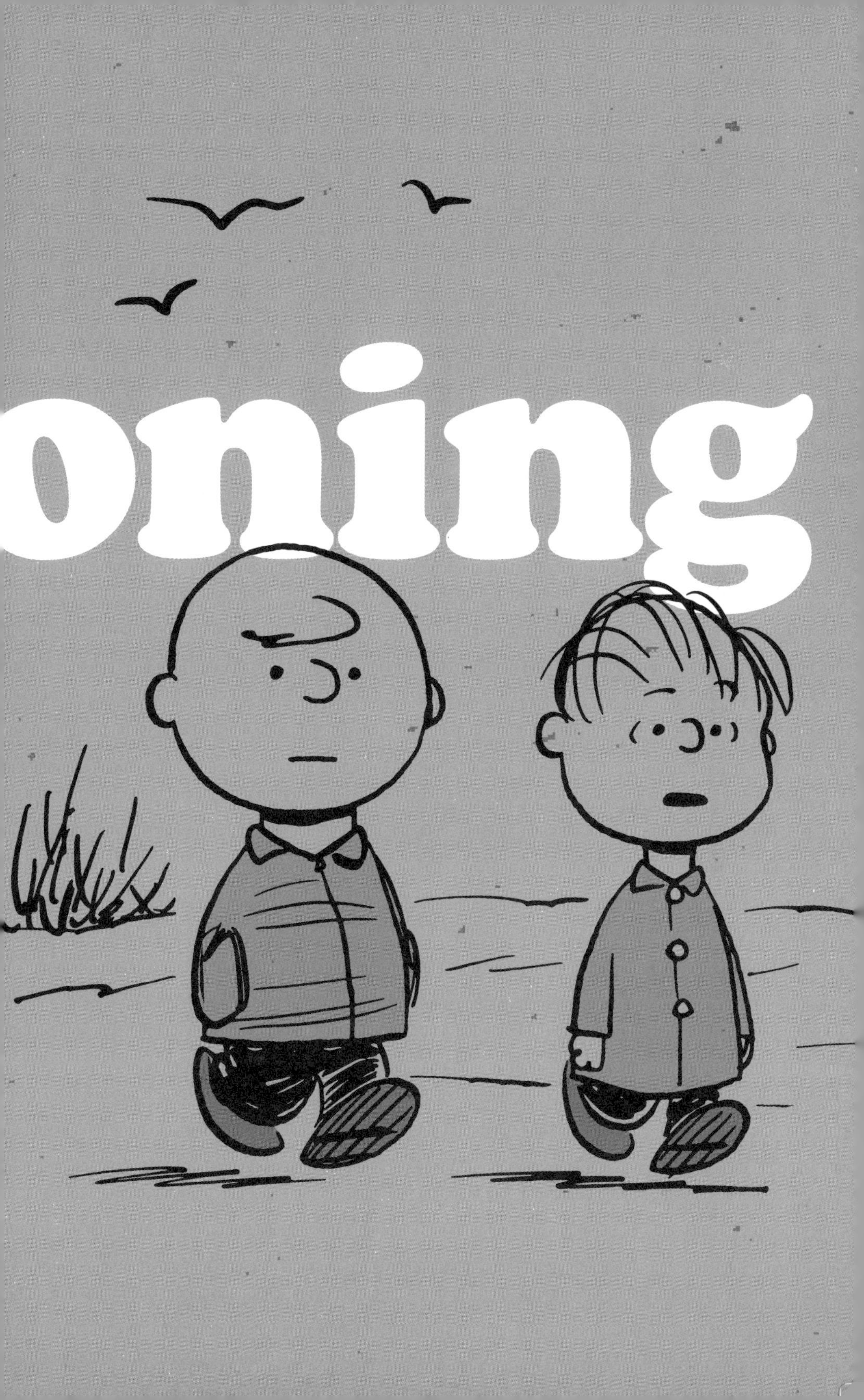
oning

Editor: Conrad Groth
Designer: Chelsea Wirtz
Proofreader: RJ Casey
Production: Preston White
Publicity: Jacq Cohen
Associate Publisher: Eric Reynolds
Publisher: Gary Groth

FANTAGRAPHICS BOOKS, INC.
7563 Lake City Way NE
Seattle, WA 98115

www.fantagraphics.com
facebook.com/fantagraphics
@fantagraphics

ISBN: 978-1-68396-382-0
Library of Congress Control Number: 2020938035
First Fantagraphics Books edition: October 2020
Printed in China

vii

INTRODUCTION
by Gary Groth

1

AT 3 O'CLOCK
IN THE MORNING
with Gary Groth

81

THIS MINOR ART FORM
HAS CERTAIN TRUTHS
with Rick Marschall and Gary Groth

117

A LITTLE JOY
AND ENLIGHTENMENT
NOW AND THEN
with Leonard Maltin

147

THE WELLSPRING
OF INSPIRATION
with Laurie Colwin

Introduction

by Gary Groth

Charles M. Schulz was born November 26, 1922, in Minneapolis. His destiny was foreshadowed when, at the age of two days, an uncle nicknamed him Sparky (after Barney Google's racehorse Spark Plug).

"My dad was a barber," Schulz recalled. "I always admired him for the fact that both he and my mother had only third grade educations and, from what I remembered hearing in conversations, he worked pitching hay in Nebraska one summer to earn enough money to go to barber school, got himself a couple of jobs, and eventually bought his own barber shop. And I think he at one time owned two barber shops and a filling station, but that was either when I was not born or very small, so I don't know much about that." Except for a misguided year-and-a-half interlude spent in Needles, California ("an eerie and eternal summer" Schulz called it), he grew up in St. Paul. "We settled in a neighborhood about two blocks from my dad's barbershop and most of my playtime life revolved around the yard of the grade school across the street from our apartment."

By all accounts, Sparky Schulz led an unremarkable, albeit sheltered, childhood. He was an only child, close to both parents. His father evidently nurtured his interest in comics: According to his biography by Rheta Grimsley Johnson, his father's "one passion was the funny papers. He loved comics and read them the way some men read box scores or racing forms—with intensity and devotion. He bought four Sunday newspapers every week, for the comics, picking up the two local papers on Saturday evening hot off the presses."

His academic career was erratic. He was such an outstanding student at Richard Gordon Elementary School that he skipped two grades, but began to flounder later at St. Paul's Central High School ("He became a shy, skinny kid with pimples and big ears, nearly six feet tall and weighing only 136 pounds")—perhaps not so coincidentally at the same time kids are going through their cruelest, most status-conscious period of socialization. The pain, bitterness, insecurity, and failures chronicled in *Peanuts* appear to have originated from this period of Schulz's life.

Schulz reproduced a report card from high school in *Peanuts Jubilee* (1975), under which read the first-person caption: "This report card is printed to show my own children that I was not as dumb as everyone has said I was." (The present perfect tense Schulz chose is instructive.) His acute sense, and resentment, of small but hurtful injustices also seem to have stemmed from this period. "I kind of resented the whole public school system at that time," he said. "It didn't cater to the many kids who weren't big and strong. The gym teachers paid attention only to the school athletes. The rest of us were shunted aside. I really resented that." Or consider this wounded recollection: "It took me a long time to become a human being. I was regarded by many as kind of sissyfied, which I resented because I really was not a sissy. I was not a tough guy, but I was good at sports. ... So, I never regarded myself as being much and I never regarded myself as being good looking and I never had a date in high school, because I thought, who'd want to date me? So, I didn't bother. And that's just the way I grew up."

Through *Peanuts*, Schulz touched upon a truth that we are perhaps too embarrassed to acknowledge but which may paradoxically account for the strip's universal popularity: that the cruelties and slights we suffer as a part of growing up, regarded by adults as inconsequential or, at any rate, ineradicable, follow us to the grave, affecting our perception and behavior in adulthood. Or, as Umberto Eco, put it: "[The *Peanuts* characters] affect us because we realize that if they are monsters it is because we, the adults, have made them so. In them, we find everything: Freud, mass-cult, digest culture, frustrated struggle for success, craving for affection, loneliness, passive acquiescence, and neurotic protest. But all these elements do not blossom directly, as we know them, from the mouths of a group of children: They are conceived and spoken after passing through the filter of innocence."

Although Schulz enjoyed sports, he also found refuge in solitary activities: reading, drawing, watching movies. "The highlight of our lives was, of course, Saturday afternoons, going to the local theater. We would buy a box of popcorn for a nickel from a popcorn shop a few stores down from the theater, and then we'd go to the afternoon matinee. My favorite movie, I still remember, was *Lost Patrol* with Victor McLaglen. I loved those desert movies, which is why I like drawing Snoopy as the foreign legionnaire."

He bought comic books and Big Little Books, pored over the newspaper strips, and copied his favorites. "Usually I tried to copy the style of *Buck Rogers*, but I was also crazy about all of the Walt Disney characters, and Popeye... and the characters in *Tim Tyler's Luck*... Clare Briggs influenced me considerably... I also thought there was no one who drew funnier and more warm-hearted cartoons than J. R. Williams." He was quickly becoming a connoisseur; his heroes were Milton Caniff, Roy Crane, Hal Foster, and Alex Raymond. In his senior year in high school, his mother noticed an ad in a local newspaper for Federal Schools, a "correspondence plan for aspiring artists" (now called Art Instruction Schools). "She came in one night and she said, 'Look here in the newspaper. It says, "Do you like to draw? Send for a free talent test."' So, I sent in and, a few weeks later, a man knocked on the door and it was a man from the correspondence school. And he sold us the course." Schulz's father paid the $170 tuition in installments. Schulz completed the course and began trying, unsuccessfully, to sell gag cartoons

Li'l Folks, December 12, 1948.

" HERE COMES GOOD
OLD CHARLIE BROWN!
HOW I HATE HIM!!"

"YOU'RE THE ONLY
PERSON I KNOW WHO
PLAYS SOLITAIRE WITH
A MARKED DECK!"

"TRY TO BE MORE PATIENT.....IF WE'RE SHORT
OF HOOPS, WE'RE SHORT OF HOOPS!"

Li'l Folks, May 29, 1949.

to magazines. (His first published drawing was of his dog, Spike, which appeared in a 1937 *Ripley's Believe It or Not!* installment.)

He was drafted in 1943 at the same time his mother was diagnosed with cancer. The timing and the circumstances made leaving home particularly excruciating for Schulz. He was home one weekend when his mother looked up at him from her bed and said, "I suppose that we should say goodbye, because we probably never will see each other again." She died the next day. His father drove him back to Fort Snelling after her funeral, from which he shipped out to Camp Campbell, Kentucky, later that day. "I remember crying in my bunk that evening," he recalled. His mother's death "was a loss from which I sometimes believe I never recovered."

Schulz was discharged after the War and started submitting gag cartoons to the various magazines of the time, but his first breakthrough came when Roman Baltes, an editor at *Timeless Topix*, a comic magazine owned by the Roman Catholic Church, hired him to letter adventure comics. Soon after that, he was hired by his alma mater, Art Instruction, to correct student lessons returned by mail. "For the next year, I lettered comic pages for *Timeless Topix*, working sometimes until past midnight, getting up early the next morning, taking a streetcar to downtown St. Paul, leaving the work outside the door of Mr. Baltes's office, and then going over to Minneapolis to work at the correspondence school."

His next break was selling 17 cartoons to the *Saturday Evening Post* between 1948 and 1950, during which time he sold a weekly comic feature called *Li'l Folks* to the local *St. Paul Pioneer Press*. It was run in the women's section and paid $10 a week. "One day, Roman [Baltes] bought a page of little panel cartoons that I had drawn and titled 'Just Keep Laughing.' One of the cartoons showed a small boy, who looked prophetically like Schroeder, sitting on the curb with a baseball bat in his hands talking to a little girl, who looked prophetically like Patty. He was saying, 'I think I could learn to love you, Judy, if your batting average was a little higher.' Frank Wing, my fellow instructor at Art Instruction, said, 'Sparky, I think you should draw more of those little kids. They are pretty good.' So, I concentrated on creating a group of samples and eventually sold them as a weekly feature called *Li'l Folks* to the *St. Paul Pioneer Press*." After writing and drawing the feature for two years, Schulz asked for a better location in the paper or for daily exposure, as well as a raise. "When he turned me down on all three counts, I suggested that perhaps I had better quit. He merely stated, 'All right.' Thus endeth my career at the *St. Paul Pioneer Press*."

He started submitting strips to the newspaper syndicates. "I used to get on the train in St. Paul in the mornings, have breakfast on the train and make that beautiful ride to Chicago, get there about three in the afternoon, check into a hotel by myself, and the next morning I would get up and make the rounds of the syndicates. ... At this time, I was also becoming a little more gregarious and was learning how to talk with people. When I first used to board the morning Zephyr and ride it to Chicago, I would make the entire trip without talking to anyone. Little by little, however, I was getting rid of my shyness and feelings of inferiority, and learning how to strike up acquaintances on the train and talk to people."

He had a near-miss at the NEA syndicate: "I opened a letter from the director of

NEA in Cleveland saying he liked my work very much. Arrangements were made during the next few months for me to start drawing a Sunday feature for NEA, but at the last minute their editors changed their minds and I had to start all over again." In the Spring of 1950, Schulz received a letter from Jim Freeman, United Feature Syndicate's editorial director, announcing his interest in his submission, *Li'l Folks*. Schulz boarded a train in June for New York City to discuss drawing a strip for them. Schulz self-deprecatingly described his successful trip thusly:

> I had brought along a new comic strip I had been working on, rather than the panel cartoons which United Feature Syndicate had seen. I simply wanted to give them a better view of my work.
>
> I told the receptionist that I had not had breakfast yet, so I would go out and eat and then return. When I got back to the syndicate offices, they had already opened up the package I had left there and in that short time had decided they would rather publish the strip than the panel. This made me very happy, for I really preferred the strip to the panel.
>
> I returned to Minneapolis filled with great hope for the future and asked a certain little girl to marry me. When she turned me down and married someone else, there was no doubt that Charlie Brown was on his way. Losers get started early.

The first Peanuts strip appeared October 2, 1950.

Prior to *Peanuts*, the province of the comic page was that of gags, social and political observation, domestic comedy, soap opera, various adventure genres. Although *Peanuts* gradually evolved over the 47 years that Schulz wrote and drew it, it remains, as it began, an anomaly on the comics page—a comic strip about the interior crises of the cartoonist himself. After a painful divorce in 1973 from which he had not yet recovered, Schulz told a reporter, "Strangely, I've drawn better cartoons in the last six months—or as good as I've ever drawn. I don't know how the human mind works." Surely, it is this kind of humility in the face of profoundly irreducible human question that makes *Peanuts* as universally moving as it is.

It's worth being reminded that Charles Schulz was one of the greatest cartoonists of the twentieth century, something that the global phenomenon of *Peanuts* by way of all the merchandising and licensing and media spin-offs may obscure.

Peanuts, October 2, 1950.

At 3 O'clock in the Morning

Gary Groth, 1997

This interview was conducted in two sessions: once in October in Charles Schulz's office in Santa Rosa, California, and a shorter one over the phone a month later. My thanks to Sparky for his generous time, hospitality, and professionalism. He copyedited the interview (in record time). I edited the interview for final publication.

Gag Cartoonist

GARY GROTH: *In every interview I've read where you make reference to them, you've said that you sold 15 gag cartoons to the* Saturday Evening Post *in the late '40s.*

CHARLES M. SCHULZ: Oh, yeah.

But you actually sold 17.

Did I?

Yeah.

That's pretty good. The odd thing is that the little kid ones went the best. But I remember this one [January 1, 1948] came about the morning after Harry Truman beat Thomas Dewey. I was so bitter and disgusted about the whole thing, and some old woman came in the room that day. She was one of the instructors, and she was all excited about it, and I remember turning to someone and saying, "Huh! I sleep well enough at night, it's living during the day I find so hard." And I sent the rough into the *Post* and they okayed it, and all of a sudden I realized that

I didn't have any drawing style. I had to draw this thing, and I hadn't developed any style at all. Because I had been drifting into drawing the little kids, and I was working on that style, and all of a sudden I had to draw these adults. It was a very mechanical style, and I wasn't proud of it at all.

You found it difficult to stylize adults because you had gotten so used to drawing kids?

Yeah. Uh-huh.

Taking ordinary things like the bed and turning them into a football field, and a race track was a good gimmick. Of course, since then I've drawn a million birdbaths. This was one of my favorites [Feb. 11, 1950], and they changed the word—it's a misprint, it should have been, "Oh, we got along swell." Rather than, "We get along swell." That doesn't make sense.

But my style is beginning to develop a little bit [at this point]. This one was quite successful, too, a gimmick I learned how to draw, and this was reprinted a couple of other places. I got $60 for this, and then I made another $15 or $20 reprinting it someplace.

I was on the right track. That's how it all started. I was very ambitious. But I couldn't sell to any other magazine. I sent to *Collier's* and a couple of others. But I couldn't sell any other magazines. Apparently, John Bailey liked them. He was very good to me, he must have been good—as I've talked to Mort Walker and others—to cartoonists. I sent him one batch of roughs once, and he tore out little scraps and corners of paper and attached them to each one telling me what was wrong with them, and why he didn't buy it. Which took time. But he must have felt it was important. I never met the man, but that was good.

Saturday Evening Post cartoon by Charles M. Schulz, February 11, 1950.

"Oh, we get along swell . . . he hasn't moved from my side all afternoon!"

He must have seen potential.

Yeah, I suppose. A long time ago.

What kind of rejections did you get from other magazines?

Just rote rejection slips.

I didn't do a lot of [submitting]. Probably *This Week*, which was another market, and *Collier's*. I don't recall sending them to *The New Yorker*, when I was at this stage, because I knew it was hopeless. So, I didn't try that. A lot of amateurs do, of course. But that's a brutal business. I used to get my mail at my dad's barber shop when I came home from Art Instruction School. We lived around the corner from the shop.

I'd open the envelope, and there'd be a little note that would say, "Here's an OK for you." The whole world suddenly became bright and cheery. But if it said, "Sorry, nothing this week," then it was so depressing. [*Laughs*] That's why I was so glad when I finally sold the comic strip, for every idea that I had thought of was used. And to have a change of pace. I think a comic strip is very important to have a change of pace. That's why I have such a good group, I've got a repertory company. And I can do things that are really stupid, and give them to Snoopy, things that are really corny, kind of dumb. But they become funny, because Snoopy doesn't realize how corny and dumb they are. Or else he and Woodstock will say something which is just silly and they'll laugh and laugh and they'll fall off the doghouse on their heads or something. I like to do things like that. Just slapstick. And then try to do things that are more meaningful. A really good range of ideas. And I've said that almost everything that I think of somehow can be turned into a cartoon idea. I'm not restricted in the ideas. I can go in any direction that I want to go.

And doing that also gives you a great latitude in terms of visuals.

Oh, yeah. Visuals are extremely important. I think a lot of cartoonists these days have gotten away from that. It's the basis of what cartooning is. I've been quoted on this many times, that cartooning is still drawing funny pictures. If you don't draw funny pictures, then you might as well be writing for live television or some other form of entertainment. But visuals were extremely difficult. I think you can run out to the end very quickly. That's what worries me lately, as I turn 75 in a couple of months, that I might have done so many things with so many situations. How many funny pictures can you get out of Snoopy looking up and watching the leaf fall out of the tree? And yesterday I think I spent almost the whole afternoon trying to get something funny out of Linus sitting in a cardboard box trying to just slide down the hill. I really like drawing that, and I came up with one idea, but I still can't decide if it's funny enough or not. So, I abandoned it. I finally went into a totally different direction. But there are so many things that I really liked having done; I would like to just keep playing on these themes and variations as much as I can. But sometimes I feel like I've run right out to the end and there are no more ideas anymore. I'm always amazed when I haven't done something for maybe 10 years or something like that, and one day I think of one. And then I wonder, "Why in the world didn't I think of that 10 years ago?" Why did it take me 10 years? This is playing on the same theme, but this is the way it is. And I think this is one of the things you learn about after doing it for so long.

That's the way I would think the imagination would work on such an organic life's work, where you're working on variations of a handful of themes over the course of a long time.

And so much depends upon your own life, too. I think critics, and interviewers, forget we still have another life we live.

The demarcation between your life and your work is often blurred because you put so much of your life into your work.

Well, yeah, and I find that people who don't know anything about it, friends of ours frequently say, "Oh, I know where you got that idea." And I want to say, "No, you don't." [*Laughs*]

What you just said about the convergence of ideas and drawings reminded me of something you said about the strip: "The type of humor that I was using did not call for camera angles. I like drawing the characters from the same view all the way through, because the ideas were very brief, and I didn't want anything in the drawing to interrupt the flow of what the characters were either saying or doing." Your respect for what you refer to as the ideas would appear to me to limit the scope of the drawings that you're able to do, and I know you take great joy in drawing. Did you ever want to draw in a way that the strip itself wouldn't allow?

I would like to, but it's too late. I've locked myself into this drawing style, and I can't escape from it. And I think it would be a mistake of course to do it because I think for me to draw the way Hank Ketcham used to draw just wouldn't work. Hank was drawing panels from wonderful different camera angles, reflections in mirrors and things like that. Which simply would never work in my strip. For one thing, it would make everything too realistic. And *Dennis the Menace* is pretty realistic. He even said to me once on the golf course—we didn't get a chance to talk very much—but one day we were playing in the AT&T together, and we were talking about the features, and he said, "Your strip is really more of a fantasy, isn't it?" And I said, "Yeah, I guess maybe it is." [*Laughs*] I didn't know he had even thought about it.

Did you admire the Dennis the Menace *panel?*

I admire the drawing tremendously, yeah. But I don't like annoying little kids. [*Laughter*]

Are you friends with Hank Ketcham?

I'd like to think so. We don't know each other that well, we've never spent a lot of time together. Those three days on the golf course at the tournament was the

"WE HAD A PARTY THIS AFTERNOON! YOU MISSED ALL THE FUN!"

most we had ever spent, but even then we didn't get to talk very much. We were too busy playing. The cartoonist whom I feel I know the best these days probably would be Lynn Johnston.

It doesn't seem like the cartooning community is very close-knit. Because Ketcham, as far as I can tell, is almost your exact contemporary.

Yeah, yeah. Of course, he got started much quicker than I did. He and Gus Arriola both worked for Disney and so were quite accomplished before they even began [drawing strips]. Ketcham was also a successful gag cartoonist before I ever got started. Gus Arriola had worked for Disney; he was drawing *Gordo* before the War, and then he picked it up after the War. Gus is a little bit older than I am.

Growing Up

When you were growing up, you were a real aficionado of both comic books and news-paper strips.

Gee, I used to buy every comic book that used to come out; I bought every Big Little Book that came out. I got the first copy of *Famous Funnies*. Some friend tore the cover off once. I lost a lot of things in a fire that took place in a big apartment building where my dad and I lived. I had a big box of Big Little Books that was stored down in the basement in some storeroom. Lost them all. The fire department came in and flooded the basement. So, I have no idea what things I even used to have.

I know that you were a big fan of comic books, but you never seemed interested in being a comic book artist as opposed to a gag panel artist or a strip cartoonist.

Yeah, yeah. In fact, we have to skip all the early days, because they were strictly amateur days. It's almost as if your life goes in little sections. And I got almost no encouragement in school and high school. Drawing was almost looked down upon and cartooning really was looked down upon. I can still remember—for some strange reason—in the seventh grade, it had something to do with social studies, and the teacher, amazingly enough, brought up political or editorial cartoons. She had a few people just monkey around with them. And I drew the best one, and she liked them. I don't know what she was going to do with them, maybe she was going to have them printed in some newspaper or something like that. But she actually took my cartoon and gave it to another kid in class, to have him go over the lines to make them darker. I was appalled and insulted by this, but I didn't dare say anything. But, you know, what a dumb thing to do. [*Laughs*] Sometimes teachers aren't very smart.

Anyway, that was my first inkling of any kind of encouragement. And then, when I got into high school, of course, high school was a total disaster for me. As was junior high school. I just failed everything. I hated the whole business. And in English once, I don't know if it was Shakespeare or what it was we were reading, but we had to do some kind of a project on what it was we were reading. And I remember thinking that I could make some drawings about this—this may seem hard to believe, but I actually thought, "Well, this wouldn't be fair." Because the other kids in the class can't draw. So why should I take advantage of something I can do that they can't? So, I didn't do it. And some other kid in the class made some nice watercolors. He must have made about ten of them, about the thing that we had been studying. And afterwards, the teacher—I don't know how she ever knew that I could draw—said, "Charles, why didn't you do something like that?" [*Laughter*] And I never explained why I didn't, either. But that was just another blow.

You learned something there.

Oh, I learned something—I learned a lot. I learned several lessons in school, very important lessons, too, along that line. Then, of course, my greatest triumph was that book of drawings of things in threes that was reprinted in *Peanuts Jubilee*. The teacher held mine up as an example. Because I batted out that whole page in about five minutes, while the other kids were struggling just making three or four drawings. All the way through school, I can remember I was, if not always the best, at least one of the two or three few that could draw reasonably well. I couldn't draw really well, but I could draw better than most people. I was the first kid to figure out how to draw a hole in the ice. Because in Minnesota, we always had to draw something that we did at Christmas vacation, we always drew kids skating. And everybody drew a hole in the ice with the sign that said "Danger" or something like that. But the kids didn't know how to draw a hole in the ice, they just made a black spot. I was the first one to discover how to show some thickness to the ice, because I had read it in cartoons and comic books. And the teacher looked at this one day, and she was amazed that I should've drawn something like that.

Then when I was a senior, the teacher asked me one day to draw some cartoons of things around school, which I did and I gave them to her. When the high school annual came out, I looked through it anxiously, and they hadn't printed them at all. That was a crushing blow. That was my first major rejection. During that period, I was taking the Art Instruction correspondence course, which was called Federal Schools at that time. A salesman came out to the house one cold winter night, I can still remember him coming up on the cold storm-doored porch. So, we signed up for the course, which I think cost $160, and my dad had to pay for it at a rate of $10 a month. Even at that, he struggled the make the payments. But I didn't have anything to do after graduating. I would stay home and work on the correspondence course. I never always had the right materials to drawn on, either. Paper was expensive. I would sometimes go downtown to St. Paul to a big art store and I'd buy maybe two sheets of smooth-ply Strathmore. That's all I could afford. And I was experimenting with Craftint doubletone because of what Roy Crane was doing with it. But I could only afford maybe one sheet, because it cost 75¢. And I could only get maybe three strips out of it. I rarely had good paper to work on. But I was always drawing something.

I used to draw a series of, like, *Believe It or Not!* panels, mostly about golf. I had become a golf fanatic, and I was drawing a lot of golf cartoons. When I was a senior in high school, I was also a Sherlock Holmes fanatic, and I read every Sherlock Holmes story that was ever written. I would buy a scrapbook at the dime store. And I would draw my own Sherlock Holmes stories, filled this whole scrapbook, just like it were a big comics magazine. The only person who ever read it was a friend of mine who lived up the street and around the corner named Shermy. He was a violinist, and I'd go listen to him practice the violin now and then, and he would read my Sherlock Holmes stories. Nobody else ever read them.

So, I filled up several books doing that. But in the meantime, I started to send in gag cartoons, mainly to *Collier's* and the *Post*, I suppose. Never sold any. My dad would take them for me in the morning to the post office, which was near the barber shop, with a stamped self-addressed envelope, and then they'd come back the next week. I was collecting a lot of rejection slips, never even coming close. But I studied gag cartooning very carefully. And one of my first jobs was working as a delivery boy for a direct mail advertising company in Minneapolis. And with one of my first paychecks, which was $14, I bought a collection of *Collier's* gag cartoons called *Collier's Collects Its Wits*. And I still have it. I used to read that

Wash Tubbs by Roy Crane, April 7, 1930.

book over and over and over, just loved looking at all the gag cartoons, and I can still remember some of the punchlines. So, I was willing to be a gag cartoonist. I hadn't really decided what direction I was going to go. And I was also drawing comic strips of my own. And of course, I was a great *Wash Tubbs and Captain Easy* fan, and I would send things in and get them rejected.

I became fascinated by the Foreign Legion, too. I read everything about Beau Geste, all of [P. C.] Wren's novels. And I used to draw Foreign Legion strips. And then, lo and behold—I might still have been in high school, I'm not sure—my mother had read in the paper something about a cartooning class downtown in St. Paul in a great big building which was an extension of the University of Minnesota. So, I went down and signed up for it. There was a young man teaching the class, who had a small comic strip running in our local paper. And he was pretty good, a very nice fellow, and he told us what equipment to bring the next week—we had to bring a drawing board, some ink, and some pencils and pens. The first night there, he had some large pieces of paper tacked to the wall. I distinctly remember that one of them was Dagwood and I don't remember what the other characters were. But he just asked each of us to copy these characters. I suppose it was a good idea just to see what level of ability each one of us had. And of course, I was used to drawing those things, because I had drawn and copied those comic characters all my life. So, I just went through them like nothing. And I was done in a matter of about four or five minutes. Way ahead of everybody else. Much better than everybody else. There was the prettiest little girl I had ever seen sitting two chairs away from me, and I wanted so much to talk to her. But there was some idiot little kid there who kept drawing Bugs Bunny and saying that it was his character. I'd get so mad at this kid, because he had the nerve to talk to her, and I didn't. And I never did talk to her. I just didn't have the nerve.

But one time, he wanted us to each start a special project and I had drawn a Foreign Legion comic strip. And of course, having the correspondence school background, I had learned to letter very neatly and render neatly, and he showed it to her. I can still remember—isn't that something? Something that happened so many years ago—and I can remember sitting there, and he showed it to her, and she looked at it and said, "Oh, that's so neat." [*Laughs*] I was so flattered, but I still didn't have the nerve to talk to her.

You would have been around 16 or 17.

I would have been 17, I guess. Six years later I had a date with her. Isn't that astounding? [*Laughter*] After the War.

Congratulations.

Now she's dead. Now she's dead, and it saddens me terribly. But anyway, that was the struggle I was going through, all before the War. And then the War came along. I remembered going up to the service club one Sunday afternoon, as we used to do if we had some time off, just to have a good lunch and dinner, and upstairs in one of the rooms they had an exhibition this one week of original gag cartoons from different magazines. And I stood there and walked around the room and looked at them, and I was admiring so much the quality of the drawing and the rendering of these things, and I was thinking, "When in the world am I ever going to get a chance to do this?" The War was still going on, and none of us knew if we were going to return. It was so depressing. [*Laughs*]

I never got to do anything during the War. I knew I wasn't that good, and I never even tried to send in things to *Yank* magazine or *Stars and Stripes* or anything like that. But after the War, I returned home and my dad and I lived in this apartment with a couple of waitresses who worked in the restaurant nearby. We shared the apartment with them. I went over to Art Instruction, in Minneapolis, and showed some of my work to Frank Wing, who was a wonderful cartoonist of his day. A man named Charles Bartholomew was the head of the cartooning part of the school, and he offered me a job as a temporary replacement for one of the other men who was going on a two-week summer vacation. So, I took it. There were about 10 of us in the room there. And then they ended up keeping me on permanently. And so that was the start of a whole new life. Because I was then in a room with people who were very bright, and had a lot of ability in many different directions. A couple of them had been commercial artists, Frank Wing was a good cartoonist, Walter J. Wilweding was in charge of the department. He was a fine animal painter. There was a woman named Mrs. Angelikas who was a practicing fashion artist. She did men's fashions several times a week for the local paper. She was very good. They were all quite cultured. They were all well read, they all listened to good music. It was a good atmosphere. It was a lot like working for a newspaper, but not quite as hectic. And so, I learned a lot being with them and, while I was with them, I had the chance in my off-time to work on some of my own things.

You mentioned comic magazines. I actually drew three pages of different comic magazine samples. One was a war episode of some men in a half-track, which was autobiographical. Another one was some little characters I called Brownies, who were just cute little fanciful things, and then another jungle type page. I sent them to some comic magazine in New York, and I got a note saying that they didn't buy freelance work like this, and that all of their work was done by hired people in New York.

I was still going around trying to get jobs. One day I was sent to downtown St. Paul to a Catholic comics magazine. They did *Catholic Digest* and some other things. I took the comic strips that I had, and a man named Roman Baltes looked at 'em and said, "Well, I think I may have something for you. I like your lettering." So, I was assigned to letter the entire comics magazine. He had three or four men who were already there on the staff. Somebody else would write the stories, and they would illustrate them. Apparently, they didn't have anybody who could letter comic strips very well, so they would give me the original pages and I would take them home at night and letter all the pages. Sometimes they would give me a French or a Spanish translation, and I would have to letter the whole thing on some kind of see-through paper in these other languages. I never thought of it as being hard work, even though I was doing it in the evening after having spent the day at the correspondence school. I would do these things, and Roman liked the fact that I could do them fast. Sometimes he'd call me up in the late afternoon, and say, "Sparky, I've got five pages here; I'd sure like to have them done tomorrow morning." So, I would either take the streetcar or my dad's car and drive downtown. He'd leave them outside the office. I'd pick them up, take them home, sit in

the kitchen and letter them. The next morning I'd get up early, drive downtown, leave them outside his office and then go on to the correspondence school. Now that may sound like Abraham Lincoln, but to me it was what I wanted to do.

And so, I became very good at lettering. I could letter very fast, I got so I didn't need guidelines or spacing or anything. That was a good training for me.

Can I ask you a few questions based on what you've said so far?

Please.

You mentioned going to the correspondence school and meeting all of these people who were involved in music and art and so on. Would you say that they represented an opening up of your world? Did that environment invigorate your curiosity about art? Was this an atmosphere you hadn't really experienced as fully before?

Oh, definitely. It was almost better than going to art school. Now, most of my friends either went or graduated from the Minneapolis School of Art, which was a fine establishment. And that was one of the first things that I did when I came back from the War—I knew that under the G.I. Bill perhaps I could finally go to a resident art school and take some actual, on-the-spot training. So, I went there and made a few drawings, which you had to make just to demonstrate if you had any talent. Unfortunately, the administrator there said that I was about two weeks too late. The classes had already started. But then she said, "We do have some night classes, if you'd like to do something like that." So, I signed up for a life sketching class. And I did that for one semester. I wasn't especially good at it, but that was the first real live training I had had.

So, I never really did go the Minneapolis School of Art. That was about it. The next semester, I signed up for another class in just drawing. But I missed two or three classes because I had these other lettering jobs to do. And then I was told that under the G.I. Bill, if you missed three classes, you were out. So that was the end of my training.

Was that disappointing to you?

No, not really. I knew what I wanted to do. This Art Instruction group of instructors created an invigorating atmosphere. There was always lots of lively conversations going on as the people were sitting at their desks. Some dictating responses, others just making corrections.

The only problem became a social problem, in that at the same time I still loved golf, and I had three or four friends with whom I used to caddy and play golf. So, on Saturdays, sometimes Sunday afternoons, we would play golf. That was one group of friends. Then there was a group of friends at the correspondence school, and I became very close with many of them—that was the second group. And then at this same time, I also became very active in the Church of God movement. I went to a prayer meeting one night—we had some nice discussions—and I went to what

June 28, 1973.

they called a young people's meeting, and I enjoyed the discussions. They were very nice people. Now, that put me in three different social groups, and they didn't overlap. They didn't meet. I was never able to solve that.

You were never able to reconcile—or integrate—these different social strata?

I was never able to find the right people in these things so I could concentrate on that. That caused me a lot of trouble.

In what way?

Well, say I liked a certain girl for instance, maybe she was with the correspondence school, but then I didn't have any girlfriends in the church group. And of course, the golf kids were foreign completely to church and art and cartooning. So, nothing worked. [*Laughs*]

They didn't connect.

Nothing connected. That made it very awkward.

It sounds like you sort of blossomed about this time. You've talked a lot about how shy you were as a kid and how you weren't really socially acclimated, but it appears as though you started traveling among three different social settings; it almost looks like you turned into a bit of a social gadabout. [Laughter]

I think shyness is an illusion. I think stupidity is a better reason. I think shyness is the overtly self-conscious thinking that you're the only person in the world. That how you look and what you do is of any importance. Not realizing if you just get out and do something and talk to people, you don't have to be shy. It's just being overly self-conscious.

You said that when you were in high school, cartooning was looked down upon. And I wonder if you had a theory as to why that was. Was there a kind of middle class propriety involved, where cartooning was considered disreputable?

I think it was the teachers' fault. Music teachers were the worst of all. Music teachers were the meanest. Art teachers were always pretty nice. But they weren't capable of either doing cartooning themselves, or even appreciating it. And they had to bring the whole class down to the lowest denominator. Because these weren't kids that especially were going to be artists, or even interested in it, but they had to create projects that would interest the whole class. So, you ended up having to make posters, or doing watercolors of flowers or silly things like that, which just drove me out of my mind. [*Laughs*] You never got to do any drawing, it was always some kind of project. Even linoleum cutting—which I never got into. I was glad I never had to do that. But as far as drawing goes, we rarely got to do any real drawing. It just had to have been the teachers' fault.

In the Army

You referred to your stint in the army, and I think you said you didn't do much drawing in the army. You once said, "I just wasn't ready, and I think Bill Mauldin's work made me realize it." You also said, "The truth is I abandoned drawing during my years of army service." Was looking at Mauldin's work so intimidating you felt you were unprepared?

It wasn't intimidating. I just wasn't even close to being able to do it. Plus the fact that after a while, we worked very hard at being good soldiers. I went in never having been away from home. Not knowing what it would be like to live with 200 men in the same building. And I can remember the first time I sat next to a water-cooled machine gun and heard that thing fire. Oh, man, it was so loud and shocking. And then the first time we had to dismantle a light machine gun I thought, "I'll never learn how to do this." I had no mechanical ability. I had never seen a gun in my life.

But as the months went by, and as we developed more in our training, and went on maneuvers and all that, I finally got to be squad leader of a light machine gun squad. We all worked very hard at being good soldiers. And we took great pride at being in the infantry. We were in the armored infantry. And to me at that point, even though I still loved cartooning and drawing, and I carried a sketchbook where I made some drawings of friends, I was still very interested in being a good infantryman. We were very proud of what we were.

Which is good, because I look back on it with some hateful memories, but also wonderful memories of the friends we made and the good guys I knew and all of that. Proud of the fact that we did what we had to do. Somebody asked me just a couple months ago, "Of all the awards you've received, what award are you the most proud of?" and all of the sudden it occurred to me: the combat infantry badge. Which is over there on the wall. I'm more proud of having received the combat infantry badge than of having won the Reuben twice. [*Laughs*]

Can I establish a context for your war experience? You were drafted in the army in 1943. Were you aware of what was at risk in that war, what you were fighting for?

Oh, yeah. Definitely.

Weren't you present at the liberation of one of the concentration camps?

No, not quite.

We spent the night out in a field—I don't remember if it was raining, but it was awfully cold and misty that night. I think there was a big swamp out in front of us. They said that we had to be ready because there may be a counter-attack by the SS. But it never happened. So, the next morning, soon as the sun came up, we moved out. And then, that day, they told us that Dachau had been discovered. Part of our division was in on that. But we had gone on towards Munich. So, we never saw it ourselves. But at least we were there.

Now, correct me if I'm wrong, but it seems that prior to your going into the army, you led a pretty sheltered life with your family in the city of St. Paul. So going to war must have been an almost inconceivable break from that kind of life.

It was. It was a terrible experience.

You referred earlier to hateful memories.

Well, just being in the army was such a desperate feeling so often. Of loneliness, and of the fear that it was never going to end. We used to sit sometimes in the evening talking, and we'd say, "They're never going to let us out. We're in this for the rest of our lives. Where's it all going to end?" It was so depressing.

But I did make a lot of really good friends. Unfortunately, many of them have died. However, my best friend is still alive. He's 85 years old now. He was our mortar squad leader, and I was a machine gun squad leader. He was like a big brother to me. He really kept me going.

But I suppose... you know, the whole world was at war. It was something that had never happened before, and undoubtedly, I think, will never happen again.

When you came home from the War, did you feel transformed?

I felt good. [*Laughter*]

But was going through that a transformative experience?

Yes, it was. I came home on the train. I don't know where I got discharged, from what camp it was. A duffel bag on my shoulder, the streetcar pulled up in front of my dad's barber shop. I put the duffel bag on my shoulder and got off the back of the streetcar. Walked around, crossed the street, into the barbershop. He was working on a customer. [*Laughter*]

That was my homecoming. There was no party. Nothing.

A little anti-climactic.

Yes, it was. I look back on it, and I think, "Well, that was robbery. I didn't get to be in a parade, no one gave me a hug, or anything like that." But I felt very good about myself those days. The other friends that I had that I golfed and caddied with were all coming home at the same time. None of us had any jobs. In those days, you could join what they called a 52-20. If you didn't have a job, the government gave you $20 a week for 52 weeks. So, most of us belonged to the 52-20 club, at least for a few months. We played a lot of golf. We had an early spring in Minnesota at that time. It was kind of a carefree life for a while. My cousin had just come back from the Marines, and he and I used to go bowling. Different things like that.

I still had some relatives around that I was very close to. But that all gradually just fell apart, as everybody went finding their different directions.

Was there a sense of post-War euphoria?

No, not that I recall. Nobody even thought much about it.

Waste of Time

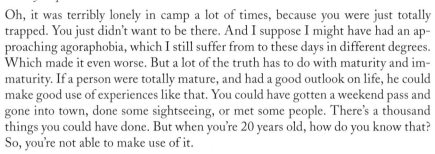

You once said, "The three years I spent in the army taught me all I need to know about loneliness."

Yes.

"And a sympathy for the loneliness that all of us experience was dropped heavily on poor Charlie Brown."

Oh, it was terribly lonely in camp a lot of times, because you were just totally trapped. You just didn't want to be there. And I suppose I might have had an approaching agoraphobia, which I still suffer from to these days in different degrees. Which made it even worse. But a lot of the truth has to do with maturity and immaturity. If a person were totally mature, and had a good outlook on life, he could make good use of experiences like that. You could have gotten a weekend pass and gone into town, done some sightseeing, or met some people. There's a thousand things you could have done. But when you're 20 years old, how do you know that? So, you're not able to make use of it.

Although you made use of it later by transforming that intense feeling of loneliness into art.

Yeah, yeah. [*Pause*] What a waste of time. [*Laughs*]

How do you mean?

To spend all of your life drawing your comic.

You don't really mean that, do you?

Sure.

How do you mean that? I would think you'd feel exactly the opposite.

Well, you know: What have you done? Drawn a comic strip. Who cares? [*Laughs*] Now I'm 75 years old.

But don't you feel like you have an enormous achievement behind you, a lasting legacy because of that achievement?

No. [*Laughs*] Because I know that I am not Andrew Wyeth. And I will never be Andrew Wyeth. But the only thing I'm proud of is that I think I've done the best with what ability I have. I haven't wasted my ability. A lot of people wasted their ability, their talents—they don't know how to do with what they have. I'm pleased with what I have done. I haven't destroyed it, I haven't misused it in any way.

Let me try and nail you down on that, because you must be very proud of what you've done. You must know you've reached the pinnacle of your profession.

I know, it's hard to believe. I'm amazed when I read *Cartoonist's Profiles* and other magazines where young cartoonists are interviewed, and they mention my name as being one of their inspirations.

November 18, 1969.

I'LL NEVER BE ANDREW WYETH..

ABOVE January 29, 1999.

OPPOSITE Calvin and Hobbes
by Bill Watterson, January 24, 1989.

That just astounds me.

Why should it?

I don't know what it was that inspired them, I have no idea. Except that I took a unique approach, as the strip developed. I think I did things that no one else had ever done.

If I may say so, I think it's because you conveyed the depth of your humanity in the comic strip. And that's a relatively rare phenomenon in cartooning.

You do some things that it's better you don't think about. [*Laughs*] You can dig your own grave by thinking you're better than you really are.

The Importance of Drawing

I think one of the reasons Peanuts *resonates so profoundly is because of your intense connection to your youth and to your childhood, especially that which was hurtful or painful. Your biographer wrote of you, "Schulz is capable of sitting at his drawing board and recalling, in all earnestness, a disappointment experienced in preschool. Not just remember it, but feeling it. His own emotional jurisdiction is immense. For him personally, there are no significant boundaries between adulthood and childhood. Not in terms of what's just, what thrills, and what hurts. Especially what hurts. A man who's built a comic empire around the skeleton of his own life is not a man to look back and laugh." [*Schulz laughs*]*

And now, of course, you're laughing. Do you agree with that?

Oh, sure.

Rheta [Johnson] was a great lady. We got along so well, right from the moment I was introduced to her on the phone and I heard her Southern accent. I think we almost fell in love right away. She came here and sat where you are now for three days. We walked back and forth to the [ice] arena and talked. And we had a good time. We became very close friends. I think she put that very well.

But again, those are things that I don't think a creator thinks of. All you're trying to do is fill in those squares. Do something good for Monday, and then do something good for Tuesday, and then you do something for Wednesday. Where does it all come from? I think you can tell that some cartoonists have no moments of reflection at all. Or else they don't use it. You hate to say they're not sensitive. I don't think I'm more sensitive than anybody else. But I suppose I just have a knack for coining phrases that can be memorable.

You've railed against cartooning that is too hyper-kinetic, and your own drawing, and the rhythms of your storytelling, had to be subtle enough to convey your experience.

Drawing is very important. To draw, you have to have a pretty good sense of design so that the drawings are pleasant to look at. This is what made Bill Watterson so good, he drew so well. Cartooning is really just designing. It's a lot like Picasso on paintings. Take the shape of Charlie Brown's head. If a cartooning style is too extreme, the artist can never do or say anything that is at all sensitive. A character that is overly cartooned cannot say anything that's very sensitive. If you look back upon all of the great comic strips down through the years, every one of them was drawn in a style that was relatively quiet. It can be outrageously funny and it can be sad, as long it's not overly cartooned. It depends on which direction you want to go.

You certainly prefer the direction of subtlety; the last panel of your strips is usually a masterpiece of understatement. You spoke very rapturously about drawing. You said, "I am still searching for that wonderful pen line that comes down when you are drawing Linus standing there, and you start with the pen up near the back of his neck, and you bring it down and bring it out, and the pen point fans a little bit, and you come down here and draw the lines this way for the marks on his sweater. This is what it's all about—to get feelings of depth and roundness, and the pen line is the best pen line you can make. That's what it's all about."

Where'd you read that?

That's from the NCS Convention keynote speech.

I got all done and I got a standing ovation. I couldn't figure it out. I was stunned. I thought, "What have I said that was so important?" They all stood and applauded. I guess nobody had ever really talked to the entire Society in that manner. And somebody taped it, and they reprinted it.

Could you elaborate on what you feel constitutes an aesthetically-pleasing line and the satisfaction you derive from creating that?

I suppose it's as difficult as explaining what a poem is about. Look at Linus's hair, there [*showing Groth a daily he'd just completed*]. See? Every stroke is perfect.

6-4

If it were too shiny or something, it wouldn't have that nice quality. Look at Peppermint Patty's hair. See the lines? Those are good lines, and that's what I'm talking about. The little fingers, the way they go that way, too. Those are nice little fingers. [*Laughs*] Those are little Picasso-like fingers, and that's important.

You can get depth from doing that, and interest. You talk about the line that comes down around the back of Linus's shirt. If it went straight down, like a lot of people would do, it loses its life. I guess in painting, you would call it its paint quality.

It has life to it. It has spontaneity.

Life to it. Yes.

The strokes in the hair that you showed me, it looks like what you were after was a messy look, which is different from sloppiness.

Yes, I don't pencil in. I draw it with the pen. I block in, so that I'll get them in the right place, and the right size, but I draw that face with the pen when I'm doing it. Because you want that spontaneity, you don't want to be just following the pencil line. You don't "ink in." Some people do ink in, but should be drawing with the pen while they're doing it.

You do very little underdrawing.

I do as little as possible. Just enough to make sure that I get the heights and the space right.

You once said, "I was a great student of pen techniques back when I worked at Art Instruction. The author of the original cartoon course was Charles Bartholomew, and he used to send out what he called 'Bart Pen Demonstrations,' which was a little card that had three sets of pen lines: very thin, medium, and thick, all done with the same pen. My friend and I used to practice making those when we had nothing else to do. We used to see if we could do three sets of perfect pen lines with a space between the pen lines narrower than the line itself."

Yeah, like a surgeon. Uh-huh.

Could you talk a little about how much time and effort you took to master your craft so that you could express exactly what you wanted to express? I think that's very important.

I won't say it was as calculating as it might have been

if I had been going to medical school and becoming a surgeon or anything, but it was certainly something I was aware of in everything I drew. And the correspondence school did place a strong emphasis on pen technique as it did upon good lettering and things like that. And the samples that they had in their textbooks were samples of cartoonists who had a marvelous pen technique. And the man who sat in front of me when I finally started to work there and who had been one of my teachers was Frank Wing, who had a wonderful pen technique. He drew beautifully in the cartoons that he had done. So, I was a great admirer of—we always mention Percy Crosby, I can't think of anybody else right now—well, Charles Dana Gibson, the Gibson Girl. Beautiful pen. He did more than just draw with the pen—he painted with the pen, didn't he? He did more than just outline the figures. If you looked at a blowup of some of the girls' faces that he drew, he could create the features with little tiny cross-hatches and things like that, and he molded the pen line in a marvelous way. And I've never been able to do that. But that was really, to me, the ultimate. Now, unfortunately, it doesn't mean a thing.

How do you mean that?

Well, people are drawing comic strips that have no pen technique at all, and I think the lowest form is to draw them with a felt pen. How in the world are you going to have a good pen technique drawing with a felt pen? [*Groth laughs*] That's absurd. You're just missing the whole point.

Did you ever master a brush?

Yes. Actually, I was very good with the brush when I was still working at the correspondence school. I had drawn a series of panel cartoons which were quite large, about a little girl named Judy. I remember taking about 15 of them to Chicago and showing them around to some of the syndicates, and my brush technique was pretty good. I used a medium-surface Strathmore, but then when I sold the *Peanuts* strip, and I had to draw these four panels, I wanted a tighter style. My whole approach requires a tighter style of drawing in most cases. Now and then, when I draw some violent action or something like that, the style is a little more loose. And that's all right. But a brush style generally from day to day wouldn't work for me.

Peppermint Patty's hair that you just pointed out to me, was that inked with a pen or a brush?

That's a pen.

OK. So primarily you use a pen in the strip today.

Yeah. Definitely. Sometimes I go back and forth. Like right in front of me now I have Charlie Brown standing with a jacket on, and he's got long winter pants on. They're going to be black. But I may scribble in some pen lines and make it black, or I may just be lazy or go for a different technique of just putting it in with a brush. I don't know what I'll do.

Talking about drawing, your biographer wrote, "He will argue that the drawing within a comic strip is more important than the writing. It is, he insists, what makes a cartoonist a cartoonist. If Schulz feels Peanuts *is getting too wordy or if he's having trouble writing a good joke, or if he just hasn't been up to standard of late, he will deliberately return to slapstick, depicting a visual absurdity that's simply fun to look at." I was wondering if, being a cartoonist, you can really separate the writing from the drawing that easily. I think that you can almost forget that* Peanuts *is drawn because, in an odd sort of way, the drawing has become a kind of handwriting. Neither the drawing nor the writing dominate because it's such a densely conceptual strip. So it's interesting that you would say that the drawing is more important than the writing since they both work in such perfect harmony.*

Well, you really shouldn't believe anything that I've said. [*Groth laughs*] A lot of times, I have to say things just to explain something. I think you can look at the comic page these days and see that there's not really much interesting drawing going on. Now, the writing obviously is important. But I'm sure that the writing has placed my strip aside from a lot of others, due to the things I've written, the phrases that I've coined and all of that. But it's a mistake to eliminate drawing. There are a few collaborative efforts these days that are doing well. If the person can draw. Now, Jerry Scott has the advantage. He writes *Baby Blues* and the new teenage one, *Zits*, because *Zits* is beautifully drawn. Anyway, Scott can draw. If the person who is doing the creating can't draw, and even if it's an adventure strip, the creating is hampered. This is where cartooning separates itself from other mediums, because we can do things that live action can't do.

And I suppose one of the best examples of that is how it would happen now and then. I'll be sitting here trying to think of something funny, and I think of

Zits by Jerry Scott and Jim Borgman, April 28, 2011.

Snoopy and his troops going out on a hike. So, I think, "Well, what are they going to do at night? They're going to sleep." So, I draw tents like this. Now, what's the next step? Bang, all of the sudden the next step is that Snoopy is sleeping on top of the tent. Everybody else would be in the tent. There's your cartoon idea. And that's funny drawing. If you can't do that, I don't know where you're going to go. Then you can think about it again. Now the birds are sleeping on the ropes that go down from the tent. That's another idea. And you go from one thing to another.

Offending People

Comics seem to me such an organic form that any strip that is written by one person and drawn by another is going to have a severe disadvantage.

Definitely. But you don't dare say that. You'll offend people. [*Laughs*]

You've said in the past that you work hard not to offend people. Why is that a concern?

I don't like to offend people. Maybe it's a desire to be liked. Maybe that's the number one reason for not offending people. And I just don't think it's right to offend people. I could never be an editorial cartoonist, because if the governor or somebody took me out to lunch, I'd never be able to do a raunchy cartoon about him. [*Laughs*]

You have a terrific strip from, I think, the early '60s, where Lucy wrote on the sidewalk, "Charlie Brown is a blockhead." And Charlie Brown asks her, "Why did you write that?" And she said, "Because I honestly, truly believe it. And I had to be completely honest." And in the last panel he said something like, "You know, I kind of admire her integrity." [Laughter] And I thought that was an interesting commentary on offense and honesty.

I wouldn't do that anymore.

Which wouldn't you do?

I wouldn't even draw that cartoon.

Because it's too cruel?

Yeah. I've gotten older. My strip is much more mild than it used to be.

It is, it is. I couldn't help but notice that the strips of the '50s and '60s are much more barbed, more acerbic than they are now.

One of the advertising agencies just sent in a rough idea for an animated commercial, and in the last panel, Lucy is saying, "Good grief, Charlie Brown." And I thought, "Oh boy." I haven't used "Good grief, Charlie Brown" in 30 years. So, this person is just drawing on something that I did years ago. Which is why nobody else is ever going to be able to draw the strip. The best they could do is come up, if they're lucky, to where I am now. But they'll never be able to take it into new areas. Because they're not me.

So, I think the strip is much more mild. Even the insults that Marcie and Peppermint Patty go through are all done in good humor. They're serious, they get really mad at each other. But nobody ever hits anybody in my strip.

And you feel that way because you think you've changed over the years.

Well, I'm older now. You see, I'm an old person.

I've read almost 47 years of Peanuts.

Astounding.

It is.

And your creativity seems to spring not just from pain but from an intensely felt and specific recollection of pain. From what I've been able to discern, you almost seem most creatively alive when feeling pain, or musing on pain. For example, in virtually every interview I've read with you, and every biography or autobiography, you mention— and you mentioned it earlier in this interview without any prompting from me—the time when you did the drawings for that high school yearbook that were not used. So, you obviously still really feel deeply about that incident.

Oh, yeah. If you're besieged with all sorts of family problems, then you have this schedule to keep up. If you have illness in the family, and you know you're going to have to draw four strips the next day, and you don't have any ideas at all, that's when it gets brutal. But what still astounds me is how you can get up in the morning, have no ideas at all, almost dread going to the studio, and then suddenly while you're driving along, you think of something. And I can never figure out how that happens. I suppose that's what makes you what you are.

In that book up there [*pointing to his bookshelf*], *Caesar and Christ*, Will Durant says about the Apostle Paul, "He had to be what he was to do what he did." And I think this is the way it is with all of us. People say, "Well, how in the world can you just sit there and think of those ideas every day?" One of the reasons is that I have no desire to go anyplace else. If I was the kind that was obsessed with having to go to Australia or Nepal or Japan or something like that, then sitting here doing these things would be a real chore, wouldn't they? I'm where I want to be. I don't want to be anyplace else. So, I'm perfectly content to come here. I love going to the arena in the morning, having an English muffin, a cup of coffee, reading the paper, and talking to my friends there. I look forward to that every day. And I resent it when these moments out of the week are taken from me. I'm satisfied with just a five-day work week. But I'm never allowed a five-day work week. I have continual interruptions.

I'm feeling guilty right now.

No. That's the way it is. It's been this way for 30 years.

DEEP DOWN I ADMIRE HER INTEGRITY..

SCHULZ

August 27, 1965.

Now, it occurs to me that part of you must enjoy engaging in those kinds of business activities. Otherwise you would turn it off.

I don't mind the interviews. Well, no. A lot of it you can't turn off. I'll bet I can name you 50 people right now whose phone messages I can't turn down. You just have to. They're good, decent people. [*Laughs*] And I have to answer the phone. Now, short interviews by newspapers and things like that are almost relaxing to me. I'm getting so I can't sit at the drawing board and draw anymore hour after hour. I had a friend of mine who could do that. As long as he had a package of cigarettes sitting next to him, he could sit at the drawing table and never get up. Just draw until noon. And then we'd play pool, have a hamburger, and then he could draw all afternoon. I haven't seen him now in years. But I can't do that anymore. That's why I don't mind answering the phone.

Do you almost regret, because of all the distractions, the scope of your enormous success?

Have I had enormous success? Do you think so?

Well, it's just a shot in the dark, but I think so. Yeah. [Laughter]

I suppose.

I don't know what to make of the modesty you convey in the many, many interviews I've read with you, a modesty that is almost hard to believe. [Schulz laughs] You're probably the most successful cartoonist in the world.

The highest paid.

Well, yes, the highest paid, but also the most recognizable. The most widely-disseminated.

Oh, there's no doubt about it. This is what amuses me, when I read about some other people, some entertainer, and they say, "Yeah, he's sold nine million books." Or nine million this or something like that. And I want to say, "Do you realize that they tell me *Peanuts* is read by an estimated 200 million people? What else has ever done that? Nobody in the history of the world has ever had 200 million readers every day." [*Laughs*]

So, you are aware of your success.

I suppose. But, success doesn't cover everything. While you're enormously successful in one area, other people don't even know you exist and regard what you do as "I don't know, I never read the funny pages." It's a low art form. It really is. In spite of people who have tried to say, "Oh no, it isn't." But to many people it really is. We don't hang in art galleries. We're not good enough. We're good if they want us to donate four originals so they can auction them off to support their art galleries. "Fine," that's what I tell them. "Sure, that's great. But you would never hang my comic strips in your gallery, would you?"

"Oh, well, uh… I guess we've never thought about it."

"Oh, sure. Because it's not good enough." It's not art.

Do you really resent that?

Sure.

If this [*pointing to a large representational painting on the wall*] were just a big white canvas with a black streak through it, I'm better than that person. But I know I'm not Andrew Wyeth. I never will be Andrew Wyeth. And I wish that I were. He is what I call the perfect artist, because he can do everything that he wants. But from reading his biography a few months ago, I realize even he gets torn apart. "Oh, Andrew Wyeth is just an illustrator. He's not even an artist." I read a review of his biography. Can you imagine some reviewer, he's reviewing the book, the biography, saying, "Of course, we know that Andrew's not a real artist"? What kind of review is that? You're supposed to be reviewing the book, not whether Wyeth is an artist or not. Anyway, those are the things that everybody goes through, whether you're an actress, a singer, a violinist, or a ballplayer. I suppose we're all hero worshippers of different kinds. I've been a golfer ever since I was 16. And I would love to have won the National Open. Or to have played in the Masters. And I've played with a lot of the big pros, and I know people like Johnny Miller and the others. I know them very well. I think it would have been great to do something like that. To watch Willie Mays when he played baseball—probably the greatest player who ever lived. To watch some of the hockey players, or to go to a concert and see a violinist performing, or a pianist playing a Brahms concerto or something like that. I feel sorry for the people then, that have to live through that, but have nothing of their own. At least I can say, "Well, I have my own career that gives me satisfaction. I know that I've done something, too." Now, that's something I mention very seldom because people just don't always understand it.

So, I suppose that's one of the values of success. One of the things that helped. And I was still regarded as kind of a nothing person. To think that I've done this, considering that everybody thought that I would never amount to anything. [*Laughs*] That's kind of fun, too, to be able to look back upon it.

But I know my limitations.

Art

Let me ask you about your attitude towards comics as art. Because you've been somewhat ambivalent on the subject. And I'd like to know what your attitude was when you were still struggling with becoming a professional cartoonist. Did you think of comics as art and, if so, what was your frame of reference for art?

I've never known much about art. I've never been a student of art. I've never found it that interesting. And to me, obtaining a comic strip was just the greatest thing in the world. Because that's what I wanted, and that's what I knew I could do. I had no desire to think, "Well, a comic strip would be a good way to make a living so that someday I can be a painter" or something. I had no desire to be anything else. I suppose that would answer that. I hope.

Well, let me follow up on that. Earlier you spoke of having your range of appreciation broadened when you started hanging around your fellow instructors at Art Instruction and that prior to that your conception of art was somewhat provincial or unsophisticated. Yet on the other hand, you obviously had a real appreciation for excellence in cartooning, because the people you looked up to—George Herriman, Percy Crosby, Roy Crane—were all masters of the form.

Yes.

So, you had an innate understanding of what constituted excellence?

Well, at that time it would have been just standard. Those were the ones that everybody liked and admired. Now, I think the correspondence course helped. Because the textbooks that we had were very strong on pen technique and all of that sort of thing. So, I began to appreciate good drawing. But art itself still doesn't interest me that much. I admire people that are good artists, I'm just astounded at what they can do. For instance, I did a whole series of lithographs where I would draw the characters in pen and ink, and then I'd have them printed on watercolor paper. Then I'd just slosh in some watercolor. And they were sold around the country. Some of 'em I'm not too ashamed of, some I just don't like at all. But when I see the really great watercolorists… I'm not going to do any more, because I just don't think they're good enough. And I hate to see somebody pay $800 for something that I did like that. [*Laughs*] I don't mind them paying for the comic strip, because I feel that this is what I do. But I don't like to do other things.

You've downplayed the possibility that comics are capable of being a mature form of expression. And I'd like to nail your thoughts down on this. You've repeatedly said you don't regard what you're doing as "great art." And you've implied that cartooning is a second-rate art. But, I felt that your phrase "great art" stacks the deck a bit.

The comic strip artist doesn't have the total freedom to do what he wants to do, because it has to be published. A pure artist can go ahead and paint whatever he wants to paint, and if no one wants to hang it in the gallery, who cares? At least he's painted it. But if a comic strip isn't published, then what good has it been? Unless you just want to hang it on the wall or something. So, we have to cater to the subscribing newspaper editor, which immediately devalues it slightly, doesn't it? Not always. This doesn't mean that some of the best things that we do don't get printed, but also I suppose I'm just being falsely modest or just protecting myself. Because the minute you start talking about what you're doing is art then you're going to get shot down. And I just like to protect myself.

Well, that was what I was going to ask you. [Laughter] *Because it does seem to me that it does a disservice to the potential of comics because although comics have had a hard time of it, their potential seems much greater than what's been realized.*

Oh, there's no doubt about it. Unfortunately, I think that other mediums have tended to gain the spotlight on us. We had our greatest attention back in the days when our only competition was radio. And that wasn't much of a competition, really. But when movies came along, and television, then we really were in trouble, because we had to compete with live action, we had to compete with that big screen—all of the things that Charlie Chaplin could do, Laurel and Hardy, and then the other great humorists. It was pretty hard to compete. Not that we couldn't do it. We could. But they got all the attention and we just kind of followed along.

You just mentioned Chaplin. And I know you were a big movie buff when you were a kid.

Oh yeah. Yeah.

And I wanted to ask you what kind of movies you grew up watching. Did you watch Chaplin?

Oddly enough, there weren't that many. We didn't see a lot of Charlie Chaplin. I never became a real Charlie Chaplin fan until I grew up. And my friends and I used to go and see his movies. As kids, I think we appreciated Laurel and Hardy more than anybody. They were really funny. We used to go to the movies mainly on Saturday afternoon. We loved the cowboy movies, and the *Tarzan* movies, and jungle movies and things like that. They always had a serial—we followed all the serials. And of course, they hadn't started filming *Buck Rogers* at the time, and there weren't any really good animated things. I think the first *Popeye* animation that my cousin and I saw together we thought was just fantastic.

That would have been Max Fleischer.

Yeah. They were really wonderful. So that was what I saw as a kid. Then later on, of course, I used to go to movies all the time, and I used to go a lot by myself. Where my dad and I lived in the apartment, the theater was only half a block away. So, I would see almost every movie that came out. Because I would have nothing to do some evenings, so I would just go to the movies by myself. I can still think of the feeling that I had when I walked out of the theater after having seen *Citizen Kane*. I knew that I had seen something great.

What was your exposure to art and culture like in your home?

Both parents went only to the third grade. I don't recall my dad ever reading a book. He read the paper every night when he came home from the barber shop after dinner. Later, I started reading a publication that came out called *Omnibook*. They abridged maybe half a dozen of the latest best-sellers; I loved *Omnibook*. I was just beginning to do a lot of reading. And I remember recommending one of these books to my mother. She read it. She really liked it. It was her first experience ever reading anything. And of course, she didn't live much longer. But, they never read anything.

If your parents weren't readers, what prompted you to become one?

I don't know. I hated the things we had to read in school. I was astounded when—I

don't know if this is the eleventh grade or what it was—we had to read Thomas Hardy's *Return of the Native*. And I can still remember saying to one of the other guys, "That was good, wasn't it? Yes." I think they assign things to students that are way over their heads, which destroys your love of reading rather than leading you to it. I don't understand that. Gosh. So, I started reading both the Sherlock Holmes stories and then *Beau Geste* and other Foreign Legion things. This was the time when paperbacks came along, but they were called pocketbooks. They only cost, I think, a dime. Maybe a quarter. And they fit into your pocket. During the War, they gave them out for nothing. All wonderful books, all in paperback, and they would just fit in your jacket pocket. So, everybody went around with one or two paperbacks in their jacket. We got into reading that way, too. And of course, by the time we went overseas, most of my friends had at least started college. So, they had a better education than I had. My assistant squad leader had been a high school teacher, so he was very bright.

At what point did you start discriminating critically?

It would have been after the War when I was working at the correspondence school. That's when I did a lot of reading. That's when I read *War and Peace* and Scott Fitzgerald. After Joyce and I got married, we only had one car. And when she finally learned how to drive I'd leave the car home for her. And I would walk up two blocks to where the streetcar started, the end of the line, and read all the way downtown, where I had my studio. I read all four of Thomas Wolfe's novels riding in the streetcar back and forth. Did a lot of reading in those days. Now, I probably read more than ever.

You introduced your son Monte to such writers as Flannery O'Connor and Carson McCullers and Joan Didion.

Yes. You'd like Monte. Monte's very well read, very bright. He's working on a novel now, which I have tremendous hopes for.

One paradox that I can't figure out is that you repeatedly refer to your lack of sophistication. I can't help but think this is some sort of dodge, because you seem to be enormously well read and, in fact, are sophisticated about many things.

Up to a certain level. Have you ever been someplace and known that you were really in over your head?

Sure.

It's an awful feeling, isn't it?

Mm-hmm.

I find this when listening to people and you discover that they have a bigger vocabulary than you do. Despite the fact that I read a lot, I still don't have a very good vocabulary. Fortunately, you don't have to have one drawing comics. But I have felt over my head many times.

But I also realize that among all the people we know, I am better read than any of them. And most of the guys that I talk to are interested in nothing except who's going to be in the Super Bowl. Which is all right, but now and then I love spiritual conversation. The best friend that I have now, a new friend, is a man named Father Gary Lombardi, who's a priest in Petaluma. I'm not a Catholic, and I never will be. But he and I have a lot in common. We play golf every Thursday together, and we just tease him unmercifully. But I do love talking about spiritual things. I don't care who I talk with about it.

A woman minister comes to the arena now and then, and I love sitting talking with her about things. I just want to know what people think about things. Who do you think Jesus really was? What made him what he was? I want to know what people think. I think it's fascinating.

Spiritual Matters

Have you read [Norman] Mailer's most recent novel?

Monte liked it. He was surprised how much he liked it. But no, it just doesn't interest me. I don't care what Mailer thinks. [*Laughter*] I can think of few people whose opinions interest me less than Norman Mailer's.

Now, when you referred to spiritual things, you mean metaphysical?

Oh, no. Definitely not. I have no interest in metaphysical things. Whatever they may be. Well, that's a whole big subject to get into. I'd rather not even get into it. All it does is get me a bunch of nasty letters. Oooh! Speaking of nasty letters, I like nasty letters. This is the prized one, here [*pulling an envelope out of a drawer in his desk*]. Although I got a whole stack of 'em.

What in the world do you get nasty letters about? I can't imagine.

Well, listen to this.

> Dear Sir:
> Received letter rejecting sending me a large signed drawing of Snoopy. I thought you had some caring and compassion for disabled veterans, men who fought in the War for people like you who did nothing but make money. What a pity. You can be sure that newspapers and veteran groups will be told of your lack of caring and lack of patriotism.
> God help you. You even had a woman write for you. Why? Mrs. Leitel, who wrote to me, says in part, you respond faithfully to most

requests. Perhaps my Jewish name does it for you. I have two purple hearts serving my country. What do you have? Nothing.

[*Laughs*] What an insulting letter, huh? Isn't that awful when you think that there are people out there who don't know you at all and they're so self-centered? I can't draw Snoopy for everybody in the world.

But a person in your position has to get used to cranks.

Oh, yeah. I just think it's kind of revealing, that's all. I had a rabbi write to me several years ago, and he says, "I have a class of young people, and they were wondering why you did *A Charlie Brown Christmas* and why you haven't done anything about Hanukkah

July 16, 1965.

or something." And I wrote back and said, "Well, you know, I don't know anything about Hanukkah." And [after I'd written him] he said my answer "doesn't satisfy the young people in our class. They just wonder if there isn't a touch of anti-Semitism here." So, I thought, "Well, I'm forced to play my ace in the hole." I said, "You can accuse me of anti-Semitism, but I was the one that spent that miserable night outside the swamp there, the night Dachau was discovered." [*Laughs*] And that ended the conversation. I hated to do it, but I felt that's the only way to put a stop to this. Because I'm not anti-Semitic or anything. And I would love to do a Hanukkah show, but they'll never buy one. Besides, let some Jewish cartoonist do it, let Art Spiegelman do it. Or if the Mormons want to do something, let the Mormons do it. That's what Ray Bradbury says. People write to Ray and they say, "Why don't you do this or do that." He says, "Why should I do it? Do it yourself if you want to do it."

You know I did church cartoons for seven years?

Yes, I knew that.

I was the first one to do them, I think.

Let me segue into that. You were, according to your biography, "born to casual members of the Lutheran Church, the largest Protestant denomination in the world, and one with an old, established hierarchy."

Who said that?

Your biographer. Rheta Johnson. [Schulz laughs]

I don't think she knows what she's talking about. I never thought of the Lutheran Church as being that enormous. But anyway, go ahead.

"Sparky found appeal in the small, fervent independent Church of God." Now could you elaborate on your upbringing in the Lutheran Church?

I only went to Sunday school for one brief period one summer. With some other little neighborhood kids. Otherwise, we almost never went. My dad worked very late every Saturday night, and his only recreation, his only sport, was fishing. It was the only thing—when he had Sunday off, or something to do, he would go fishing. And it never bothered him. Later on, oddly enough, after the War, and after my mother died, he remarried. His wife was Lutheran, and they attended a big church. He got involved so that he was one of the ushers and he would pass the collection plate. He was very proud of that job. And I was always pleased that he did that. I should have told him, but I never did.

But anyway, the Church of God appealed to me in its basic message. It's a non-denominational movement, and I think the message that it had was very strong, which was that if you want to get into this, you did not have to join a denomination. By your belief, you were already a follower of the Way. You were already a member of what the New Testament called the Church of God. Paul writes to the Church of God, which is in Corinth, and so on.

Your beliefs and your actions made you a member of the Church of God. And that's what the teaching of this movement is. We had a wonderful minister, I became very close to him. He died a few years ago. I was just wrapped up in it. I was very active. Became very close friends with some other people in it. And that's how that went.

When we moved out here, there wasn't any [church] that I really went to. But a doctor came by our house and brought us some apples and invited me to their Sunday school class at the Methodist Church. And like I always do, I speak up too much in those classes, and the next thing I know they invited me to teach a class, which I did for about 10 years. And I just finally figured I'd run out of things to say, let somebody else take over. I would never teach a class again. I'm not a teacher. I kind of like leading discussions, but I don't like teaching anybody.

Did you feel uncomfortable in that position?

I don't feel that I know enough. I'm not obsessed enough with anything to be a teacher. I love the discussions, I took people through the entire Bible, chapter by chapter, three or four times. I find so many people are interested in biblical things, but they've never really studied it. They've probably never even read the Bible. And I just wanted to get them to become acquainted with it. And to make a few connections. I didn't like always having to hear, "Well, I think maybe it says somewhere in the Bible such-and-such." I want them to be able to know where it says it and why it says it. That was my only purpose. As far as teaching anything, I don't care. I don't even care what they believe. I don't really care what anyone believes as long as they behave well.

Now, you drew youth-oriented cartoons from 1958 to 1964 that were consolidated into a series of books by Warner Press. Can you tell me something about those? Were they single-panel gag cartoons?

A fellow named Kenny Hall was editor of their youth magazine, and we became acquainted. He knew what I did. He asked me to do a panel every two weeks. It took me a while to develop a style. I'm still quite proud of the way they look. But I did things that no one had ever done in church magazines before. It opened up a whole new field. Since then, others have followed.

I was the first person ever to draw a nun in a protestant youth magazine. And I was the first person, I think, ever to draw a black person in a cartoon like this. But nobody knows it. I just had so many things to do those days. That two weeks would come around in a hurry, and then I was doing Hallmark cards and I was doing Ford advertisements, helping them to write those commercials and drawing the storyboards. Plus, the fact that I was growing more and more away from youth meetings by then. I was in my forties, and I was just going on memories.

Comic Books and Syndicates

The only time that I've known you to relinquish writing and drawing your characters was for Dell Publishing's comic book version of Peanuts *in the '50s. I was wondering why you allowed that.*

Because it gave me a chance to have a couple friends do something.

Were you satisfied with the results?

Only when Jim Sasseville was doing them. But it gave me a chance, when we moved out here to California, to have somebody else in the studio to help run to the post office and to take care of things. And we got $45 a page for doing these stories, which enabled them then to earn their salary. They weren't assistants, because they never did anything on the [newspaper] strip.

What did they do?

Just things around the studio. Whatever was necessary. But they had to work hard drawing those comic books. We usually had four pages in *Nancy* comics. Eventually we got a 32-page comic book ourselves. At first, I had two men come out with me from Minneapolis. Jim Sasseville was really good. He and I did that feature called "It's Only a Game" for a while. Boy, nobody could draw better than Jim Sasseville. But his wife hated it here, and he finally had to quit because she couldn't stand living here. It was just disrupting his family life. There was never another guy who worked that good. [*Laughs*]

You're quite adamant about not having assistants work on the strip.

Oh, yeah.

Do you still letter the strip?

Sure.

I heard a story that I couldn't verify, but that I thought I'd run by you. Ten, 12, 15 years ago the syndicate actually had an artist by the name of Al Plastino draw a lot of Peanuts *strips. The story, as I recall it, was that you hit the roof when you heard this. And the syndicate did this in case you decided to drop the strip. I understood you were not happy with that. Is there any truth to that?*

That isn't quite true. I only heard it secondhand. There was a man named Bill Payette who was head of the syndicate at the time. He took over from Larry Rutman, who was the first president when I signed up. I became very dissatisfied as the years went on, and decided more and more that I wanted ownership of the feature. No big blow-ups or anything like that, but it was getting closer and closer to it. And for some reason, I didn't know about this until it was all over.

Can you give me a timeframe on this?

Well, we were in this studio at the time. And we didn't really achieve a showdown until he finally retired. He had a vision problem. And I don't know if it forced him to retire, but when he retired Bob Metz took over. And I told Bob Metz what I wanted. And he said, "Well, that's reasonable enough." And we settled it in a five or 10 minute conversation. Then he told me that he went back and was going through some files, and he found some strips that maybe Al Plastino had drawn that Bill Payette had asked him to draw, unbelievably thinking that if I had decided to quit he would have somebody ready to take over the strip. Which was absurd. And Bob Metz was so embarrassed by the whole thing, I couldn't believe that he could do this. So, he said, "I took all the strips, and I burned them." [*Laughs*] He said, "I don't want anybody ever to see those things." So that's the story as I know about it.

How'd you feel about that when he told you?

Well, I couldn't believe that Bill Payette would be so dumb.

It strikes me as a betrayal.

It's disappointing that somebody thinks that it's that easy. Of course, that's been traditionally what comics have been down through the years. Just hire somebody else. Look at *Nancy* and all the others.

That's the traditional point of view of a businessman who doesn't respect the artist.

And the most disappointing thing is when people say, "Oh, you're still drawing the strip?" [*Laughter*] Here I am trying every day to draw the best I can, and doing little experiments and trying to make it better, then they ask me that. Who do they think is drawing it?

How do you feel about something like Garfield, *which must have been drawn by assistants for something like 15 years now and it doesn't make a bit of difference.*

I don't know Jim Davis that well.

I'm interested in nailing down your attitude about—well, for the lack of a more subtle way of putting it—art and commerce. For example, you've had a lot of really harsh things to say about the rapacity of newspaper strip syndicates. Which surprised me.

Do I?

*Oh, yeah. I'll quote you in a moment. [*Schulz laughs*] In your biography, Johnson wrote, "One difference between Schulz and hundreds of other aspiring cartoonists, noted Harry Gilburt, United Feature Syndicate sales manager at the time, was his willingness to compromise. Syndicate executives considered such an attitude a sign of maturity and professionalism. 'He went along,' says Gilburt, 'he was smart enough to.'"*

And then later she wrote, "As already mentioned, Schulz earned an early reputation around the syndicate as a reasonable, adaptable young artist. This reputation arose however not from a pliable personality, but from a calculated willingness to swallow whatever was necessary to reach his goals." Can you comment on that?

Well, I think I've always been a reasonable person. And getting back to is this art or not, I realize that this is still a business. And for a long while, I figured that the syndicate people knew more about it than I did. They were the ones that had to go out and sell it. Harry Gilburt was a remarkable man. I don't think he knew as much about comic strips as he thought he did. We talked just a little bit last year. Very knowledgeable. He knew every editor in the world. He could go into a room and introduce you around, and say, "This is so-and-so from *The Wyoming Press*." He was remarkable and very well respected in the business—as a salesman. And so, I cooperated with all the different things they wanted. And just went along, until finally, as the years went on, I could see that I should stand up for a few things.

That you should exercise your authority.

No, because they knew I was right.

It took you a while to reach that point.

Oh, yeah. It took me a long time. Plus, it took a long time to achieve the power to do it. The power is either I get my way or I quit. And that's the only language they understand.

Wouldn't you have had that power by around 1960?

No.

The strip was pretty phenomenally successful by then, wasn't it?

Bill Payette wouldn't have had the vision. But when I finally did get my way, it was because they realized that nobody else could do it. [*Laughs*] And they'd better keep me.

Did you think the contract you signed with the syndicate initially was fair?

At the time, I thought it was. I can see now that it probably wasn't.

Do you think that was a little naive?

Yeah. But it was typical of everything. You go to Hollywood, you're going to have to take this role of the waiter, or else you're not going to get any role at all. And you have to take it, and you're going to get $40 a day for doing it. That's it. You have no choice. And if you're an athlete and you join the ballclub, and the manager wants you to play right field but you'd rather be pitching, you're stuck with playing right field. This is the way it is in all these things. You have to work your way out of them. And I think you have to learn how to be cooperative. That's just the way it is.

Isn't there a sense, though, that—and I understand this is true of virtually every business relationship in America—those who are in a position of power routinely take advantage of those who are subordinate, and that at the time you signed with the syndicate you were the weaker of the two. And isn't that use of advantage wrong?

Well, that depends on motive. Now, if you look upon these people as being evil men, that distorts the whole discussion. But a syndicate invests a lot of their reputation and money when they take on a new feature. And cartoonists are notorious for not making their schedules on time and not keeping up the quality of their work and all of that. Syndicates, as I can see, had to be firm. I suppose that the best thing they could have done would be to put a clause in there that after maybe two or three years, the contract could be renegotiated or something. There was no renegotiating those contracts at all. They had an option for another five years, another five years, and you just took it or you were out. But if you became so good that nobody else could take your place, then you finally developed some power. I think that's the power that you, the cartoonist, has that the syndicate does not have. They're kind of trapped, too. They're at your mercy, the same way as the owner of a ball club is at the mercy of Willie Mays. [*Laughs*]

Like I said, you had some pretty harsh things to say about newspaper syndicates and the businessmen who run them.

But I always got along well with them.

I find that… Of course, I'm of a different generation. [Schulz laughs]

Yeah.

And I'm interested in how your generation viewed the people for whom you were working. It seems like there was a much more compliant attitude among your generation, that there was a greater willingness to accept their authority. Or their superiority, as the case may be. But it does seem like over the years you have accepted their authority less and less. For example, you said, "The comic strip profession is a deadly serious business. And someplace up there [some metaphorical corporate upstairs]—"

Back to my NCS speech again.

Yes. [Schulz laughs]

"—there are some people that you will never know existed. They don't care anything about you, so watch yourself. They don't even read the comics. They could not possibly care less what happens to you. I don't know who these people are up there, but I'm sure that every newspaper, every organization has this group of mystery people. Like the people who run the ballclub, like the man who owns the theater. He doesn't really care about the actors. He likes the bottom line."

Do you question that ethos more now than you did then?

Well, I didn't know it. Let me tell you something. The man that signed me up initially was named Larry Rutman. A very fine gentleman. He still was very narrow in his view of how it all should work. There was a certain point, after having drawn the strip clear up into the '60s, I remember saying to him, "Larry, I think I want something more."

"Oh no," he said. "We can never do that."

You see, this was beyond his scope. Nobody had ever asked for anything like this. And yet, now, two years ago, I suppose it's been, maybe a year and a half, the phone rang one day and the person said, "This is David, Larry's grandson. I just wanted to let you know that Larry died last night."

I said, "Oh, gee, that's too bad." Larry after he retired moved out to Monterey, and we used to see him once a year when we'd go down for the golf tournament. Jeannie and I would always take him out to lunch or breakfast, just to renew acquaintances.

He said, "Larry died last night. I have a little list of people here that he told me to make sure, of all the people, that I call Sparky first." That is something, after all those years… That's what being cooperative will get you. The love and respect of a man like that. Which I'll cherish forever. To think that somebody thought that highly of me who was just another one of his cartoonists. But, he always used to tell me that he had the right to make some of these major decisions. I found out later that he didn't. That the president of the syndicate is still under the control of the board of Scripps-Howard. And up there, that's the mystery people. So, when the man came out here to discuss my eventually getting total control and everything, I said, "How old are you?" He said, "Well, I'm 57." I said, "You know, all my life I've been pushed around by your kind and told, 'You have to do this, you can't do that,' and all that." I said, "No more. From now on, I control the licensing myself and what I say goes. Either I get exactly what I want, or I quit."

Wow.

It worked. [*Laughter*]

And I wasn't being nasty, but this is the truth, you see? These people, they don't care anything about you. They like all the money that you make and all of that. But if you don't produce, nice knowing you, so long, we'll get somebody else.

But it takes a long time and, as you know, only the superstars can do that. Only Tiger Woods can do it.

What did you mean when you referred to him as "your kind"?

The big shots. When you're young, you have to listen to them and all their nonsense. And you don't have a chance. I went through too many interviews and talked to too many people who wouldn't even listen to me. I took some comic strips down to the *Chicago Sun* once. The editor was a guy named Walt Ditson, nice fellow. He looked at my *Li'l Folks* things and he said, "Boy, these are really good. I can't say no to this. But we'll take them in and show them to Harry Baker here." Harry Baker was on a coffee break, and when he came back, he took me in and introduced me, and said, "Harry, I just want you to see the work here of this young man. I think he's really good." And Harry looked at it, and said, "Well, no." And that was it. [*Laughs*]

And my other classic story is going into a syndicate also in Chicago. I bring in the strips, and this was a nice presentation. They were well drawn, and all of that. I always knew I was getting better all the time. I came in, and the guy didn't even get up when I came in. He goes, "My name is (whatever it was)." I sat there and handed him these things. This is the way he looked at 'em. [*Indifferently rustling through papers*] "Not professional." And then went back to his work. I thought, "You idiot. You don't even ask where I'm from. Did I have a nice trip down?" All the niceties of life. So [that's what I was referring to] when I said, "I've been pushed by your kind all my life, but not anymore."

Without prying unduly, may I ask you who actually owns Peanuts*? Could you change the strip's name to "Charlie Brown" if you wanted?*

Yeah, but it's been discussed many times. It would create so many problems with the licensees. So many products out there with the name *Peanuts* on it, and it has become so prominent. And it would cause a lot of trouble, and a lot of expense for the people that are making the products and all of that to make a change like that. And at this point, I suppose it really doesn't matter, and a lot of people think *Peanuts* is a great name. So, it's just one of those things that humble you and you accept, and that's the way it goes.

So, do you essentially own the strip?

I don't own the copyright. Which is not necessary. But I have total control over everything. I can do virtually anything that I want, as long as it doesn't damage the property. And the syndicate can't do anything with the property without my permission.

Aesthetics

In re-reading the Peanuts *strip, I was trying to focus on what made it as rich as it was. The central reason, it seems to me, artistically as well as commercially, is because you've created not one but several archetypes who all interact within the strip. Charlie Brown is the perpetual loser, Snoopy is the romantic, Lucy is the quintessential curmudgeon, Schroeder is the artistic conscience who cares only for his art, and so on.*

He still plays catcher, though. [*Laughter*]

I was going to say: None of them are one-dimensionally so. Because Snoopy's also a loser—albeit a deluded one—Charlie Brown can be acerbic, and so on. I can't imagine you had all this planned out when you started the strip. Can you tell me how it developed so organically over the years?

It depends on what ideas you have and who in your repertory company will play the role, that's all. The characters themselves provide ideas just because of the nature that you've given them. So, it works both ways. But none is consistent, as none of us is. I think they go in all directions.

I find that coming up with ideas never ends and never gets any easier. And you find yourself going in a certain direction just to survive. Now lately, Rerun has almost taken over the strip. He's been in the strip for—gosh—20 years.

In fact, you thought he might've been a mistake when you introduced him.

I think he was a mistake when it first began. I was looking for something that was different. I put him on the back of his mom's bike, and the only time he ever appeared was riding on the back of that bike. I like those. And then, we had a few grandchildren who had to start preschool and kindergarten, and I see little kids at the arena, too. I began to get some ideas, and so he was the perfect one to have start kindergarten. He's different from Lucy and Linus. He's a little more outspoken. And I think he's going to be a little on the strange side, the way he is already. [*Laughs*] I just had him expelled from school for another day recently, just because he spoke up. I did a strip where he's painting. And he says, "This is a border collie, see, and these are the sheep he's guarding. Suddenly a wolf comes. So, the border collie gets on the phone and calls in an air strike." And a little girl

January 22, 1974.

says, "You're supposed to be doing watercolors of flowers." He says, "It all takes place in a meadow." He's perfect for that. The other kids are too old for this, really. So, it's worked out. Which gives me an idea for another I've thought about. He's going to complain that he couldn't do watercolors anymore because the fumes were overcoming him or something, I don't know. I'll have to think about that. But you have to be careful that the strip doesn't run away from you. So, whenever I get going on these stories, I always realize that that week is over—now I've gotta bring 'em back to the regular *Peanuts* stuff. Charlie Brown and Snoopy: They're the ones that count. So, I always try to bring 'em back. I thought of one Charlie Brown idea last week, and I couldn't of any others.

And I love doing Snoopy as a World War I Flying Ace, but I almost feel that it's dated, that I've done it too much. So, I have him doing other things. I've had him serve as a soldier at Valley Forge. I did a big Sunday page on that a couple of weeks ago. And that's kind of fun to do. But again, it's quite limited. And of all the things that I've done, that probably got more attention—his Flying Ace adventures—then anything I've ever done.

You once said that you didn't want to portray him as the World War I Flying Ace because it was inappropriate during the Vietnam War.

Yeah. I quit doing him at that point.

Can you tell me why?

Well, because everybody was suddenly realizing that this was such a monstrous war. It just didn't seem funny. So, I just stopped doing it. Then going into bookstores and seeing the revival of war books, mostly World War II, Korea, World War I books,

I thought, "It's coming back again," so then I started doing some more. But I didn't do him fighting the Red Baron. Mostly, it was just sitting in the French cafe flirting with the waitress. Then it turns out that he's not in a French cafe at all, he's in Marcie's kitchen! [*Laughs*] Which was a real twist. He's drinking all the root beer.

Well, that brings up an interesting aspect of Peanuts. *You've said, "The strip has become so abstract that the introduction of an adult would destroy it. You can't have an adult in a strip where a dog is sitting on a doghouse pretending he's chasing the Red Baron." You've also said, "I don't know where the* Peanuts *kids live. I think that originally I thought of them living in these little veterans' developments, where Joyce and I first lived when we got married out in Colorado Springs. Now, I don't think about it at all. My strip has become so abstract, and such a fantasy, that I think it would be a mistake to point out a place for them to live."*

I don't even draw houses anymore. [*Laughs*]

Right. You've really whittled it down, so that the strip can encompass almost anything. And one of the things I've noticed over the years is that the fantasy elements—I don't know if it's right to say they're taking over—but they're becoming more prominent.

Oh, they are. No doubt about it. I never do Lynn Johnston things, and I never do *Family Circus* things. And I never do *Dennis the Menace* situations. The fantasy elements just make it much more flexible. I can do things they can't do.

And this was a gradual change.

Oh, yeah. The strip was fairly realistic when it first began. Little kids doing little kid things. They rode tricycles. Of course, Charlie Brown hasn't even flown a kite for a while. Maybe I've reached the end. [*Groth laughs*] That's a problem. This can happen to a lot of people. You use up all of your life

ABOVE November 10, 1997.
RIGHT August 28, 1988.

38

experiences. And you get finally to the end. And now you have to wait for new experiences, you stay alive and read a lot, and hang around with a lot of people and try to stay in tune with things. If you don't, you're going to use up all those experiences. I just read a review of Kurt Vonnegut's latest novel, and it said he has nothing left to say.

Do you fear that happening?

Sure. But it's a living. [*Laughter*]

Since we were talking about the abstract elements of Peanuts, *let me ask you about another formal element: There's an aesthetic fragility that's an integral part of the* Peanuts *strip, by which I mean there are very clearly defined boundaries which can't be transgressed. For example, you once said, "Adults have been left out because they would intrude in a world where they could only be uncomfortable. Adults are not needed in the* Peanuts *strip. In earlier days, I experimented with offstage voices, but soon abandoned this, as it was not only impractical but actually clumsy."*

Could you explain why the strip needs these boundaries? And are there any boundaries other than not depicting adults that you adhere to that might not be so readily apparent?

Well, the main thing is that the kids seem to accept Snoopy's actions. Now, it's totally absurd that this dog is on top of this pointed doghouse all the time. And he's afraid to go down inside it. But if you go back to the earlier strips, where you see the doghouse from a three-quarter view, immediately the doghouse becomes too real. Snoopy can't really lie on top of that doghouse, because you're looking at it from the proper angle. But if we don't show it from the three-quarter view, we just keep the side view, then the reader eventually accepts that as being the doghouse, but we don't care if it's the doghouse anymore. And he can sit there, and he can type on the typewriter and it doesn't slide off, and he can lie on his

back, and all the other things, so we accept that. Then, all of the things that he thinks and does are so fanciful that the kids again accept it.

Now, in my strip, Snoopy never talks to the kids. You'll notice that. And the birds never talk to them. They think to each other. The animals do, but the kids somehow are aware of what he is doing without actually knowing what he is really thinking. And they accept that, because I suppose we could say children live different lives. And they probably do. The more I talk with my own children now that they've become adults, I find out that they were doing things around the house which I never dreamed about. I never knew they did some of those things. Children, I suppose, are like animals. They have to survive. And they have to keep things from the parents that they do. Nothing serious, but just things that they do that the parents never know about. Especially if you've gone away for the evening, or something like that, then they do some things that they normally wouldn't do. And I like to think that animals do the same thing. And this is what Snoopy does. He has to retreat into his fanciful world in order to survive. Otherwise, he leads kind of a dull, miserable life. I don't envy dogs the lives they have to live. They're trapped living with families that they never knew anything about [*Groth laughs*], and so Snoopy survives by living this extra life. Now, we can go any direction with Snoopy. Woodstock, too. It's absurd to think of this dog and this bird wandering through the woods going on hikes and camping out. So, as soon as an adult is in the strip—bang, the whole thing collapses. Because the adults bring everything back to reality. And it just spoils it.

Now, we have another even more practical solution or reason, and that's the fact that there's no room for adults. When it was given to me, my strip was about the size of four airmail stamps. Well, you remember Fritzi Ritz and Nancy. Fritzi Ritz could never stand in the same room as Nancy, because she was too tall. So, Ernie Bushmiller always had to fake it. This is what is done in so many strips. There's just no room for adults to stay. Besides, they don't interest me. And also, it's kind of neat to have the reader create some of these characters in his or her own mind. What kind of a teacher was Miss Othmar really? And what did she look like? And why did she run away and give up teaching to get married? And who are the principals that the kids are always going in and talking to? And the little red-haired girl appearing offstage. We never see her. It's almost too late to draw her, because I could never draw her to satisfy the readers' impression of what she's probably like. So, it's good to establish a group of offstage characters.

But size is very important. I just didn't have the room to draw kids—with the

ABOVE November 5, 1953.
BELOW October 24, 1980.

result that I brought the camera right down on level with the kids. I have never drawn the kids from an adult viewpoint, looking down on them.

Have you ever been tempted to do a strip about adults?

Oh, I've been tempted to do a lot. I did a comic feature for three years called *It's Only a Game*. And that had adults in it. They were playing all different kinds of sports. And they played bridge all the time. And of course, I did the teenage youth cartoons, which I was pretty proud of. I didn't like the drawing of them for at least a year or so. But after that, I think the drawing really came along quite nicely and I'm quite proud of the way those things appeared.

Were you as comfortable drawing teenagers and adults as you are drawing the children?

I think they're harder to draw. [*Laughs*]

In a peculiar way, Peanuts *taps into the fantasy lives of children; Snoopy and Charlie Brown communicate even though the reader is never quite sure that they're aware they're communicating.*

Yeah.

For example, when Snoopy bangs on Charlie Brown's door for a cookie in the middle of the night, Charlie Brown knows exactly what he wants and comes out screaming at Snoopy.

The theme of this business goes all the way back to… did you have a dog or a cat or anything like that?

Yes, I had a dog.

And I'm sure you have done like almost all adults. We see our dog in the morning and we say, "Good morning, Tommy. Did you sleep well at all last night?" We then kind of give a voice to Tommy, and we say, "Yeah, I slept pretty well. I wanted to bark a little bit, but I didn't want to disturb anybody." We give the dog answers, don't we?

Right.

I think it's just a common thing that everybody does. And this is really what Snoopy's thinking is all about. This is where all of that started.

LEFT *Nancy*
by Ernie Bushmiller,
October 13, 1944.

OPPOSITE
September 17, 1974.

So, when you did that, you were that conscious of your strategy?

Mm-hmm. But not taking it that seriously, of course. None of this is that calculated.

I guess that was my question. To what extent are these creative strategies calculated?

Well, I think about it a lot and I consider everything carefully before I do it. But of course, I've made a lot of mistakes down through the years doing things I never should have done. But fortunately, in a comic strip, yesterday doesn't mean anything. The only thing that matters is today and tomorrow.

There's almost a slippery slope to the fantasy quotient of the strip where the strip started off being more realistic, and then slid more and more into fantasy. First there was Snoopy acting more and more human, and then Snoopy's fantasy life, and then the children actually entering into and coexisting in Snoopy's fantasy life. Such as when Snoopy is Peppermint Patty's attorney or Marcie appears as a French lass in his World War I fantasy. Things like that. And then more recently I noticed that the inanimate objects are actually talking to the children. Sally's school building talks to her, Charlie Brown's glove and ball talk to him, etc.

But the children don't hear them, do they? The schoolhouse used to think things all the time like Snoopy did. But Sally never heard what the schoolhouse was thinking.

Is that right? I guess I felt that was ambiguous. I wasn't sure.

No, I don't think she ever heard what the schoolhouse was thinking. I haven't done one of those in a long time.

No, I think I read those in the late '80s. But as the strip progressed, there was less and less of a demarcation between reality and fantasy, and I was wondering why you increased the fantasy quotient.

I suppose a lot of it is just the struggle for survival, Gary. [*Groth laughs*] The days come and the days go; you send in one batch, and you need another batch. And it just goes on and on and on. What are we going to do tomorrow? It never ends. And then you get caught up in something that works, and all of a sudden Snoopy's pursuing the Red Baron, next thing you know, he's in the French cafe, and then the next thing you know, his brother Spike is in the trenches. [*Laughs*] Something works, and something doesn't work. This is what it is, just a constant pursuit of something new.

Do you think that you would be less creatively fertile if you didn't have the pressure of a daily strip? If someone were to say, "Stop doing the strip, and just do whatever you want, whenever you want to do it," would you find that…

Probably would be a handicap, wouldn't it? Because you might think about it too much. You might lose some of the spontaneity. It'd be like the argument that musicians have all the time: Should they leave in the bad notes? If they're playing some very intricate violin concerto and they play as fast as they can. So, they miss a note now and then. Who cares? It's the risk you take when you draw these things and you gamble on certain things. Some things work and some things don't.

You said once, "I don't know which story has been my favorite, but one that worked out far beyond my expectation concerned Charlie Brown's problem when, instead of seeing the sun rise early one morning, he saw a huge baseball."

Oh, that was great.

That was one of your most outrageous strips in terms of combining reality and fantasy. Do you have any recollection of how you came upon that idea? You'll recall his head was turning into a baseball.

Yeah. It was kind of a head rash.

ABOVE
June 15, 1973.

OPPOSITE ABOVE
June 23, 1973.

OPPOSITE BELOW
July 5, 1973.

Well, I don't know how you think of those things, but then, when you do them, I let the stories go where the daily strips take me. I discovered that if you try to plot out a story, you'll end up with some weak daily strips. And it's more important to try to make each daily strip as good as you can, no matter where the story goes. And fortunately, I sent him to camp. And there he was ashamed of it, so he put a sack over his head. And he became a leader. Nobody knew who he was. There was a lesson there. [*Laughs*]

Had you planned that?

No.

Because it was so thematically perfect for Charlie Brown to be recognized as a leader only when he wore a bag on his head. [Schulz laughs]

It just happened, that was all. And then, of course, I needed an ending, and that's when "What, me worry?" came up. And I called *Mad* magazine, and they said, "Well, I guess we should let you do it, because we've been parodying you for so long."

I've never understood why they mispunctuate "What me, worry?" It should be "What, comma, me worry?" But they don't do it that way.

Well, it was probably just a mistake the first time they did it, and then they had to repeat the mistake forever.

I think so. A lack of education.

The Sundays and the dailies have diminished in size over the years.

The dailies haven't. They got bigger. The Sundays diminish because some of the editors won't give me a bigger size. Our local paper gives me the whole half page. But the *Chronicle*'s really insulting. They trim it down to about a sixth of a page. But it depends on the editor, how prejudiced he is.

Wasn't the size of the dailies changed around 1988?

We made them bigger.

I see.

Because you changed your format considerably. You had a very rigid format of four square, identically-sized panels.

I was given that. That was one of the things that

Harry Gilburt wanted to see. That was a sales gimmick. The strip was not an instant success by any means. It took a long time.

You once referred to the format of the strip as a "space saver." Can you tell me what that was?

It meant that an editor could buy it and put it wherever he wanted in the paper. He could run it in the want ads, this way, or he could run it over on the side next to the crossword puzzle this way

Vertically.

Or he could run it in a square. He had three choices. It was just a sales gimmick.

So, that's why you had to have a rigid four-panel format.

Yeah. But again, I think they lied to me. It was just their sales gimmick, because about two or three years later, they came out with *Twin Earths* and *Long Sam*, which were big strips just like other ones. Of course, *Long Sam* was Al Capp, and he had his way about whatever he wanted. He gave them so much trouble. And *Twin Earths* was the dumbest idea for a strip there ever was. [*Laughter*]

You really created a beautiful visual and temporal rhythm within that strict four-panel format.

Mm-hmm. But I'm glad I got rid of it.

Are you?

It was restrictive.

It was beautiful in its way, though.

Yeah, but like this strip here [*shows a long, single-panel strip*], which isn't quite finished. Four panels would ruin that.

So, you were really very happy when you could change the size of the panels and do these large single-panel illustrations.

I was just leaving a cartoonists meeting with Mort Walker and Mell Lazarus one evening, and I said, "You know, it's very strange. I drew my strip for years in four panels and now I can have one long panel. I can have characters talking here, here, and then finally ending up over here." I did that, and then all of a sudden I realize,

"Mell, this is what you've been doing for 30 years." [*Laughs*]

Let me ask you this: Being a newspaper strip artist is unusual in the sense that most artists have a sense of completion about what they do, but strip cartoonists can't. A painter paints a painting, it's finished. A novelist writes a novel, it's finished, and he moves onto the next novel. But it seems to me like there's never a sense of completion with your work. Do you see this as one long, lifelong piece of work?

Sure. Sure. But I think there are quite a few strips that I'm very proud of that I think stand absolutely on their own, and they look real good. The more I look at them, the worse they get. [*Groth laughs*] But I'm very proud of a lot. So, I think each one will stand by itself.

Well, you've had many terrific stories. Your stories don't last more than three or four weeks as far as I can tell.

They used to last longer. But lately I haven't been able to make them last that long for some reason. But editors are becoming more impatient. I think there's a market for longer stories, if editors would just give us a chance.

Are you optimistic about the future of the newspaper strip?

No, no. Not the way it's going. They're getting worse all the time.

There doesn't seem to be much room for optimism.

And it shouldn't be that way, really.

Do you think there's something anachronistic about a strip appearing in the newspaper every day?

Well, maybe so. Just like I imagine newspaper columnists are having trouble, too. But I think I know what has happened. Years ago, when comic strips first began to develop, the cartoonists were all newspaper people. They worked usually in newspapers, they made spot drawings and they illustrated things that were going on. Photographers weren't as prevalent as they are now, and so cartoonists all drew pretty well. Because if they didn't, they would never have gotten hired. So, they had a lot of drawing to do. And then, we drifted into the '40s when gag cartooning began to become so prominent. And I think you'll find that most of the cartoonists that were drawing came from animation or gag cartooning. Walt Kelly came from animation.

Did Mort Walker come from animation?

No, he came from gag cartooning. And I came from gag cartooning. There's a whole bunch of us who developed from gag cartooning. Then gag cartooning began to diminish as the magazines disappeared. Now where are they going to come from? They've gotta come from someplace. Newspapers don't employ cartoonists anymore, there's no gag cartoonists, so where are they going to come from? They're coming from college. Colleges have lousy cartoonists because they'll take anything. They don't learn how to draw, and they come up with radical ideas—they're going to save the world and all of that. And I think that's where it's falling down. Now even that's disappearing. Now housewives are becoming cartoonists. [*Groth laughs*] I don't know where it's going to end. You find so many amateur cartoon strips. Before, it took a lot of training, you had to work your way up until you finally got a comic strip. Now they jump from nothing to drawing a comic strip. They have no training at all, no experience at it. And that's deplorable.

Development and Style

You just mentioned how gag cartooning became prominent in the '40s, which remind-ed me of something you said about the beginnings of Peanuts. *About the early creative evolution of the strip, you said, "What has to be realized is that the characters I drew then came out of a style of gag cartooning that was prevalent at the time. Tiny children looking up at huge adults and saying very sophisticated things. This was the professional school from which I graduated and which formed my style. And it took me several years to break away and develop a style of drawing that would allow the characters to do new and special things." Could you talk a little about the creative process involved in breaking away from the gag style and into a style more suited to a continuity strip? And can you define the differences between those two styles?*

I think we always have to remember that gag cartooning is different from comic strip cartooning. And it's a mistake if you don't realize that early and you never do go away from that. Now, comic strip cartooning allows you much more of a change of pace. You develop characters and from those characters you develop themes and ideas and, of course, discussion, too. The characters can talk to each other. You don't have to come out with one lone punch line. Now, the characters also have to be drawn so that they can do different things. Gag cartoon characters don't necessarily have to be really doing anything. They only have to pose in the action that is relevant to that gag. But comic strip characters have to be a little more flexible in the way they're constructed so that they can run and talk and hold books and throw baseballs and do all sorts of different things. And do them consistently. I think that's the difference.

I love the old gag cartoons that were back in the '40s, with the little kids with the great big heads. They were funny.

You said the characters you drew came out of a style of gag cartooning. But you were also passionately interested in comic strips at the time. Why did you choose a style from gag cartooning rather than from comic strips like Gasoline Alley *or something like that?*

Probably because I just wanted to get started. This was what sold. I tried all sorts of different things, and could never sell anything, and it was the breakthrough to the *Saturday Evening Post* with the style, then, that I was working on. Which was little kids with great big heads saying things that were a little bit out of context. And it was just, I suppose, being commercial, that's all. Just trying to please the editors. [*Laughter*]

You also said, "The cartooning of the characters, with their large, round heads and tiny arms, came frequently to prohibit them from doing some of the more realistic things that a more normal style of cartooning would allow. Nevertheless, this was the direction I wanted to take. I believe it has led me to do some things that no one ever attempted in a comic strip."

Now, it seems to me that Peanuts' *"intellectual" status as a comic strip derives from its talkiness. The fact that there's so much conversation between the characters, so much philosophizing. Was that something that you were consciously aware of from the very beginning? Was that something you purposely wanted to do, or is that something that just evolved?*

I was aware of it to a certain extent. I remember discussing this when I first went to New York and signed the contract and I was introduced to the man who was the sales manager. His name was Harry Gilburt. Still lives in Florida. Very nice man, very knowledgeable in those days and considered one of the best sales managers in the business. And after I was introduced to him and we talked a little bit, he said, "Now, I would suggest that you don't try to make the strips and what you're doing too subtle." Being a young, wise-cracking kid, I said, "Well, if you're expecting another Nancy and Sluggo, you're not going to get it." [*Laughter*] I've often regretted saying that, because it was a kind of a smart-aleck thing to say. But I knew that I didn't want to draw Nancy and Sluggo. To me, there was nothing wrong with Ernie Bushmiller's work. He was wonderful. But that's not what I wanted to do. I knew that I wanted to go on what I would consider a little higher plane, but I didn't know how it was going to happen, or where, or anything like that. So, a lot of it just came natural. As I've said before, what the characters say and do is really me. These are the things that I say all the time.

I think that was really something of a new direction for comic strips, where the characters were almost talking as much to the audience as they were to themselves.

Well, I wanted to break away from the old kids' strips which were so prevalent in the earlier days, the "What are we going to do today?" sort of strips. Where the kids are just hanging around. Do you remember *Reg'lar Fellers*?

Yeah, yeah.

And there was also *Just Kids*. They were good features, but they were never very subtle. The kids were usually just bouncing around the neighborhood, jumping over fire hydrants while they were talking and doing that kind of thing. Sort of meaningless stuff. And I just knew that it was possible to go beyond that. But there were some other wonderful strips with little kids in them at the time. Of course, *Skippy* would be the best example.

And Percy Crosby was something of an influence, wasn't he?

Skippy by Percy Crosby, December 28, 1927.

Oh, yeah. Definitely. I didn't know enough about the business to realize what was happening, but I was appalled at his seemingly careless attitude sometimes. And I read later on that he would bat out a whole bunch of scripts in one day when he would get behind. He'd get involved in many other activities. I don't know about drinking, that's beyond me, but I would look at them when I was very young and wonder why he drew so carelessly and why he didn't even use a ruler to draw the panels. [*Laughs*] I didn't realize he was just trying to draw as many as he could.

Pogo started in '48, I believe.

Yeah.

And in a way, the two strips developed similarly, because Pogo *is also very talky with a rich cast of characters. Were you an admirer of that strip? Did you know Walt Kelly?*

I only met Walt Kelly twice. I introduced myself to him at one of the Reuben dinners, and we only said, "Hello," and that was about it. And I met him later at a meeting of cartoonists where we were doing something to raise money for war bonds or something like that. So, we never had a real conversation. But I certainly thought his work was wonderful. I used to buy every *Pogo* comic book that came out, and every reprint book and all of that. And I thought they were just great. Now, unfortunately, as the years went on, I found myself buying the *Pogo* books and then not being able to read them. They became boring. He got so political and so involved in things that they just weren't funny anymore.

But they were beautifully done.

How About a Doc?

I'd like to get back to your work. It occurred to me reading over all of your work that you have a lot in common, artistically, with Robert Crumb. Which is kind of an odd pairing, I'll admit, but I rather like the parallels for that very reason.

Really?

Yeah. You're both wrestling with similar demons: resentment from your youth, insecurity, injustices, rejection by the opposite sex. And you're doing it in very, very different ways. You went in diametrically opposite ways to deal with these issues. And I was wondering if you saw that connection or how you feel about Crumb's work, because in some ways you're so similar, and in other ways you're so radically different.

I think he's great. I'm appalled at the vulgarity of the so-called underground cartoonists. I only met Robert once; it was at a big convention downtown. He was just

WHAT IS THAT YOU'RE PLAYING, SCHROEDER?

THIS IS "WALTZ OF THE FLOWERS," LUCY...

IT'S FROM THE "NUTCRACKER SUITE"

"SWEET"! HE CALLED ME "SWEET"!! I'VE NEVER BEEN SO HAPPY IN ALL MY LIFE!

ABOVE January 27, 1953.
OPPOSITE December 4, 1963.
BELOW February 14, 1992.

coming out of the building, and we were going in and somebody said, "Oh, there's Robert Crumb." And I said, "Hi, Robert. I'm Charles Schulz. Glad to meet you." And he was just stunned. He said, "Oh, really?" just as if I would hate him or something. [*Laughs*] And I really thought it was laughable that he would think that I would hate him. That I must be some kind of a wishy-washy, goody-goody two-shoes person. I think his drawing is great—he does funny things.

But he also deals with sex very overtly.

Which is all right if it weren't so terribly vulgar. There was a young underground cartoonist, who came up to see me once here several years ago. And we sat and talked. And I said, "The trouble with you guys is that you think that you are so free in what you do, and we are inhibited." I said, "You couldn't do what I do." I said, "You guys, you all do the same thing. You all think you're free, but you all do the same jokes, the same vulgarities." And I said, "I defy you just to do what I do. You'll never be able to do it."

Because I'm not in the business to offend people.

But someone like Crumb doesn't do it to offend people. What he does certainly can offend people, I'm sure it does offend people—but you know, in an odd way, another parallel is that you don't care if you offend people using Scripture [Schulz laughs], whereas Crumb doesn't care if he offends people with his political or sexual expression.

No, I know.

So, in a way, you both are compelled to do what you have to do. Regardless of the consequences.

Yeah. I always wonder what made me like that. I think there is some kind of a weird connec-

HERE, SWEET BABBOO... I BROUGHT YOU A VALENTINE

I'M NOT YOUR SWEET BABBOO!

WELL, TAKE IT ANYWAY, YOU BLOCKHEAD!

I LOVE VALENTINE'S DAY... IT'S SO ROMANTIC..

tion there. I've never been able to figure it out. I've thought about it. You know that I have never sworn in my life. I never use vulgar phrases, and I don't know why. Now, as I get older, I find that I don't use vulgar phrases just because I'm trying to be more cultured or something. I like the niceties of language. My mother and dad were never crude, but my dad would say "damn" or "hell" or something now and then. But I never heard them tell dirty stories that way. I don't know. I went through the army, three years of the worst vulgarities imaginable. Although I think it's worse now. But I don't know whatever made me that way. Maybe there's some kind of a fatal flaw or something. I don't know what it is. [*Groth laughs*] But that's just the way I am.

Did it have to do with your upbringing in the Midwest?

It was just the way we lived.

One way or the other, though, you do have an upbringing, whether it's vigorously or dogmatically imposed or if it's simply part of your environment.

Yeah, but I was surrounded by it all the time…

But you never…

Never. Maybe I'm competitive, that's all. I wasn't going to be dragged down.

Well, you're very competitive, apparently.

Yeah. You have to be. That's why I'm competitive in drawing the comic strip. I want to make the playoffs. [*Laughter*]

The parallel between you and Crumb also brought to mind one other related question, which is about sex. He deals very directly with sexual impulse and his sexual impulses. Whereas you skirt sexuality per se *and*

deal with a much more romanticized or idealized version of love: Charlie Brown and the red-haired girl and his unrequited love for her, Peppermint Patty's interest in Charlie Brown is oblique and touching, Lucy's unrequited love for Schroeder, etc., but you don't deal directly with sexuality. Since the strip is one of the most personal ever done and sexuality is such an important part of one's life, I was wondering if you ever felt like you wanted to do that but couldn't because of the newspaper strip format and the restrictions of the newspaper audience.

Well, in the first place these are just little kids. That really puts a lid on it right there.

Did you ever feel constricted by that self-limitation?

Oh no. I never feel constricted at all. Not in the least. I can do anything that I think of.

Have you seen the Crumb documentary?

I saw the movie. That's all I know about Robert. I admire his drawing. I think he draws beautifully. Very creative and all that. But also, don't forget I raised five children. I also have 16 grandchildren, which separates us, doesn't it?

Well, I don't know. He has two children.

Does he?

Mm-hmm.

Well, how about a dog? [*Laughter*]

Right. I don't think he has a dog.

It's a difficult comparison. One that's valid, I suppose, from a journalistic state. I don't know. I'm getting too old to worry about those things.

You definitely don't feel comfortable expressing things like that.

No.

I wonder if that's generational, or if it's simply a different worldview irrespective of generational differences. Have you grown older gracefully or have you fought it?

No, no. I'm fighting it. [*Laughter*]

One thing I wanted to ask you is that I know your hand shakes.

It's been shaking for a long time.

Is that getting worse, is it getting more difficult to draw the strip?

It's just the same as always. It's leveled off now. I don't even think about it. But it bothers me sometimes, like if I'm going back over the top of Peppermint Patty's hair or something like that...

Politics

Now, this is something that I became more and more curious about as I immersed myself in your life—

[*Laughs*] It's a boring life.

No, no, I think that's a superficial view. One thing that fascinated me was that the shortest section of notes I have about you is on politics.

Oh, yeah.

You don't like politics in strips. I might have ferreted out a little bit of political content in the early Peanuts, *but you're very adamant about not putting political content into strips. And my impression, based on various things I've read, is that your bent is somewhat conservative.*

No. I'm very liberal.

[Surprised] Huh. [Schulz laughs] You were over-joyed to have dined with Ronald Reagan.

Well, so what? I mean, the man was governor. You get invited to have lunch with the governor, why not? [*Laughs*]

Well, Jules Feiffer may not have been quite so eager...

Well, Jules Feiffer... gosh. We don't want to talk about him. Feiffer and I wouldn't agree on anything.

My point is that a liberal might not be quite so eager to dine with Reagan.

Well, there's a difference between being a liberal and being kind. By being liberal I mean being kind. Generous. I don't want to brag about it, but you'd be astounded by the amount of things that Jeannie and I do. I don't know Jules. I heard him speak once. And I thought he gave a wonderful talk. I haven't seen him since.

July 8, 1968.

I mean, he's the kind of person who if Ronald Reagan invited him to dinner, he might be so opposed to Reagan's point of view that he would not do that.

But that's insulting. That's beyond politics, isn't it? One of my favorite stories is about Joanne Greenberg, who wrote *I Never Promised You a Rose Garden*. She said, "I was with my father, sitting on a park bench one day, and a man came walking up. My father said, 'Stand up.' I said, 'Stand up? Why should I stand up?' And he said, 'This is Senator So-and-So coming by.' So, he said, 'Good morning, Senator,' and he said, 'Good morning,' and walked on. Her father said that the position deserves respect. So, I think to use your own personal views to say to the President of the United States, "I'm not going to come," that's childish. Again, I don't want to get into that.

I would have given anything in the world to have met General Eisenhower. What an honor. What a tremendous feat he had commanding D-Day. The decisions he had to make were just unbelievable. And a lot of other people I'd like to meet just for that... Reagan was a very thoughtful person.

That's hard to believe. [Laughs]

No, extremely thoughtful. Very personable, and he would never forget you. Now just in the little bit of contact I had... Joyce and I had lunch with him and Nancy—I didn't arrange it, he didn't arrange it—some press secretary said, "They should have a *Peanuts* day in California or something." So, we went up there and had lunch with them.

Now, would you have done that with a public figure with whom you completely disagreed?

Like Barbara Boxer? [*Laughter*]

There you go.

I don't know, because she's never invited me. I suppose, just out of curiosity—well, I went down to see Clinton, and I've attended things for Senator Feinstein, and things like that.

But getting back to Reagan. Just to show what I'm talking about, several months later, after he was no longer governor, he and I and a few other people were honored as fathers of the year. We went down, and he was surrounded by some people. And I was led over there. And he looked down and he said, "Sparky, it's good to see you." He said, "Nancy. Come over here. Look who's here. Sparky's here." Now, how many politicians and governors are going to do that? He remembers.

I don't want to sound too cynical, but couldn't that just be the kind of professional schmoozing that politicians...

No, that's just the way he was. And he called me when I was in the hospital and had heart surgery.

So, you think it was genuine.

He's taken a terrible beating from the press and other people, just nastiness. [Jimmy] Carter was the same way. I was Easterseals Chairman. We went to Washington and had some friends that went with us, and they had to hang back as I went in to meet Carter. We had our picture taken with the little girl who was on the poster. And then we said thank you. He asked if there were any folks with me. And I said, "Oh, this is my wife. And her son. And some friends." And he said, "Well, I'd like to meet them." He went over and shook hands with them. Again, that was the sort of person he was. I don't think I've met any others. Shook hands with Clinton. I talked with Bush on the practice tee at the AT&T. But I'm out of that whole realm. Comic strip artists are not regarded as celebrities in that way. We don't get the Medal of Freedom and all of that sort of thing. They proposed it for me; I don't think we even came close. Last year, on the 100th anniversary of the comics, all the cartoonists wrote to Senator Feinstein to promote it.

But that's all right. I know my place. [*Laughs*] And it doesn't bother me.

What I meant by conservative or liberal was ideologically speaking. And it just seems like you're more on the conservative side ideologically. Of course, I could be completely wrong.

I want to ask you what you meant when you referred to that syndicate executive as "your kind." It seems to me that people of "his kind" run the corporations, run the government, and I'm curious as to whether you've become increasingly skeptical of that kind of arbitrary power.

Well, I'm out of it. I don't have any connection with it outside of some of the licensees. Mr. Hall, who runs Hallmark, seems to be a fine gentleman. Joyce Hall was a remarkable man. Other people like that. I've never met anybody, except the very first one when we signed up with Metropolitan [Life Insurance]. I don't know anybody with Metropolitan. I'm just out of all of that. I don't know any of the network people as far as television and that goes. By conservative, I think the only definition of a conservative that I would accept would be responsible living. I live a very conservative life. I don't drink, I don't smoke, I'm not mean to people. I built that arena, cost me a fortune. I think it costs me about $140,000 a month to keep it up. And I built this roller hockey rink for the neighborhood kids. I saw them playing out in the parking lot, and I thought, "They shouldn't have to play in the parking lot. They should have a nice rink to play on." But somebody said, "You want to put a fence around it?" Put a fence around it? It's supposed to be for the kids. Oh, well...

Lee Mendelson had a meeting with the CBS people a couple of months ago, because they're going to have to do a big show about my 50th anniversary, and he said he was astounded. He said the head of the meeting said, "Do you realize the scope of what this man has done? The things that he has touched? Literature, music, art, and all of these things. No comic strip has ever come close to touching all of this." He said, "We've got to do this. We've got to put these in the show somehow." And I hadn't even thought about it. But it's true. Everything from Vince Guaraldi's Linus and Lucy on down to Snoopy going to the moon.

And I love looking at the golf tournaments where Snoopy is on the big dirigible floating overhead. Look, it's Snoopy the World War I Flying Ace. So, that's what I mean when I say that it's difficult to label somebody liberal or conservative. I think I'm very liberal in my outlook on life and how I treat people, and all of that sort of thing.

I've always been Republican—at least up until a certain point—because my dad was. But you see, my dad was a Republican because he ran his own business. And of course, he grew up in that era where it was Calvin Coolidge and Hoover, until Roosevelt came along. But I think owning your own business will turn you into a Republican in a hurry. [*Laughter*] Because you have to start paying all the bills and doing all the things that are required of you.

How did your father feel about Roosevelt?

We never talked much about it, but he always voted against him. He voted for Hoover I'm sure, and I'm sure he voted Republican. Now, the odd thing was that my mother's brother was a radical Democrat. In Minnesota, they were called Farmer-Laborites. He worked for a creamery; it was a cooperative creamery. So, he was extremely for Roosevelt and an extreme Democrat. But my father would never get into arguments with anybody. They saw each other as families every Friday night, but I can remember them getting into a discussion about something only once. My dad just never got into discussions like that.

Were there discussions at home about what was going on in the world, politics?

Not really.

So, you developed your own attitudes and so forth by osmosis. By just picking things up.

I became fascinated by Wendell Willkie when I was young. I was downtown with my mother and I saw a little book about Wendell Willkie. And I read it, and then I used to hear him on the radio. I used to love to listen to him speak. I have his biography, and I read it every now and then. He was a remarkable man. He would have died in office, had he been elected.

Were you ever attracted to someone like Norman Thomas?

Oh, no.

That would have had no appeal to you.

No. Not at all. I think, well, communism has proven to be a disaster. And I think socialism, too, simply doesn't work. Not that anything ever really works. [*Laughs*] But there was a lady who ran for governor here a couple years ago. And Jeannie and I went to a reception for her. She was a liberal. We discussed the surtax. I said, "Who is going to put a level on my income? Who is going to do that? Who is going to support Canine Companions? We built that whole building over there, and we pay to keep it going so those people in wheelchairs can have dogs. Are you going to pay for that? Is the government going to pay for it? They're not going to pay for that." And I listed all of the things that Jean and I do. Just because it's the right thing to do. And I said, "If we don't do it, don't tell me you're going to do it. Because you're not going to do it. [*Laughs*] But you're going to take all my money, and the government is going to do it all." This is my only argument with Clinton's whole philosophy. He just thinks that government can do everything. I've never seen a president who wanted to run so many different things.

You're being hired by a newspaper editor, and he buys your strip because he wants to sell his newspaper. So, why should you double-cross him by putting in things that will aggravate him? That's not my job.

What do you think of Lynn Johnston's putting in the gay stories?

If she wants to, I don't care. But Lynn is a different person. See, Lynn is a problem-solver. Lynn loves to get involved in all of these things. But I think I have introduced and done things that nobody else ever did, too. Who else ever did something on Amblyopia and sleep disorders? I've done a lot of medical things. I've done more theological things than anybody. And done them deeper. You never see Charlie Brown praying, saying silly things.

[Joking] Your quotation of scripture could offend atheists.

Oh, who cares? We're going to offend somebody. But at least I know what I'm talking about there.

I always wanted to do something where Linus is going from house to house, passing out pamphlets about the Great Pumpkin, and he mentions in passing,

For Better or For Worse by Lynn Johnston, April 10, 1993.

"Who are the two guys out there with the white shirts and the neckties riding those bicycles?" Because I know most of the Mormons will laugh at it. They have a pretty good sense of humor. But some of the editors are afraid of things like that. My daughter is Mormon, so we laugh about those things all the time.

I love Amy. I think her beliefs and mine have brought us even closer together. We can discuss spiritual things and our love for the gospel songs and all of that. And I really appreciate what she has done with her life and the way she's raising her family. It's a marvel. So, who am I to criticize that?

Philosophy, Intellectuals, and Al Capp

I wanted to ask you if you could comment on a couple of things that other people have said about you and your strip. There are three people specifically—Al Capp, Umberto Eco, and Bill Mauldin. Al Capp said, "The Peanuts *characters are good, mean little bastards. Eager to hurt each other. That's why they are so delicious. They wound each other with the greatest enthusiasm. Anybody who sees theology in them is a devil-worshipper."* [Schulz laughs]

Of course, that was a long time ago. That came from the first *Time* magazine article, and I don't think he would say the same thing about them anymore. But I think he was right on target at the time. Of course, that was typical Al Capp talking. But I don't think that would be a fair description anymore.

For that very reason, he would probably not think they are so delicious now.

You know, I knew Al quite well at one point. Until we had a falling out, which was just a complete misunderstanding. But I liked him. I liked being around him. Because he was funny. But he and I never would have got along in the long run. We were just total opposites.

I was going to say, I'm surprised you got along because, in a way, he too was a mean little bastard. [Laughter]

And of course, I think real jealousy came in because I took over his number one spot at United Feature. And so, when he decided to leave, Larry Rutman at United Feature was just plain glad. He didn't miss him at all, because now he had me to fill his place.

Right, right. Well, you just agreed that he wouldn't have said the same thing about strip today. Could you tell me a little about how you think it's changed over the years? You said earlier that it's gotten less cruel.

Well, I've simply gotten older, that's all. And I don't say sarcastic things to people anymore. If I can help it. If I can catch myself. If I find myself making some kind of smart-aleck remark to somebody, now I kind of hold back and don't say things like that anymore. I just don't think it's a nice way to be. I think that's just the direction I've gone with the strip, too.

Well, I have to tell you that occasionally, and there was a recent example of this, you'll have a masterpiece of sarcasm in the strip. [Schulz laughs] *My favorite was about seven months ago, where Lucy walks up to Charlie Brown on the mound and asks him something like,*

"Would I fall off the planet if I stepped far enough back in left field?" And he said, "Well, the planet is actually round, just like a ball, but you wouldn't know that because you've never touched a ball. You've never caught a ball." It was a masterpiece of sarcasm to the effect that since she's never caught a ball she wouldn't know that a ball is round, like the planet. Which leads me to believe you are really capable of incredibly sharp sarcasm.

Oh, yeah. And I don't think it's a good quality to possess. I'm not proud of it. I've had a few incidents down through the years, when I was younger, and said things that I never should have said to people. I don't think it's a good trait to have. But it's good for creativity. That's why it's nice to have a comic strip where you can have an outlet for these feelings that you have.

But it also requires a wit, which you obviously have.

Yeah, but what he was saying is funny. It's not really mean, is it? [*Groth laughs*] He's not insulting her black hair, and saying, "Your hair looks stupid, and you've got a funny look on your face." Or "Why do you walk funny?" or something like that.

No, no. But he is insulting her ineptitude.

Well, she deserves it. [*Laughter*] Totally inept. But I love that relationship, because in other areas she's totally superior to him. And the same way with all the characters. I love the little relationship, which took a long time to develop, between Marcie and Peppermint Patty. They insult each other all the time, yet they still appreciate each other.

It appears in that relationship that it took a while for Marcie to screw up the courage not to be deferential. To give as good as she got. Was that pretty much how it happened?

No. Again, it just goes back to this search for ideas, Gary. You can't keep hitting the same note all the time. You have to try to advance. And so, one thing leads to another…

Another quote is from Umberto Eco. And I'm sure you read his essay about you.

Yeah.

It was actually written as an introduction to a Peanuts *book published in Italy and reprinted in one of his books in English. And he said, "These children affect us because in a certain sense they are monsters. They are the monstrous, infantile reductions of all the neuroses of a modern citizen of the industrial civilization." Now that's a pretty heady observation.* [*Schulz laughs*] *I was wondering what you thought of that.*

I had breakfast with Umberto in Paris. Jeannie was there, and some other friends. We hit it off real well. And we didn't waste any time with small talk. We got into theological discussions. When I'm with somebody like that, I don't want to waste time telling him all about myself and discussing where we live and all of that. I want to find out who they think Jesus really was. Did Jesus have a dog, and

August 7, 1996.

all that sort of thing. We had a good time, though it didn't last very long. But I'm sure that when I'm with Umberto Eco, I'm in over my head. [*Groth laughs*] He's too intellectual for me, and I don't understand the things that he wrote, but I like reading these things, and I'm very flattered that he should say things like that.

Do you think that he was correct in saying that your characters represented...

I don't know, because I don't understand it. [*Laughter*]

I see. OK. Finally, Bill Mauldin said about you, "He's a preacher at heart. All good cartoonists are jack-leg preachers, reading stories, drawing morals from them."

Mauldin's quite a guy.

Do you agree with that?

I used to do a lot of preaching. But I'm no good at it. I never was any good at it. And I would never do it again. I don't mind giving talks. I give talks, and I may do it again, down at Barnaby Conrad's writer's conference in Santa Barbara every year. And it's kind of fun. I like talking about cartooning, and I love questions and answers, just talking to people about writing and all of that. But I would never want to be a preacher. Because I don't have any axes to grind or beliefs that I want to convince people of. But Mauldin's right there. Cartooning is preaching. And I think we have the right to do some preaching. I hate shallow humor. I hate shallow religious humor, I hate shallow sports humor, I hate shallowness of any kind.

It's funny, because I know what Mauldin is talking about but, in a way, you're doing the exact opposite of preaching. You're raising questions that are unanswerable.

I suppose that's good.

Did you ever read *The Gospel According to Peanuts*?

Yeah.

You'd like him. Robert Short. Wonderful guy. We didn't even know each other when he wrote the book. We didn't meet until about a year after it came out. Of course, I haven't seen him for a long time, because I think he's in Arkansas now. He's a Presbyterian minister. He finally joined the ministry after all those years.

But he writes to me now and then, and sends me copies of his sermons. He loves preaching. But you'd like him. He's a very nice man.

Short once said, "Tolstoy believed love is what it was all about, that people are capable of this, that the spirit of love was inherent in people. Culture causes people to be mean and shortsighted. So, Tolstoy wanted to withdraw from culture, live very simply, work with his own hands." And he went on, "I think Sparky's religious orientation is typified by Tolstoy." Would you agree with that?

I don't know. It's beyond me! That's too deep for me. [*Laughs*]

I'm not going to accept that.

I think *War and Peace* is the greatest novel ever written. Tolstoy was a remarkable man. But he sure went through a lot of turmoil. And at one point, he felt that he had to give everything away, didn't he? And he also had what Scott Fitzgerald talked about once, "the dark side of the soul," didn't he? He had a terrible experience once on a trip, where he felt a darkness kind of overwhelm him. I think perhaps a lot of us have gone through that in different ways. And I don't even know if it can be explained. But I'm just astounded that he was able to write the way he did. It's a society that I don't understand at all. I can't comprehend the whole Russian way of living, and the way he lived, did everything that he did, and was still able to write this monumental book.

I had dinner with my heart surgeon. We had played in a golf tournament, and afterwards we were talking. We only see each other about once a year, but I had bypass surgery—gosh, I think it was back around 1980 or so. He was the one who did it—and here is the man who [saved my life.] And I said, "What do you think

June 27, 1993.

really are the important things in the world?" He loves music, and I said, "Do you think what you do is really the greatest thing in the world, to be a great surgeon?" He said that writing a great symphony or a piano concerto, that's the great thing. To be able to write something that's so great that thousands, millions of people enjoy year after year. That's the real accomplishment. [*Laughs*]

And I did a strip about that once where Charlie Brown was wondering out loud. He was sitting on a bench with Linus. [They were discussing] *War and Peace* or Beethoven's Ninth, or something like that. Then he gets up and strikes out. I think he sits down and say something like, "And I'll probably never write *War and Peace*, either."

I always think about things like that. What is of importance? I suppose the most important thing is just to do what you can do best. You have no other choice, do you? You have a certain amount of ability, and you do the best you can with your abilities.

You made reference to something you've quoted before. It was either by Tolstoy or Fitzgerald, and it must be a favorite quote of yours: "In the real dark night of the soul it is always three o'clock in the morning." And that's an incredibly harsh quotation, the sentiments of which fuel your strip because, in a way, it's always three o'clock in the morning in Peanuts.

Well, Napoleon said you didn't have two o'clock in the morning courage: I mean unprepared courage. A military man has to have that. The attack is planned all night long, and all of a sudden, it's dawn, and you think, "What have I done? I can't do this." The brave man has the courage of the early morning. And he does it anyway. I think we all have that bridge to walk and make the trip that we don't want to make, or to see somebody that we don't want to see. That takes the courage of the early morning.

Do you feel that you have that courage?

No. Oh, I don't think about it. I just do it because I got nothing else to do. [*Laughter*]

Speaking of the dark night of the soul, I wanted to ask you something about your philosophical disposition, if I can put it that way, and how it manifests itself in the strip. You've said a couple of things that I thought were incredibly demoralizing or nihilistic. [Schulz laughs] And of course, the strip is very melancholy in a way. You said, "It is

April 12, 1995.

a virtual miracle that we've existed over these millions of years against such deplorable odds. When everything is against us." And I was wondering if you could expand on what you meant by that.

Well, it is astounding that we have survived, isn't it? Just look at what's been going on over in Algeria these last couple of months. How these soldiers go into small villages and just murder everybody. Why? That's totally absurd to do that! How in the world can people become so monstrous?

With the kids in the strip, it's kind of a parody of the cruelty that exists among children, too. Because they are struggling to survive. How many were in your family?

I was an only child.

I was, too, so we didn't have to go through that. But as one child comes along in a family, and another, there's a struggle just to survive and to try to make your parents like you more than they like your sister or your brother or something like that. And then, of course, the struggle in the neighborhood when you grow up is a brutal one.

You started the strip in 1950 at a time when the kinds of familial difficulties you're talking about were not acknowledged. In fact, they were, I think, hidden or disguised.

Well, yeah. And I think I was the first one to bring them up.

Yes, yes. I mean, there was a lot of sociology from the '50s that tried to counter the widespread, post-War Eisenhower view of America, where everyone had a plot of land and a white picket fence in the suburbs and families were too busy consuming to have problems.

But pop culture is always slow to acknowledge these social realities. And what you actually came along and did at that time was say, "That's not entirely true. There's a lot of dysfunction and neuroses and problems under the veneer."

Oh, yeah. Well, I remember that we could never really go to a playground and have any fun. We could very seldom, unless we took a whole baseball team over to play another baseball team on a playground. Then, we could survive. But as far as just going to a playground to have fun, it didn't happen, because there were always other kids there that would ruin everything. And so most of our playing was done within maybe a block or two of where we lived. And there were some blocks that we never dared go to, because we knew that there were bigger and uglier kids that lived around there. Maybe a lot of it was our own imagination. But we just didn't do that sort of thing. We kept within our own little area. And that is one of the things I was talking about. Because I despise bullies, and I just hated them when I was a kid, and I still do. Now, I don't draw them much in the strip, because they're hard to draw and it's hard to get any humor out of it. If I was drawing a more serious strip, I think I would bring them in, but I've tried to touch on it a couple times, and it just doesn't work. I do want to do an animated show, and I know we're going to do it, eventually, about Charlie Brown challenging this kid who is stealing everybody else's marbles because he's a better player. And Charlie Brown ends up like Shane; he's the gunman who beats the kid.

Guns down Jack Palance, right. Well, this goes right back to what Eco said about the kids being infantile reductions of all the neuroses of a modern citizen of the industrial civilization. How conscious were you in the '50s that this was your point of view?

Oh, virtually not conscious at all. I think once I got married and we began to raise a family, that was our whole life. You know, we lived out there on Coffee Lane, and we had our life out there. We didn't pay much attention when people talk about the '50s and '60s and '70s, I frankly don't even know what they're talking about. We lived kind of an isolated life. And that's all there was to it.

Yet the social trends, the social zeitgeist, did effect you because you were aware of it if only on an unconscious or intuitive level.

I suppose if you look back, your life goes in different sections. My most influential section of life as a child was living within about three blocks of the barber shop, down around the corner on a quiet street. We used to play cops and robbers, and cowboys and Indians, and run around the neighborhood and go to the movies and all of that. But there were also unpleasant episodes. There were always some nasty kids around that would spoil things. But there were some good kids, too. And if everybody left us alone, we did have fun. But then later on, I moved away from there and became a teenager, and then my whole life was just reading comic books and drawing pictures and playing sports. I loved playing baseball, and touch football, and hockey, and that sort of thing. But again, there were always invariably little incidents where nasty kids would come around and spoil things. And I just hated that. Which is, I suppose, one of the reasons that I loved golf. Because you were out on the golf course yourself and your struggle was with you and the course. It was a great relief.

Do you ever reflect that the kind of society we've created actually encourages the kind of cruelty and predation in adults that you see in children?

Yeah, and I don't think it's something that can be avoided.

You don't?

I think it will always be with us. I do feel strongly, however, that parents should watch more carefully over what is happening to their children. And I think teachers should watch more carefully. Now, a perfect example of this was when one of my grandchildren who lives in Utah came home and was disturbed by school. He got so he was apprehensive about going to school each day. And my daughter Amy, his mother, asked him why. And he says, "Well, my fingers hurt. This so-and-so twists my fingers back. That hurts." So, she said, "I wasn't going to stand for that." So, she went right in and told the teacher, and I think his father told their father. "Your stupid kid [will] leave our kid alone, or I'm going to pound you myself." [*Laughter*] And that's what you have to watch. You can't just say, "Well, let it go. It'll be all right." It won't be all right. The bully kid will keep twisting your fingers back until someday he breaks one. And I think we have to watch out for that all of the time. I remember when my one daughter, who was in about the fourth grade, came home one day and said, "Out at recess, that stupid kid, Tom, comes around and pulls the girls' skirts up." And I said, "Well, has he done that to you?" And she says, "Well, not yet." And I said, "Well, if he does, kick him in the stomach." [*Groth laughs*] And so, the next day she came home, and she said, "I did what you told me to do." I said, "What was that?" She said, "He tried to pull my skirt up so I kicked him in the stomach." But Meredith was the kind you could tell that to. She wouldn't take anything from anybody. But one of the girls might not. I think we have to be very careful with our kids and watch over them and protect them.

Animation

You said one other thing I wanted to ask you about. And it struck me as possibly revealing and terribly despairing in a way. You were referring to the animator drawing the little red-haired girl in It's Your First Kiss, Charlie Brown, *but noting that you never drew her in the strip. And you said, "Somehow you always sell out for a cheap victory somewhere along the way."*

Yeah. It's almost inevitable when you do as many things as we have done, drawing the strip every day for all these years, and then doing all those animated shows... To try to attract attention, and keep them on the air, and keep getting good ratings, and keep people at the networks interested, you have to do things that will attract some kind of attention. And there's no doubt that that was just one of those stupid stories we never should have done. But it happens. It happens all the time.

What struck me about what you said was the sense of inevitability about selling out for a cheap victory. The sense that you feel that that's impossible to avoid.

The story I liked better was when Charlie Brown sees this girl sitting in the stands at a football game, when they used to have what they called "honey shots." They don't have them anymore. The camera used to wander around until they picked out some real beautiful woman sitting in the stands. They don't do that anymore. Which is kind of dumb that we should become so sensitive to things like that.

Anyway, Charlie Brown sees that girl and just falls immediately in love with her and [the story's about] how he goes to find her. That was a good little story.

But again, animation is different. It's almost impossible to talk about the characters and the feature and everything and talk about animation and the comic strip. Because it is different.

You write all of the animation material.

And then I'm at the mercy, however, of the animators. I am not like a playwright, who can write the play, and then have it tried out in New Haven, or rehearsed and rehearsed and rehearsed until they get it just right. Once I write it, it's gone. And I don't see it until it's finished. And I'm at the mercy of the animator, who's probably freelance and working at home and isn't as good an actor as I think he should be. So, he blows all my scenes, because he doesn't animate the characters the way I think they should be animated. It's very aggravating.

Is that how you feel about a lot of the animation?

Bill Melendez knows that. And he's got some good people, some of them can really draw. And Bill himself is a great cartoonist. But this doesn't mean an animator is always a good actor; and that's what an animator really is, he's an actor. Or he should be.

Licensing, Abortion, and School Prayer

There must have been a period where your success was just phenomenal. How did you handle that?

No, it all happened very gradually. One thing after another, just step by step by step. While all these things were happening, I was still drawing the strip. All the time.

How did you maintain your equilibrium amidst this success that must've been growing exponentially?

I just did it. That was all. But there did come a time when I called a halt to some things. I was drawing the dailies, the Sundays, the youth cartoons for the church thing. And I did some of the Hallmark cards, and then we sold the advertising rights to the Ford company. So, for seven years I had to help those guys write their ads and I had to draw all the Ford ads.

You didn't really like doing that, did you?

It was hard work, yeah. I could be doing a whole Sunday page, and now I have to waste it on one of these ads.

Why did you do that?

I thought it was just the thing to do. There was a lot of money involved, and the syndicate was strong for it. That's when we first started making what you'd call a lot of money. And finally, I just said, "No more." Also, I had done *Happiness Is a*

Warm Puppy. And I did five or six books for Determined. And I also illustrated three books. I did two books for Art Linkletter, *Kids Say the Darndest Things* and *Letters to President Johnson*, which was easy to do.

What's Letters to President Johnson?

They took kids' letters, and then I illustrated them with funny drawings. It was easy to do. But I didn't want to do any more. I said, "I don't want to be a book illustrator. I'm a cartoonist. I have my own work to do." I just said, "No more." [*Laughs*] In the meantime, I was raising five kids.

It sounds like as soon as you felt you could say no, you said no.

Yeah.

Can I ask you why you license the characters to corporations like Metropolitan Life Insurance? You obviously don't have to.

Well, but they pay a lot of money.

But you don't need a lot of money. I mean, you already have a lot of money. Right?

How would you like to keep this place going [*gesturing at his ice skating rink*] at $140,000 a month? [*Laughs*]

But realistically, you make enough money to support this without licensing your characters to Metropolitan Life Insurance, don't you?

Yeah, but I couldn't do all the things that we do. If you turn that off, I'll recount some of that. [*The tape recorder is turned off and Schulz recounts some of his philanthropic work.*]

In the course of my research, I came across what I thought was an interesting wrinkle regarding the question of licensing, which involves a complicated question about that.

LEFT October 20, 1963.
BELOW August 9, 1976.

You did two strips in the '70s that struck a real nerve politically. One of them was a strip where Linus asks Lucy, "What would happen if there were a beautiful and highly intelligent child up in heaven waiting to be born [Schulz laughs] and his parents decided that the two children they already had were enough?" And then Lucy replies, "Your ignorance of theology and medicine is appalling." And that created something of a controversy over whether that was implicitly about abortion. You got letters from both pro- and anti-abortion advocates assuming you were on both their sides. Then another strip you did was one where Sally whispers to Charlie Brown, "We prayed in school today."

Yeah.

And you got a lot of letters from people believing that you were either pro- or anti-prayer in school.

That one disturbed Larry Rutman of the syndicate very much. See, it disturbed him when both sides wanted to reprint the strip to promote their beliefs, so we talked about it, and he decided that we wouldn't let anybody reprint them. Now the other one, on abortion, it never even occurred to me. I don't know what I was thinking about, but there is a thought among some brands of theology that souls are waiting up in heaven to be born. How in the world anybody comes up with that is beyond me, and how you can be so sure of that is also beyond me. I always like to go back to Snoopy's theological writings, which he called, "Has It Ever Occurred to You That You Might Be Wrong." And that's the way I feel. These things fascinate me, and I like to talk about them with other people and hear what they think. But I'm always a little bit leery of people who are sure that they're right about things that nobody's ever been able to prove and never will be able to prove.

You said that Larry Rutman decided not to let either side print the strips. Did he make that decision, or did you? Who made that decision?

I used to do whatever Larry wanted, generally. Larry was a decent person. He and I got into, oh, a couple of discussions about things. The worst was over Franklin.

The black character?

Yeah, when he was first introduced. Larry didn't mind the fact that Franklin was in it, but he was disturbed about the strip where Charlie Brown said, "Come on over to my house someday, and we'll play again." He wanted to make some changes. And we talked about it and talked about it. And finally, I went back to my 1950 smart-aleck mode, and said,

"Well, Larry, let's put it this way. Either you print the strips exactly as I draw them, or I quit." And that ended the discussion.

But Larry and I were very close. He was a good man. He was like an uncle to me.

His objection to that strip you cited sounds racist. Do you know the basis of his objection?

The syndicate at that time were—and maybe they still are, I don't know, maybe syndicates rightfully are—terrified of [newspaper] editors. They never wanted to do anything that would offend an editor. Although Larry would stand up against some of them. And he told me a few stories about some editors that he just stood up against. And wouldn't let himself be pushed around, either. But it's a hard business. Salesmen are out there and they're driving around in their Dodges trying to sell these features. And I always felt sorry for the syndicate salesman who had to be out there, trying to sell a feature, and the cartoonist is doing something stupid. And he doesn't realize that if it wasn't for the salesman, he wouldn't even exist.

Do you think he was afraid that it would cause problems, say, in the South?

Oh, sure. There's no doubt about it. In fact, I did get one letter from one Southern editor who said something like, "I don't mind you having a black character, but please don't show them in school together." Because I had shown Franklin sitting in front of Peppermint Patty.

Good God.

But I didn't even answer him.

Well now, this seems to be an instance where you really took a stand and said in effect that you didn't care if it offended people, you thought it was the right thing to do.

Yeah, yeah. I've done that now and then. [*Laughter*]

I don't mean to imply you didn't.

Let me get back to my question about licensing. The strip where Sally whispered to Charlie Brown, "We prayed in school today" stirred up a little controversy.

I don't believe in school prayer.

You don't?

No, I think it's total nonsense.

You said that both sides wanted to use that strip in their own political campaigns, and you said the simplest solution was to deny everyone the right to reprint the strip. And you just told me you actually don't believe in school prayer. Now, my question is basically this: You would allow for Peanuts *characters to sell cars or front an insurance company, but you wouldn't allow them to be used to present a serious political point of view that you believe in. [Schulz laughs] And I was wondering why you would allow them to do one and not the other.*

Well, I think one is more personal than the other.

But shouldn't that be why you should allow the one and not the other?

To me, the school prayer thing is more personal. I feel very strongly about that. Now, the licensing thing has always been around. Percy Crosby did all sorts of licensing. *Buster Brown* was licensed like mad. It's always been just traditional. Al Capp did a lot of licensing with *Li'l Abner*. It comes upon you so slowly, you're not even realizing that it's happening. And also, you're young, you have a family to raise, you don't know how long this is going to last. Larry Rutman was very anxious to try and promote something that would guarantee me some kind of a reasonable income for the rest of my life. The first licensing we did almost came along by accident. I was in New York one day, and he said some chocolate company wanted me to draw a special strip with some kids drinking their chocolate. And they didn't want the *Peanuts* characters, but just some other little kids. So, I did it. And that was our first licensing. And then the

Eastman-Kodak company came, and they wanted me to do a special little booklet showing the characters using the new Brownie camera. Which I did. Didn't make a lot of money, and it was hard work, but these just came along little by little by little. And then one day, some company wanted to make these little rubber dolls of the characters. Well, what was wrong with that? Those were cute. And then Bill Watterson came along later with his stand against licensing, which is really ridiculous. But I don't know Bill, and I'm sure his life is different from mine. And he didn't have five kids to support and a lot of other things like that. It's always risky to take a stand on some things like that.

Disregarding the issues involved in licensing per se, *it seems to me that the very reason you would let the* Peanuts *characters be used in a political campaign is because you personally believe in the morality of the proposition in a way you can't believe in the Ford Motor Company.*

Yeah, I suppose.

And yet you didn't. So, I was wondering why…

You know, Gary, I don't even remember. That was so long ago. I knew it was an issue at the time. And I just thought that this was kind of a comment on it, that's all. It wasn't even that funny, as far as I was concerned.

But I did write a letter condemning promoting school prayer to the church publication I was very active in. It was called "Vital Christianity," published in Anderson, Indiana. And there were people writing in saying how important it was to have school prayer. I wrote a letter that was published in their letters to the editor saying how ridiculous I thought the whole thing was.

Does that belief stem from a belief in the separation of church and state?

I just believe that it comes from an absurd use, a ridiculous use, of prayer. [*Laughs*] This runs us off into all sort of thoughts, Gary.

Prayer should be a private act rather than a group activity?

And all of that business. And who is the teacher there that is going to have them pray? And is the teacher going to be Catholic or Mormon or Episcopalian or what? It just causes all sorts of problems. And what are the kids praying about anyway? What are you doing it for? The whole thing just opens up all sorts of elements of discussion.

I think it's crazy.

That seems like a very sensible attitude. The idea that prayer should be turned into the equivalent of an organized sport is odious.

I do feel strongly about one other thing, though. And I think it's too late for me. But I think kids could be taught right from the very start that when the teacher comes into the room in the morning they should all stand. And I think the teacher should be referred to as whatever their name is. And I see nothing wrong with pledging allegiance to the flag and whatever it is they want to do. I think that kids don't mind being polite, if they're taught that's the thing to do. And I think that they wouldn't mind. And this business of teenagers going to school with jeans and a white t-shirt is ridiculous. There are a lot of things that could be taught at a very early age, and kids wouldn't even mind it, as long as they were taught that this is the proper way to conduct yourself.

I remember that when I first went into the army, calling officers "Sir" was so hard to learn to do. And saluting. Some people just thought saluting was so demeaning. But as you learn to be a good soldier, saluting is almost fun. It's a matter of dignity. "Good morning, Colonel." You're saluting the office, that's all, nothing wrong with that. We need more dignity.

Yes. That would be a good title for the interview.

Yeah. [*Laughs*]

Licensing has become such a ubiquitous part of our culture... I wanted to ask you if you didn't think that the public perception of your work and your strip could be transformed in the public consciousness as a result of the saturated level of licensing and merchandising that Peanuts *achieved.*

No. I've already proved that to be wrong. This is what people were telling me 20 years ago, and I've proved that to be wrong. The strip is more popular than it's ever been. I remember back in about 1968, Al Capp said, "Well, it's just about run its course, you know. Little kids talking like adults. It's just about run its course." Well, since then, we've added about 2,000 papers to our list. Al Capp was pretty jealous of me. [*Laughter*] But I always got along well with him. He was funny.

Didn't you guys have a bit of set-to over his parody?

Oh, yeah. That was so stupid. He just didn't understand. That's all. It was just one of those misunderstandings. Which is unfortunate, because I always liked him. I didn't know him that well. But when I was around him, we always got along well. All of that. But he had things to be bitter about, anyway.

You're opposed to injecting politics in the strip, but have you ever thought about the political dimension of licensing? By allowing the Peanuts *characters to promote Ford, for example, in a way you're promoting private vehicle ownership over and against public transportation, which in turn harms the environment.*

But those things happen so gradually! Larry Rutman [the president of United Feature], whom I got so close to, treated me really like a father. He had no vision, as none of them did, that this was going to last this long, and the scope of it. This had never happened to them before. The biggest thing that they had ever had was *Li'l Abner* and *Nancy*, but it never compared to this. What he wanted was to establish something for me that would last the rest of my life. He didn't want it to drift out, and then I'd be stuck when I was 45 or 50 or something. So, that's one of the reasons he took on the Ford thing. He thought it was a good, lasting arrangement, and it lasted for seven years. He was always looking for what he called an annuity, something that would last the rest of my life. But it's hard to go back and realize how slowly all of this developed. One step at a time. Some things fell off, and some other things worked. And it was not like *Star Wars*, an overnight success or something like that. And you know, you look at other people. Bill Cosby does commercials. He sells things. Look at Tiger Woods! [*Laughs*]

Is he doing it?

Tiger Woods is the most phenomenal thing in the history of licensing. Nothing in the world has ever compared to Tiger Woods. But if he doesn't win some golf tournaments, he's in trouble. [*Laughter*] And the fact is that I watched over it all very carefully. I always had control. There were a lot of things we turned down. I get to see everything. Make sure that it's all done properly.

But then, on the other hand, we have things that the others have never been able to do. Ellen Zwilich, the most famous woman composer in the world, Pulitzer Prize winner, concertos, symphonies, everything. She wrote a *Peanuts* piano concerto last year, and it was premiered in Carnegie Hall. What's wrong with that? There you are, see? That's wonderful to think that my characters can be part of a classical piano concerto. That's unbelievable. And who went to the moon? Snoopy went to the moon! [*Laughs*]

Now, also, we must never forget that while all this is going on, who's drawing the strip? Who has thought of 16 or 17,000 ideas and has drawn all of them himself? I've been faithful to my first client. Which is the newspaper editor.

Fellini, Andy Griffith, Isabelle Adjani...

Something you just said reminded me of an observation you once made about creative inspiration: "I can almost guarantee it, if I attend a symphony concert and see a violinist perform as a soloist in a concerto. Or if I merely watch a great conductor, my mind will begin to churn up all sorts of ideas that will have no relationship to watching a violinist or a conductor. There will be an inspiration there."

I suppose it's the activity. Almost anything that I do will provide me with a cartoon idea. Sometimes directly applicable to what we're doing: When we're playing golf, or listening to the symphony, I'll think of something. But sometimes, just the activity of what you're doing gets your mind going and kind of wakes you up and you think of things.

I like that, because there's such a subtle connection between a piece of beautiful music and the inspiration for a medium quite distant from it. I know that you used to listen to country music.

Not anymore. I just don't know where to find it anymore. Of course, I never listen to the radio anyway.

You said that you don't listen to music anymore. You can't enjoy music anymore?

There is no more music. [*Laughs*]

But even if you don't like what's being done now, there's a wealth of old music.

But I never listen to the radio. I have two stations on my car radio. One is PBS, the public radio, the other is a local classical station which most of the time I turn off because they don't play enough Brahms. I never listen to the radio at home.

July 31, 1965.

You can buy Brahms on CD.

Yeah, I bought 'em all. [*Laughs*]

Do you derive pleasure from listening to music now? Because I got the impression you didn't.

For a long while after my separation and my missing of the kids for a little bit, it was so depressing that I just didn't listen to any. It would make me sad.

Right now, you'll be stunned to discover that the tape I've been listening to the last three days is Andy Griffith singing gospel songs. [*Laughs*]

My God!

I like gospel songs.

Is it good?

Sure. I don't think he's as good as Ernie Ford. I knew Ernie Ford, but he died. Ernie Ford had a wonderful, rich voice. He used to sing those gospel songs so beautifully. And Sandi Patty was here once. We had lunch. I like her a little bit. None of it means much anymore.

Why do you think that is?

I don't know. I keep saying, "I'm getting old." And you don't believe it. But that has a lot to do with it. Things change. Your friends change, and everything else. I like Jill, who you just met. Jill is a delight.

Your daughter.

Yeah. She was with the Ice Follies. She's a rollerblade expert. She and her husband have their production company and they produce rollerblade shows. She's really good and she's fun. We have a lot of fun around her, because she's very witty. But she can't draw. None of my kids can draw! [*Laughter*]

Is that right? That's pretty funny.

But they all like to laugh, and they're all quite witty in their own ways. Jill is very funny. I always enjoy being around her.

Well, it sounded like you had a really good family life.

Yeah, yeah. I really did. That's sad, too. To think you're getting old. You could die any day. That's very depressing.

That's true. That's true.

I was interested in the authors I heard you read. I was surprised you liked Flannery O'Connor and Carson McCullers.

They were great.

They are great. But they also deal in grotesques.

To a certain extent. But not like some of the really grotesque writers.

I can't imagine you're a big Bukowski fan.

Who?

Charles Bukowski.

I don't know him at all.

Who are some of your other favorite authors?

Well, let's see. What have I read lately? I'm just finishing John Grisham's first novel, *A Time to Kill*. But as soon I finish it, I want to read *Underworld*.

By Don DeLillo.

Yeah. I'm going to read that.

Really?

Oh, yeah.

You like Don DeLillo?

No, I've never read much of anything of his.

Underworld *looks great.*

This thing has been getting rave reviews. Monte and I were talking about it the other day.

I'd be very curious to know what you think of it. Because he's not the kind of author I'd expect you to gravitate toward.

Who knows? There's a couple of women authors from England that I like. Margaret Drabble. She's got a new one coming out. And, of course, crime novels. Everyone likes Elmore Leonard. I've met him a few times. Oh, and I like everything Anne Tyler writes. I call her on the phone to tell her, but she never says anything. I don't think I'll call her anymore. [*Laughter*] I guess she doesn't like to talk to people on the phone. Like Fred Couples, the golfer, who says he never answers the phone because it might be somebody who wants to talk to him. [*Laughter*]

I know a professor of English literature from South Carolina, Matthew Bruccoli. He's an expert on Scott Fitzgerald. He sends me a lot of things. I mention Fitzgerald in the strip every now and then.

I assume you like Fitzgerald a lot.

Yes.

We did a *Great Gatsby* number here on ice. We do some things in our Christmas ice show that nobody else ever does. It was a wonder.

My impression is that you read a lot of dead authors.

Not necessarily. I try to keep up on everybody.

In addition, do you also track down the Classics?

Yeah. Oh, yeah.

So, you're really very self-taught.

I did a term paper on Katherine Anne Porter. I did one on *Pale Horse, Pale Rider*. I really enjoyed that. That's the only college course I ever went to. I took a course in the novel, and I got an "A" in it. So, I've never gone back. I don't want to ruin my grade average. [*Laughter*]

Right, right. Nowhere to go but down.

It's kind of amazing that a man in your position would do that. You did that about 10 years ago?

At least. The older I get, the more self-conscious I get about my lack of real education. But like I said before, I have a host of friends around town here who are all college graduates, and they don't know half as much as I do.

Do you find that lamentable?

Yeah, it is. Terrible.

I feel like a fish out of water a lot of times.

Sure.

I'll talk to my insurance adjuster or a doctor and discover they can't talk about anything but jet skiing or something.

I know. It's terrible. [*Laughs*]

It's hard to have a literate conversation.

Yeah, I know. You'd like my son Monte. Monte's an expert on a lot of things. Once he gets hooked on something, he becomes an authority.

LEFT December 29, 1976.
RIGHT May 22, 1980.

Now how old is he?

He just turned 45 this year. It's hard to believe he plays senior hockey now.

I can't imagine my son at 45.

I know.

I'd have to imagine me at 85. [Schulz laughs]

Well, I hope you make it.

I do, too.

I know you watch foreign films as well as domestic ones. Do you have any favorite foreign film directors?

I don't pay any attention to that.

People like Fellini…

I knew Fellini.

Did you?

I have a cartoon upstairs over in the other building that he drew for me.

Is that right?

Yeah.

Tell me how you met Fellini.

Let me see. I was going to Rome to be given a medal by the Rome government and have a one-man show. And the lady who was in charge of it invited lots of people. And she invited Fellini, because she said, "I heard that Fellini likes your work and has always liked cartooning." He couldn't make it to the opening, but he did come to the hotel. And we sat in the lobby one afternoon and had tea and talked. I found it difficult to talk with him, though. Here's this great man, and I just didn't know what to say to him, and we had a little language barrier. But I asked him about Charlie Chaplin and Orson Welles, and he only met them briefly, and then I had drawn a cartoon to give to him. He seemed pleased, and I said, "Would you draw something for me." He said, "Oh, no, no." He says, "I am not in your class," and all of that. But, "I will think about it." The next day, we had gone out to play golf, and he came into the hotel again. Jeannie met him and had tea with him, and he brought me this cartoon that he had drawn of himself and Snoopy, so it's a real collector's item. He died about a year later. But at least we can say we met him.

So, that was a few years ago.

Yeah. Not too long ago. A few years ago.

Do you like his films?

Oh, sure.

I saw one film I loved about a sculptor whose love for art finally destroyed her…

Do you mean Camille Claudel?

Yeah. That was a good film. I think the best movie I have ever seen about the creative process. And of course, the girl that did it...

Isabelle Adjani.

She's my favorite.

I think she is one of the most stunning women in the history of film.

She really is. I saw her in another one where she played the violin. Which was a good one. Anyway, we try almost all of those. This Japanese film that's in town now is a real gem.
    Do you watch *Masterpiece Theater* at all?

No, I don't.

They have something on there now which ended last year called *To Play the King*, which was one of the best things I've seen anyplace, anywhere. It was three separate showings. The first one was three episodes, and then the other one is three. And they brought it back, and then they brought three more. And it is marvelous... One of my girls gave me a set for a present. I never look at videos, but this has been rerun a few times on different PBS stations we have. And I always watch it. Because it's so wonderful. *To Play the King.*

400 Million Books

Lynn Johnston wrote an introduction to one of your books, 45 Years, *and she related an anecdote. She wrote, "Last Christmas, Sparky and I wandered into a bookstore to buy a gift for his daughter. Only one of his books was on the shelf in the humor section. 'My books aren't number one anymore,' he told me, 'its hard to step aside.'"*
    That struck me as being a very melancholy moment.

It was.

I was wondering how you...

I made a lot of money for a lot of bookstores. You know how many books I've sold?

I can't even conceive of how many books you've sold.

I used to hear 300 million? Lately, I've heard 400 million books. And yet, we are still treated so shabbily. We have a new book program going now, but there's no market for cartoon collections anymore. No matter whose collection it is. What's appalling is to go to the airport when you're going to fly to New York, and you go into the book store, and there are no cartoon books anymore. There used to be all the Fawcett reprints, you had *Tumbleweeds*, and some of the ones that you normally didn't see. And they're gone. Cartoon books are just regarded as nothing.
    Except, of course, for Gary Larson and Bill Watterson. They were the only ones that sold. I went into one bookstore once up in the northern part of the state. And I said, "Do you have any *Peanuts* books?" "Oh, no," she said, "we just don't have much call for them." I said, "Do you have any call for *War and Peace*?" [*Laughter*] Why couldn't they order 30 copies and put them up in the front of the store? They'd sell. Nobody's going to come in and say, "Do you have any

Peanuts books?" So that's what I was talking about there. We made a real revival last year, but that's a long story.

A cartoonist by the name of Seth, who's a big admirer of your work, wanted me to ask you a question. He wrote, "Peanuts may well be the last great strip of the twentieth century. Does this idea please you or sadden you?"

Well, if it's true, I'm glad that I was the last one. [*Laughs*] But I doubt that it's true. Somebody is going to come along… I suppose Bill Watterson could have been it, if he hadn't quit. He certainly rose to the top in a hurry. He deserved it. And then he quit. So, I don't know who will come along these days.

How did you feel about his terminating the strip?

Didn't bother me. Because I never met him. I think that the guy who is really good these days is Patrick McDonnell. *Mutts.* He's great. We like each other. We're both followers of *Krazy Kat.* I think what we do is very, very similar to each other. A lot of times, we do things very, very similar. We draw differently. But he draws so funny. I think he's the best thing around these days.

Mutts by Patrick McDonnell, January 19, 1998.

This
Minor Art Form
Has Certain Truths

Rick Marschall and Gary Groth, 1987

This interview with Charles Schulz was conducted in late 1987 in Schulz's studio in Santa Rosa, California. It originally appeared in *Nemo: The Classic Comics Library*, a magazine devoted to newspaper strips, cartooning, and popular illustration, in January, 1992.

Growing Up

RICK MARSCHALL: *I'd like to ask about your background. I know you grew up in St. Paul. Your name is Schulz. Isn't that German? Do you have any ethnic flavor in your background, or has your family been here for many generations?*

CHARLES M. SCHULZ: My dad was born in Germany, but he was the only one in the family who was. Apparently, his parents went over on a year's vacation or something back to Germany, where he was born, but his brothers and sisters were all born in this country. My mother was one of nine children, and I always regarded myself really as being Norwegian and not German. I think I was a little bit ashamed of being German, due to World War I, and always played that down. I never think about nationalities, and I know my own children don't think of nationalities: If you were to ask them what nationality they are, I think they are probably the first generation who would now say American.

My dad was a barber. I always admired him for the fact that both he and my mother had only third grade educations and, from what I remembered hearing in conversations, he worked pitching hay in Nebraska one summer to earn enough money to go to barber school, got himself a couple of jobs, and eventually bought his own barber shop. And I think he at one time owned two barber shops and a filling station, but that was either when I was not born or very small, so I don't know much about that. I was raised during the Depression struggle, which didn't affect me personally, because I don't think little kids are into what's going on. If you have pancakes for dinner, you think that's wonderful because you like pancakes. You don't realize that you're probably having them because your parents can't afford anything more.

But my dad ran a three-chair barbershop...

Ran it through the Depression?

Right through the Depression. I know at one point he was seven months behind on his rent, but he told me years later it didn't matter because the big building where his barber shop was had so many empty spaces in it that the landlord didn't really care, as long as he kept up as much as he could on the rent. I always admired him for being a self-employed person who loved his work. I remember his telling me several times that he loved to get up in the morning and go to work, and I think he was as totally at home in the barber shop as I am off doodling in my studio. Years later, I began to realize that a lot of this being at home in your place of work is not necessarily because you love it so much, but because you're secure there, and he probably had the same travel fears that I have. But he was incapable of expressing them and I knew about it, and I never had a chance to talk about these things with him. I don't know how much my dad made, but I never felt that

I wanted anything. I had a baseball glove and a bicycle, for which my dad paid $24 and paid for it at the rate of four dollars a week at Western Auto. And we had a car. We never had a new car, but we had a car.

Did you have friends whose families suffered through the Depression?

We never knew. You're just little kids and you're playing cops and robbers and cowboys and Indians and you organize your baseball games. There was no little league at that time, so all our baseball games were between neighborhood teams. We would make up our own teams and challenge another neighborhood. We literally did lose a game once 40 to zero, which is where I got the idea for Charlie Brown's string of losses.

   The highlight of our lives was, of course, Saturday afternoons, going to the local theater. We would buy a box of popcorn for a nickel from a popcorn shop a few stores down from the theatre, and then we'd go to the afternoon matinee. My favorite movie, I still remember, was *Lost Patrol* with Victor McLaglen. I loved those desert movies, which is why I like drawing Snoopy as the foreign legionnaire. We never went downtown to a movie at a first run theater. I think first run theaters were about 35¢. If we went downtown on Sunday night to a movie, it was always to a double feature where the theater only charged 15¢ per person.

Was St. Paul in the '20s and '30s anything like Garrison Keillor or Jean Shepherd's stories about growing up in a Midwestern town?

I don't know Shepherd and I've only heard four of the Keillor tapes, but that was different. He's talking about small towns. St. Paul is not a small town. I always thought of myself as growing up, really, in the city. So, I always regarded myself as a city boy. I grew up on the sidewalks, not in the country.

You were never tempted to make Peanuts *a city strip?*

I don't know where the *Peanuts* kids live. I think that, originally, I thought of them as living in these little veterans' developments, where Joyce and I first lived when we got married out in Colorado Springs. Now, I don't think about it at all. My strip has become so abstract and such a fantasy that I think it would be a mistake to point out a place for them to live.

Your backgrounds are pretty sparse, too. You've never committed yourself with tract homes or anything.

No, I've never been able to reconcile just how those backgrounds should be drawn, or even the interiors. I admire people who can do that well. I'm never quite sure how it should be done. I fight it all the time.

Segar used to do that little roof just hanging a little bit over the horizon—every horizon. Speaking of Segar, I would like to draw you out a little bit on the strips you grew up with, the special favorites of yours.

Well, *Popeye*, of course. I could draw a great Popeye when I was a kid. And I could draw Mickey Mouse. I could draw the three little pigs and, strangely enough, I used to like the black panthers that Lyman Young drew in *Tim Tyler's Luck*. I was thinking about it today: When I was about 11—maybe 12, I'm not sure—I didn't really realize the value of drawing. I remember one night visiting some relatives who lived down in Stillwater, Minnesota, or Hudson, Wisconsin. Our parents were talking and the boy, who was a couple of years older than I, showed me his loose-leaf binder. He had drawn some cowboys on the front of it and he was proud of them and I looked at them and thought, "That's kind of neat." And all of a sudden it occurred to me, I could do that. Why hadn't I ever thought of drawing something on the cover of a loose-leaf binder? I started to do that and, of course, when the other kids in my class saw me draw these things, then I had to draw them for everybody. It was a lot like autographing these days; it drove me crazy. So, I didn't really know the joy at the time of drawing, or what you really could do with it.

And I remember, when I was in the 10th grade, in high school, one of the other guys in class—who was a much better student than I—had illustrated the essay that we were supposed to write. He had done some watercolors and the teacher posted them around the room. And somehow she found out that I could draw, and she said, "Why didn't you do that, Charles?" The reason I didn't do it was because I didn't think it was fair. I really thought that maybe me and a couple of the others were the only ones in the class who could draw and it wouldn't be fair to do something like that. And I was stunned that this teacher gave me a mild dressing

down for not doing it. So, it took me a long time to realize the value of drawing.

I'm always surprised at how few people can draw. Down through the years, there were never more than two or three people in any of my classes that could draw fairly well. And in my three years in the army, I bet I never saw one person in any of the companies or platoons I was in that could draw better than I could—and I've never considered myself that good. There aren't very many people who can draw. I don't think you can learn how to draw. I think you can be given a few tips. Thinking about comic strips, you can learn a few things that can make your strip look better and give it a better appearance and all that, but I don't think you can learn how to draw, just like I don't think you can learn how to sing. Either you have a voice, or you don't have a voice. It's not learning how to play tennis or golf or anything like that.

Did you ever use your talent for drawing as some sort of power over your fellow students?

No. Never.

I used to love to do caricatures of the kids who'd pick on me. They would walk into the classroom and they would see, anonymously of course, a caricature I'd done of them on the board. I thought it was a great power over them.

I never really liked caricatures, and I still don't to this day. I never did caricatures. If somebody has a big nose, I'm sure that they regret the fact they have a big nose and who am I to point it out in gross caricature? So, I don't do it. But, knowing how to draw has brought its moments of attention. I worked once at Northwest Printing and Binding as a delivery boy and office boy, and one day I drew a cartoon of the man who worked the big cutting machine and how proud he was when he got a new board to stand on. I was inspired, of course, by J. R. Williams and that down home type of humor. And I brought it down and showed it to him and, oh, he was so pleased with it and all the people that worked with him in the place came and looked at it. And, for the next hour, I got lots of attention and that made me feel good. It did demonstrate a little bit of this kind of power that perhaps you were talking about.

Popeye by E.C. Segar, November 9, 1932.

LEFT
Buck Rogers
by Dick Calkins, 1932.

OPPOSITE TOP
Terry and the Pirates
by Milton Caniff,
December 13, 1940.

OPPOSITE BOTTOM
S'Matter Pop?
by Charles M.
Payne, 1911.

Early Cartooning Influences

You mentioned Popeye *and* Tim Tyler's Luck *and I know you've written about being a fan of Roy Crane's. Were you drawn as a kid to the continuity strips?*

I read them all. I liked every comic strip. *Skippy*, of course, was fantastic. Although I couldn't understand why Percy Crosby was so careless in his later years. He didn't even take the time to rule out the panels that were on the strip. That baffled me. There were a lot of things that baffled me when I was smaller which I didn't understand. I loved *Buck Rogers*. That was one of my favorite strips. Years later, I read one of the reprint books and discovered how terrible it really was. It wasn't a good strip at all. But it was ahead of its time and that puts some value into it, being ahead of your time.

Later on, as I grew older, in my last year of high school in the correspondence school, I became acquainted with some of the other great cartoonists. If that course did nothing else, it taught me to value good drawing in comics and good pen work. I thought Clare Briggs was wonderful and, as far as writing, I always thought *The Bungle Family* was a great strip. A couple of months ago, I spoke at a meeting or gathering here in Berkeley of some people who wanted to become syndicated and I opened my little speech by saying, "How many people have ever heard of Charles Payne? Raise your hand." Nobody raised their hand. I said, "Charles Payne drew *S'Matter Pop*, and if you don't know *S'Matter Pop*, frankly, I don't think I even want to talk to you." Because *S'Matter Pop* is obviously one of the great strips of all time, beautifully drawn and so funny. I like that and *Hairbreadth Harry*, I remember I loved *Hairbreadth Harry*. It annoyed me because Rudolph Rassendale was always so mean. And then, later on, Al Capp came along with *Li'l Abner* and I loved *Li'l Abner*. And then when Milton Caniff came along and put

in the wrinkles where the wrinkles were supposed to be and shot all the camera angles and drew German Lugers the way they were supposed to look, it was a real revelation. There was nothing wrong with the way Chester Gould drew *Dick Tracy*; that was wonderful, too. But Caniff had this unique approach. As I look back upon it now, I don't think his strip was as witty as it could have been, but the drawing was marvelous. It was pure comic strip drawing, which we've never had quite enough of. It was marvelous. So those were all my heroes.

Is there anyone else, maybe a certain period, whom you wanted to draw like?

I emulated Roy Crane when I was in my late teens, before I went into the army. I tried to draw a strip which was similar to that. I used to observe downtown areas in St. Paul as I walked around delivering packages for these printing companies that I worked for—where would be a good setting for some action—and I would try to draw it that way. My drawing was improving, but I had a long way to go. Then, after World War II, when I came home, *Krazy Kat* became my hero. I had never seen *Krazy Kat* up until then. Neither one of the papers in the Twin Cities published it, so I didn't know *Krazy Kat*. But then it became my ambition to draw a strip that would have as much life and meaning and subtlety to it as *Krazy Kat* had.

Before we leave the first period of your life, when you took the correspondence course, was it the Federal School then, or...

Yes. It was the Federal School. I was sitting at home at night and I used to draw on the dining room table. I had to push back the beautiful tablecloth my mother had made, put the newspaper down, and draw. I remember I fooled her one time.

I brought a magic inkblot and pretended the ink bottle had fallen over and she came rushing in and I said, "Mom, look." She screamed and ran out to get a dishtowel. When she came back in, I laughed—great sense of humor.

She came in one night and she said, "Look here in the newspaper. It says, 'Do you like to draw? Send for a free talent test.'" So, I sent in and a few weeks later,

a man knocked on the door and it was a man from the correspondence school. And he sold us the course.

They went door to door?

Yeah.

Did you ever finish the course?

Oh, sure.

I don't think I've met a cartoonist who's had the Famous Artists course who actually finished one. They thought the world of them, but...

I may be wrong, but the percentage of people that finish the course was very low, because it just takes a lot of drive to do this on your own at home. Now, this is a good course, and they were all good instructors, dedicated people. They were always sending out material to encourage you to do your work and all that sort of thing. All my friends work there.

And you worked there, eventually.

After the War, yeah.

Correcting the students?

Yeah. See, I was afraid to go to art school. I could not see myself sitting in a class with 30 other people who could draw circles around me. It just didn't interest me. So, I didn't do anything after high school. I had a couple of jobs. And then, of course, the War came along, and that was the turning point for all of us. I remember visiting the service club one Sunday afternoon and seeing a show of originals of gag cartoons that had been in *Collier's* and *The New Yorker* or wherever they were, looking at them and admiring how beautifully drawn they were. And before that, when I was still a teenager, drawing some kind of adventure strip, my mother noticed in the paper that there was a show of originals in the downtown library. We went down there that afternoon, and I walked around the room and I saw Roy

LEFT
Hairbreadth Harry
by C.W. Kahles, June 15, 1924.

BELOW
Wash Tubbs and Captain Easy
by Roy Crane, April 25 & 26, 1933.

Crane drawing boats in the water, then went home and took all my work and tore it up and threw it away and started over again.

I knew I had a long way to go. But I used to go over then to the correspondence school, which was in Minneapolis, although I mailed in all my lesson work. I didn't even have the nerve to take that over in person, although we were allowed to do it. But then, later on, after I got my diploma and graduated, I used to take my comic strips over and I would show them to an older man named Frank Wing and he used to draw this thing called *Yesterdays*. He was a great believer in literal drawing. He could draw beautifully and he tried to encourage people to draw from life—you know, if you have to draw a shoe, put a shoe down on the ground and learn how to draw a shoe. You can't draw a cartoon shoe until you learn how to draw a real shoe. And he would look at my work, but he couldn't really tell me what was wrong with it. I used to say, "Well, look at *Popeye*. He doesn't draw real people." He never could explain to me why *Popeye* was good. And that always puzzled me.

Did he really think it was?

Oh, yeah. He liked *Popeye*, but he couldn't tell me what marvelous quality was there. So, later on, after I got a job, he used to sit with me and we used to laugh and joke about things and talk about comic strips and stuff. But I learned a lot from Frank Wing.

Breaking into the World of Gag Cartooning

You sold gag cartoons to the Saturday Evening Post *and, am I right, no other magazine?*

No, nope...

That's incredible—I mean, just starting out...

The [other magazines] just didn't buy the things.

Yeah, but if you're going to sell to some magazines, it's going to be This Week *or* American Legion *or something like that. The* Post *is the cream of the crop.*

I did it all wrong. I drew this little cartoon of a boy sitting out on the ends of a chaise lounge, with his feet on the little stool. Then I finished it up and just sent it in all by itself.

As a finished...

Yeah. I'd been sending things to other magazines. And I came home—I used to get mail from my dad's barbershop, when I lived in an apartment around the corner and upstairs. It said, "Check Tuesday for spot drawing of boy on lounge." So, I put it away. My dad and I went out for dinner that night, as we usually did, and I said, "I got a note today from the *Post*. Gee, now I understand that. They're going to send me a check on Tuesday. I thought it meant I should check the mail on Tuesday, they were going to send it back." And, sure enough, that Tuesday, I got a check for $40 and it was my first sale, my first major sale. I had been selling cartoons, *Li'l Folks*, to the *Pioneer* for two years and I had been doing lettering for the Catholic comic magazine *Timeless Topix* for several years.

That was located...

That was in St. Paul. I used to letter the whole comic magazine by myself: I would letter it in French and I would letter it in Spanish and it seems to me once I lettered the whole thing in Latin, sitting in my kitchen at night. I didn't know any of those languages, but they gave me the translations. I loved it.

Did you do any other drawings for them, maybe fillers?

Once, I sold them two pages of little gag cartoons, four to a page, called *Just Keep Laughing*. The editor was going to run them regularly and then, after the second one, he said, "No. The priest that runs the place doesn't like it, so I have to tell you we don't need any more." And then, one day, I had done a special rush job for them. I went down after work, picked up these pages, went home, lettered the whole thing, and had it down there the next morning for him. As a show of gratitude, he let me do a four-page story, and that was the only thing I ever got to do for him. You know, I saw him last year down in Santa Barbara and we reminisced about this.

[Showing Schulz some old roughs from his collection] After you made that initial sale to the Post, *did you then start submitting roughs like these...*

Yeah. Where are those from?

I think I got them from Jim Ivey.

Yeah, but where would he get them? You know, David Stanford sent me some Xerox copies of things like this several months ago. Where did it come from? Because if they are *Post* submissions, they should have been sent back to me—I mean, they were rejected.

And if they'd been bought, they would have been sent back with notes on them or something.

No matter what. But they weren't bought. Isn't that weird? Better keep them. So, I sent in ten every week and over a period of two years, after a couple of years, I hit a terrible slump. You know, John Doly was kind enough to tear off little notes and clip them to each cartoon and tell me why he didn't buy it. I've never met the man, but I've been told that he was very kind that way and very considerate of cartoonists. And then I began to get on track and I made most of my sales using the gimmick of little kids using something the way it shouldn't be. Like they're playing football on the bed and one of them says, "We're close enough. Let's try for a field goal!" and the bedposts are the posts. And in another, they're going to have a race down this long davenport and the davenport is made to look like a racetrack. In another one, they're playing hockey on top of the birdbath. I've had Snoopy do that now for years. That was the kind of idea I sold.

Props?

Yeah. And the first good line I thought up was one that was jotted down on the wall over there. Somebody permafaxed it for me;

OPPOSITE, RIGHT, AND FOLLOWING PAGE
Saturday Evening Post cartoons, c. 1948–1950.

"We're close enough. . . . Let's try for a field goal!"

it was a girl standing in front of a desk talking to a guy and she says, "We're taking up a collection for one of the girls in the office who isn't getting married or leaving, but feels that she's stuck here for the rest of her life." I think that was my breakthrough of doing something that was reasonably literate. Anyway, I sold 15 over a period of two years, and then I sold *Peanuts*, and when I went to sign the contract, I said, "Would it be all right to continue to submit ideas to the *Post*?" And he said, "No, I don't think you should. Because an editor who buys your strip usually buys your name and your work, and we think he should have exclusive use of your work." That was all right by me. I wanted to draw a strip. I couldn't stand that freelancing and that bitter blow of opening the envelope and seeing a note that said, "Sorry, nothing this week." It was so crushing.

Well, it's got to be like baseball players, when a successful ball player fails two out of three times at the plate. No matter how much you sell to the magazines, most of the gags are rejected.

Right. And I never got into the real professional pattern, which you have to do, I think. You have to have a lot of markets and be very practical about it. I never got that far in it. I just sold the strip too quickly so I never became a real gag cartoonist.

The Genesis of *Peanuts*

You've said that a lot of Charlie Brown's school experiences come from your school-age experiences.

Oh, yeah. It took me a long time to become a human being. I was regarded by many as kind of sissyfied, which I resented because I really was not a sissy. I was not a tough guy, but I was good at sports. I was a good baseball player. When I was 15, I instantly became a good ball-player. I was good at any sport where you threw things, or hit them, or caught them, or things like that. I hated things like swimming and tumbling and those kinds of things, so I was really not a sissy. We never had the chance in those days to do some of the athletic things we wanted to, because the coaches were so intolerant and there was no program for all of us. So, I never regarded myself as being much and I never regarded myself as being good looking and I never had a date in high school, because I thought, "Who'd want to date me?" So, I didn't bother. And that's just the way I grew up.

I was telling somebody, I think it was just yesterday, that it wasn't until I came back from the War that I really had self-confidence. I went into the army as a nothing person, and I came out as a staff sergeant, squad leader of a light machine gun squad. And I thought, "By golly, if that isn't a man, I don't know what is." And I felt good about myself. That lasted about eight minutes, and then I went back to where I am now.

You've said it, and Al Capp and a lot of text humorists have said it: "The basis for humor is pain, suffering, or humiliation." You can intellectualize about that now, but when the strip started, did you see that as a formula?

No. When my strip first started, it was so totally different from what it is now that I don't even know what it was when it first started. I had experimented with many different types of features. I used to get on the train in St. Paul in the mornings and make that beautiful ride down to Chicago, get there about three in the afternoon, check into a hotel by myself, and the next morning I would get up and make the rounds of the syndicates. My first few trips, I really didn't have enough to show them and only one man treated me nicely. I met him years later and we talked about that and I was able to express to him my appreciation of how polite and nice he was, because some of the other syndicate people were very rude and most of them didn't even let me in the door. But as my work improved, I began to sell this thing called *Li'l Folks* to the *St. Paul* [*Pioneer*]. While I was doing this, I was also working at the Art Instruction correspondence school, drawing funny little figures, and I developed this three-panel strip which was unique in that what happened in the story was an incident that was only a couple of seconds. And so, when I sent in the panels that were finally accepted by United Feature, I hadn't...

Excuse me; it was a panel? It wasn't a strip?

It was unique. This was something that nobody knew about, and it annoys me that the editor lost my original submissions. For years, he kept promising me he'd send them back and he never sent them back. Somebody had them someplace, and I would love to know who has them. Either that, or they got thrown away.

But I was looking for an angle. I figured if I'm going to break into this business,

I've got to do something that is a little bit different. I had developed this very simple style of drawing, and I took all the best ideas that I sold to the St. Paul paper and I re-drew them in a panel format. I took *Grin and Bear It* as my size to pattern after and, instead of drawing one single panel, I drew one above the other. I figured I'll be smart: I'll give the editor two cartoons for the price of one, and this will be a good sales gimmick. So, I sent it in and they were really good and I was very proud of them. And this is what the syndicate editor finally said to me: "We kind of like it. Would you like to come to New York and talk about it?" So, when I went to New York, I brought along a half dozen of these comic strips that I had been working on that I have been telling you about, which were really unique…

These were two tiers?

The panel was two tiers. It was called *Li'l Folks*. And that's what the syndicate editor saw in my submissions. But then when I went to New York, in person, I brought along these other things because I wanted to show what other things I could do. And they opened up that package while I was out having breakfast, and decided that they would rather have a strip. And then, like syndicate people do, they began to fiddle around with it. The sales manager said, "How about if we make it even broader in its appeal and we have one little kid strip at the top and a teenage strip at the bottom?" So, I thought about it and said, "Oh, all right, I have to do what they tell me." So, I did that and they really didn't care for the teenage thing. And then they said, "We'll just have the kid thing." Somewhere in there, they decided that they'd rather have a strip, and right then was when they made this fateful decision that it was going to be a space-saving strip, which I have resented all my life. Now it may have gotten me started, but I had to overcome the fact that I was drawing a space-saving strip under the title *Peanuts*, which was the worst title ever thought up for a comic strip. It's totally ridiculous. It has no meaning, is simply confusing, and has no dignity—and I think my humor has dignity. Those are two things that have hung over me and I've resented my whole career.

Thirty-seven years hasn't softened that?

No, no. I hold a grudge, boy.

By "space-saving strip," you mean that it was reproduced smaller than the average comic strip?

It was reproduced smaller; it was drawn in four equal panels so that it could be run vertically, horizontally, or in a square, two below two. Now, the ironic part of it is, about a year later, they came out with *Twin Earths*, which was enormous in its size, and *Long Sam*, which was also enormous. Then they told me that newsprint is kind of short and we're having trouble and we think having this as a space-saving strip will help. Well, you know where *Long Sam* is and you know where *Twin Earths* is. I've always been proud of the fact that quality won out over size and space.

You've kept to that four-panel square format, though you don't have to now. [Editor's note: Schulz later converted the strip to three equal-sized panels

Li'l Folks
BY SPARKY

"MEOW,...MEOW,...MEOW!"

"BROWN'S THE NAME...
CHARLIE BROWN... ALWAYS
GLAD TO GREET A FELLOW
CONSTITUENT!"

"WHOOPS!...
PARDON ME!"

"IT ALL STARTED WITH AN
ARGUMENT OVER WHO HAD
THE WORST TEMPER"

ABOVE *Li'l Folks*, May 30, 1948.
BELOW February 8, 1951.

DO YOU WANT ME TO CARRY
YOUR BOOKS, VIOLET?

I ALREADY HAVE
SOMEONE

FOILED!! AND BY MAN'S
BEST FRIEND!

2-8
SCHULZ

and then began varying the panel size from strip to strip, a format that continued throughout the rest of the strip's run.]

I'm a great believer in loyalty. I'm not a believer in dictating to the newspaper editor how he should run my strip. And I've had some papers with me now for 36 years and they have run my strip in the same spot all this time. Who am I suddenly to say, "I'm too good to draw a small strip like this! I want more room, I want more space, I want more this or that." I just think that would be too egotistical. I believe in being loyal to these editors who have been loyal to you. And that's just the way I look at things. I don't want to break this agreement here and cause the editor to have to shuffle around everything that he's done and to change all of it.

GARY GROTH: *How do you feel about [Garry] Trudeau's demanding more space [for* Doonesbury*]?*

[*Pause*] That he's not professional. He's never been professional.

How do you mean that?

I don't think he conducts himself in a professional manner in the things that he does.

MARSCHALL: *You're not just talking about the artistry on the strip?*

It's his whole attitude toward the business.

GROTH: *You don't admire the strip.* [Schulz shakes head]

MARSCHALL: *You were just talking about the title* Peanuts. *You've written before that Bill Anderson made a list of 10 names and "Peanuts" was chosen. Do you know where he'd come up with that?*

Well, he told me, a couple of years afterward, "I never saw the strip. Somebody came to me and said, 'We're gonna start a new kid's strip and we need a title. Can you think of anything?'" He said, "I wrote down 10 ideas and one of them was 'Peanuts' and that's what they took."

Do you know where he got "Peanuts" from?

No.

He told me it was because thinking of a kids' strip, a kids' milieu, Howdy Doody *was the hottest thing on kids' TV at that time and where the kids sat in* Howdy Doody *was the Peanut Gallery. That seemed logical to him.*

But you see what bothers me. In the first place, it has no dignity. I don't even like the word. It's not even a nice word. They didn't realize that I was going to draw a strip that I think has dignity. I think it has class. But, of course, and I've said this before, when a young person goes into the syndicate president's office, what that president is buying is the potential of this young person. He's not even buying the work that he is looking at; he's buying the potential 10, 20 years down the road, and how does he know? They didn't know when I walked in there that here was a fanatic. Here was a kid totally dedicated to what he was going to do. And to label then something that was going to be my life's work with a name like "Peanuts" was really insulting.

Now we'll go to the next step, which is that little kids are never called "peanuts" as they said they were. They never are. The only "peanuts" that are referred to are insignificant; something with no color, or else it might be the nickname of a ball player or some little kid. And I said they're going to confuse Charlie Brown with the name "Peanuts." "No, no, no, no," they said. "No, no, it's just a catchy name that will attract the editors." So, what happens the very first year, I begin to get letters saying, "I love this new strip with Peanuts and his dog." Oh, jeez! That aggravates me.

I never mention [the name]. If someone asks me what I do, I always say, "I draw that comic strip with Snoopy in it, Charlie Brown and his dog."

Characters, Storytelling, and the Evolution of the Strip

Peanuts *really was the renaissance—do you agree with this?— of the intellectual strip. Growing up,* Peanuts *played a large role in my not being embarrassed about using big words in front of the other kids, and the Beethoven thing made me interested in Beethoven and Mozart. Do you agree with that definition of the strip? Did you have something like that in mind when you started the strip, or was this just a next generation* Skippy?

I didn't have anything in mind. I was just drawing. [*Looks at promo brochure*] This came out later, though. See, Violet didn't come into the strip for at least a year and Schroeder didn't come in for over a year. [*Editor's note: Actually, four and a half and seven months, respectively.*] I never did figure out how to draw Schroeder's hair. Why did they buy that? That looks terrible.

But it's marketed here as a little kids' strip.

Yeah. Well, I've fought that all my life, too. And I fight it with licensees today. I don't draw for little kids. I draw for myself, which is who I think we all draw for. We draw for ourselves and hope that people like it. But the licensees keep driving it down for little kids. We did the first television show, *A Charlie Brown Christmas*, we did the best show we could do and what happens? We win an Emmy for the best children's animated show of the year. We didn't draw it for kids. We drew it for grown-ups. I just draw for myself, and draw it as well as I can. I'm not pretending to be modest. I know I'm not an intellectual. I don't even think I'm very smart. I really don't. I think I'm witty and I think I know how to skim the surface of a subject and take out enough for me to use and to make it look like I know a lot about the subject. You really don't have to know much to be a cartoonist. So, if it's an intellectual strip, I've never really even thought about it. I'm glad. I never thought about it, but I did want to draw something that was good.

You've never pictured adults, parents or otherwise, in the strip. Maybe once or twice you've had the hand of an adult at a magazine counter or something like that. Was that something you set out to do?

Oh, I never thought about it at first. It was just the way I drew the characters. They filled up the strip, and I drew them from the side view. The type of humor that I was using did not call for camera angles. I liked drawing the characters from the same view all the way through, because the ideas were very brief and I didn't want anything in the drawing to interrupt the flow of what the characters were either saying or doing. So, there became no room for adults in the strip. At one point, years and years ago, I drew a whole bunch of adults in a gallery where Lucy was playing in a golf tournament, which is something I never should have done. But it was an experiment.

In the background...

Yeah, in the background. I drew these adults. I never should have done that. And then I used to have off-stage voices, which again was simply because I didn't know how to handle it. Now, the strip has become so abstract that the introduction of an adult would destroy it. You can't have an adult in a strip where a dog is sitting on a doghouse, pretending he's chasing the Red Baron. It just doesn't work. So, it's taken all these years really to learn some of these things. You make mistakes, but fortunately it's a medium that allows for mistakes if you recognize them right away. It's possible—I think—to make a mistake in the strip and, without realizing it, destroy it. My best example, I think—and this will surprise you—I think Eugene the Jeep was a mistake. I think Eugene the Jeep took the life out of Popeye himself, and I'm sure Segar didn't realize that. I realized it myself a couple of years ago when I began to introduce Snoopy's brothers and sisters. I realized that when I put Belle and Marbles in there it destroyed the relationship that Snoopy has with the kids, which is a very strange relationship. And these things are so subtle when you're doing them, you can make mistakes and not realize them. You've got to watch that very carefully. What made Popeye great was that he solved all his problems by whopping somebody. But then by having Eugene the Jeep be able to predict the future and do all of these things was just the wrong direction. And once you go there, it's almost impossible to pull back. I think the Jeep was a great idea, but it shouldn't have become as dominant as it became.

*Comic strip history breaks down into the pre-*Peanuts *era and the post-*Peanuts *era. It seems to me one of your main contributions is a technical construction of the strip. You started with a small cast of characters in the beginning, and then it got large. You drew*

BELOW Popeye by E.C. Segar, April 1, 1936.   **OPPOSITE** May 16, 1954.

*them all with very, very strong personality traits, and then established a lot of premises
and a lot of situations for them to fit into. So many strips before that were basically sit-
uational—"What are we going to do next?"—or humorous continuity. Since you established this type of strip—large cast, strong personalities as opposed to situations—virtually everything since that has come down the pike has been in that format; Doonesbury,
certainly.*

Few people give me credit for having started this, but I think a lot of them don't
realize that I did start it. I think, too, they used to say *Peanuts* has brought humor
back into the comics page, because there is no doubt that, during the War, we had a
lot of adventure things, and gag strips and humor strips had virtually disappeared.
I think the great tragedy is now we have lost the continuity strip. We've lost, especially, the humorous continuity strip. They're all turning into gag strips. They're all
saying what they think are meaningful statements—they're not meaningful at all;
they're just dumb. And that's a tragedy, too. A lot of it is due to the shrinking of
the size. Poor Al Capp would die if he had to draw at the size of these things these
days. Now, we have this terrible trend, which has just suddenly burst upon us, of the
one-panel comic strip. I don't know where that's going to lead.

It's cheating.

And boring. Not only that, but it's robbing a creator of a chance to develop a group
of characters and some good situations. Now, I like what you said before, the way
you expressed that about how from the characters, we went to certain situations,
and I think this is the key to the whole thing. I created Beethoven's birthday, I
created Linus and his blanket, I created the pursuit of the Red Baron, I created the
pulling of the football, I created the Great Pumpkin—all of these, these are the
things that make up a comic strip. You can't sit down and say, "I think I'm gonna
draw a comic strip and this will be my main character." The main character has
nothing to do with it. What you really need are the situations and that's where you
should start. Nobody wants to start with that. They want to start by thinking up
a character, which will be a good gimmick and will make good plush toys. That's
the wrong direction.

It seems to me that one thing that could revive the newspaper comic strip, the humor strip, would be the return of humor continuities. And you use them. How do you plan them? Do you know the ending before you start, or do you just let it run and surprise yourself when it comes to an end?

I never have any idea where I'm going with it. I discovered something, which is why I don't think—and why, I suppose, I'll always offend somebody someplace—that you can write a comic strip on a typewriter. I think you're robbing yourself of the ideas that come from drawing. So, what I'm more interested in is a good, standard, day-to-day group of ideas, which is more important than where the story goes. I'm doing a story right now and I have no idea where I'm going with it, but I'm very interested in trying to make each day funny. If you think of an overall story, you're liable to end up with a weak strip on Tuesday and Friday or Saturday, and I don't want to do that. I'm more interested in making each day as funny as I can. I've had some stories run five weeks, five or six at the longest. I haven't had any lately. They're awfully hard work, and you have to have time to think about them. But I do agree that certain kinds of stories and strips can bring the reader back so he doesn't want to miss the next day's strip. It's very important in building circulation.

You once said in the development of character, "I don't think the cartoonist can show a character. He's got to expose a character, maybe through situations, and explain it as you show it." When Snoopy started thinking, that told more about him and the things you had him do. Did that just evolve, too? Snoopy didn't think at first.

No, he didn't think. He actually barked and ran around on all fours and was just kind of a cute little puppy. I don't know how he got to walking, and I don't know how he first began to think, but that was probably one of the best things that I ever did.

Linus and the blanket: Was that just—

My own kids all had blankets, so that was something I observed. And I said many times that I was glad I did, because I know if I hadn't done it Mort Walker would have come in with it a few months later for sure. Since then, I've seen other comic strips with blankets, and they've used the same ideas I had already drawn. In fact, lately,

I'm beginning to see ideas in comic strips that I drew 20 years ago, which makes me happy to know I beat these guys. But I remember being beaten by J. R. Williams by 30 years, and I was beaten by Gus Arriola by 10 or 15 years, so that happens. But I do see people using ideas that I've done for a long time. Well, it's just a pattern of thinking; I don't say that it's stealing. I know it's not stealing; it's just a pattern of thinking.

The sincerest kind of flattery.

Yeah.

OK, we mentioned Snoopy and the blanket. Charlie Brown evolved. Wasn't he almost a bit of a wise guy, at the beginning?

Yeah. Little by little the characters begin to fall into place. I think there is a similarity to the lead characters in a lot of scripts. There is one simple character who is kind of innocent. He's not too strong in his personality; if he were, then he would dominate the strip. He's the one that holds everything together, and it's the other characters who have the unique personalities. He can't be a terrible character, but he has to be somebody that you like that holds things together. And that's what Charlie Brown is there for. Although, sometimes I think I should use him more—but I've got so many characters now that it's difficult to know who I should use the most. For a while, I received a couple of letters from somebody that said, "Don't use the dog so much. Get back to the little kids." I never pay attention to letters like that. But maybe he was right: Maybe I was using Snoopy too much. I'm always trying to be selective. I'm always trying to do different things. And I always wanted to have some girls in the strip, which is why I have drifted more toward Peppermint Patty and Marcie.

There is something else here worth mentioning, which is important towards building personalities and characters, in that Peppermint Patty calls Charlie Brown "Chuck." She's the only one in the strip that does that. Marcie

ABOVE September 24, 1953.
OPPOSITE November 18, 1959.

calls him "Charles." Everybody else calls him "Charlie Brown." Those are the little things. If you have enough of those little things, then I think you take on some kind of depth. I'm not a believer in funny names. I think a funny name is fine for one gag or one idea, but I don't think people are going to laugh at that funny name every day. You can't count on that. That's why my strip doesn't have many funny things like that in it, where you're trying for that extra laugh all the time.

In that vein, were you planning for the April Fool to take off like the Great Pumpkin did?

No. That was just a one-time strip. I didn't even like the way I drew it. I like the Easter Beagle. For a long while, I wouldn't do anything on Easter. I'm very sensitive to not offending anybody, and I thought I shouldn't do anything with Easter. But then I thought, "Oh, the heck with it. It's fun—the Easter Beagle," so I did it anyway.

You've got characters with neuroses—Charlie Brown with his inferiority complex and Linus being insecure and Lucy kvetching and all that. Does anyone advance the observation that you have done sort of Yiddish humor in WASP clothes?

Not really. I have become a fairly good friend, through the mail, of Leo Rosten. He sends me all his books, and I think *I'm the Captain* is one of the greatest humor books ever written. Otherwise, I don't know much about it.

There is one thing I do resent. I resent the fact that when we talk about America's great humorists, comic strip artists are never mentioned, not even the great people that draw for *The New Yorker.* Where's George Price?

A couple of characters—Frieda and Faron. Are you a fan of country music?

I was. I'm not a fan of any music anymore. It's very personal, but when Joyce and I were separated and divorced, and I was living alone and I was very unhappy, and I was separated from my children for a few months there, I couldn't stand to listen to the radio or any music. So, I stopped listening to music and I really have not gotten back into it. I used to love country and Western music. The whole business of Charlie Brown and the red-haired girl came from listening to a Hank Williams song. I was home alone one night listening to it, and it was so depressing that it occurred to me that I would do something with Charlie Brown and the little red-haired girl. That's how it all started. [*Laughter*]

You'll never show her, right?

No. And I think it was a mistake to even show her on television, but you make a lot of mistakes when you do a lot of media. But I could never draw her into the strip now. You reach a point where the reader has already drawn her. And you could never live up to the way the reader has drawn her in his or her imagination.

Was that a temptation because of the animated format, or...

I'm not good at drawing pretty little faces. That would be the number one fear. I could probably be tempted into drawing her, if I could draw a real knockout of a cute little girl, but I don't think I could. So, I don't think I will. I like the little face on the girl that keeps telling Linus, "Aren't you kind of old for me?" Even that face was a struggle to draw.

You named Woodstock during the Woodstock era. Were you speaking of your readership, or did you just hear the name and think it was neat?

I had been reading the *Life* magazine article about the Woodstock festival and I had the little bird in the strip. It was a she and she was Snoopy's secretary and I was doing secretary jokes quite often, so then I thought Woodstock would be a good name for this bird. And, also, it will get the attention of these people that liked that kind of thing. Suddenly, she was not a secretary; she became Woodstock, the boy. [*Laughter*] It just happened. But that's what's good about a comic strip—you can just do it.

ABOVE March 23, 1966.
OPPOSITE April 11, 1971.
BELOW June 9, 1986.

March 4, 1992.

Philosophy, Spirituality, Politics

I wonder if you realize how deep an impact Peanuts *has had on your readers.*

No. Actually, I'm very surprised. And I always worry about it because I realize that I'm in a medium where it's dangerous to stick your head out because there are so many people that simply don't read the comics and still don't regard it as worthwhile entertainment. There's nothing that annoys me more than somebody coming up to me and saying, "My 19-year-old daughter really loves your strip and she still reads it," because that's the audience that I'm really going for. And another thing that bothers me are the parents who come up to me with their two- or three-year-old child on their shoulder and say, "Look, you know who this is? It's *Peanuts'* father!" and the poor kid and I look at each other and the kid has no idea what the mother and father are talking about, and it really bothers me. Beyond that, I kind of keep to myself and try not to think about that. When people say to me, "I really admire your philosophy," I literally and honestly do not know what they are talking about because I don't even know what my philosophy is.

They try to read something into the strip.

Which is all right. I think that even minor art forms like this, as Robert Short tried to talk about in *The Gospel According to Peanuts*, do have certain truths in them, and I think that's important. I think that people should be able to read whatever they want to into what they're looking at or reading. But as far as an overall philosophy goes, I'm really not sure what it is. Although I try to draw a gentle strip. I try to draw a strip that doesn't have any real cruelty in it, outside of things like Lucy pulling away the football. And it's not as insulting a strip as it used to be. Of course, I've gotten older, and I'm not as insulting as I used to be myself.

Do you think Robert Short went too far in analyzing the strip?

Well, I don't know if he really analyzed. I think what he was really trying to do was use a comic strip as a springboard toward some kinds of spiritual ideas. Robert's a great guy. We didn't even know each other when he wrote the book. I think the book had been out for a year before we finally met, but since then we've become close friends and we love being together and talking about different things. I think he likes to just draw little spiritual thoughts from everything that goes on in his life, and it occurred to me *Peanuts* was providing some spiritual jumping off place. Now, I know it didn't come off that way, but I know that's what he was intending. The book was never mine and it was never meant to be my idea. That was part of the original agreement: Sure, he can use the strips, but it's not my writing.

It's his interpretation. You just talked about readers being offended—you've probably gotten complaints when you've used Scripture, which you have more than any other artist.

I think I've done more authentic scriptural strips than anybody. I hate cheap spiritual innuendo. I hate strips showing the kid praying, talking about what mean things he did in the daytime. I just despise that kind of thing. I'd like to think that mine was done on a better level than that. I'm a reasonable student of the Scriptures, a typical Midwestern scholar. I think I use the Scriptures very well in the strip in ways nobody else has ever thought of doing it, or would have the nerve, or even has the scholarship to do it. I'm proud of that and also very sensitive to it. I've always done it in a nice way, never offensive. I was amazed when we put out the book called *The Beagles and the Bunnies* that we had enough to fill out the whole book. I never dreamed of that.

You're a committed Christian?

I think I'm becoming a secular humanist [*laughter*], but I don't want to get into that.

I've heard that term applied to you. Did I read once that you were a lay preacher?

Well, I was very active in the church group right after World War II. We were all in our twenties and we went to Sunday morning services. We went to Sunday evening youth meetings—although we weren't really youths—and Wednesday night prayer meetings and we were all very dedicated to the church. And now and then, I might be asked to speak on a Sunday evening. I have even spoken out on street corners, which I never should have done. I would never do it again, because I no longer feel I'm in a position to tell anybody anything. But, anyway, I did all those things and it was a good group; they were nice people. I still have contact with a few of them and I'm in contact with the minister, who is now retired. We studied the Scriptures and discussed them avidly. That's where my background for all those biblical things comes from, and I have an honorary doctorate from Anderson College, which is the Church of God College.

When you go from your knowledge, or maybe you turn to Proverbs or some of those parables, you don't do it in a subversive way to get a point across.

I'm never grinding an axe. I'm never doing it to teach anybody anything, or very seldom. Maybe if we looked through them I could point out a few where I might be trying to say something against hypocrisy, I really don't know. It's hard to say overall. It's just that certain phrases pop into my mind that I think would be funny, so I look up the Scriptures or else I remember a Scripture, and suddenly I find that something comes into my mind. A certain way of using it, that's all.

GROTH: *You said something earlier that I thought was potentially fascinating, that you were becoming a secular humanist?*

Well, I don't go to church anymore. I taught adult Sunday school class in Minneapolis and came out here to a local Methodist church, but I never became a

Methodist. They were just a nice group of people and they were all quite educated. I enjoyed the class and I did it for about 10 years. Finally, I just ran out of things to say and it became an effort to do all the studying. Besides, this business of always having to think of something gets to you after a while. It got so that I could never be invited to a banquet without having to get up and say a few words. I have to think up a daily strip and I have to think up a Sunday and I was drawing youth cartoons for a church magazine and trying to think of a Sunday school lesson and studying and oh, gosh… Finally, after a while, I just had to say, "Let somebody else do it," because I just don't have any more to say. So, I haven't been back to church.

Is there a sense that you're questing for…

No, I'm not questing for anything. I don't know anything, frankly. I think it's all a total mystery. I have no idea why we're here, and I have no idea what happens after you die. My class wasn't one so much of teaching as it was just getting people to say things. I know I led them through the Bible verse by verse four times, and each time I would learn something more. I was not at all anxious to teach them what I thought about. Every now and then, someone would say, "Well, what do you think?" and I would say, "It doesn't matter what I think. I just want to hear what you think and get you to talk about these things and actually read the Scriptures instead of saying, 'Well, I've heard about that in this or that.'"

MARSCHALL: *An awful lot of people haven't.*

Oh, I know, I know. I don't even know what secular humanism is. Have you ever heard of the book, *I Never Promised You a Rose Garden*? I know the author very well. She asked me what I believed. I said what I thought I believed in, and she said, "You are a secular humanist, that's what you are," and I said, "I am?" and she said, "Yeah, that's what I think you are." [*Laughter*] But she's a marvelous lady.

GROTH: *Was there ever a time when you questioned your religion?*

Well, it's not a matter of questioning… My religious thing must have been a matter of gratitude. I was brought up Lutheran, but my dad liked to go fishing on Sundays, so we almost never went to church. I was never really brought up in church. But my mother was extremely ill with cancer when I was just turning 20. She was just coming out of the hospital. She suffered terribly. I used to wake up at night and hear her down the hall crying in pain. It was a terrible time. I got drafted as soon as I turned 20, and I had to report. I got to go home a couple of weekends as they were deciding what ought to be done and one Sunday night I was home, she was so ill. I was saying goodnight to her to her back and she said, "Well, goodbye, Sparky. We'll probably never see each other again." It has to be one of the most heart-breaking things in my life. It's bad enough to get drafted, but to know that your mom will die… She was only 48. And sure enough, she died the next day. Then I came home from the funeral and the next thing I knew, I'm back with the army on a troop train and I'm traveling through the night with a bunch of guys I've never seen before in my life without knowing where I'm going. And I started going to church just out of a feeling of gratitude that I survived all of that. I felt that God protected me and helped me and gave me the strength to survive because I could have gone off in all sorts of wrong directions. I always felt that I was helped to live through those three years and come home, because I never got shot or anything.

I knew about this Church of God—my dad and I used to go now and then—but one night, it was a Wednesday night, I was feeling very lonely and I knew they needed a new sign out in front of the church. It was a very poor church, so I walked all the way down several miles through the snow to the church. I told the minister I would make him a new sign if he wanted me to. He was a great man. I made a lot of friends there. That's how it all happened. And then we came out here and my first wife didn't care much about getting involved in the church once we got out here, so we sort of drifted away from it. But now, I've ended up with one daughter becoming a Mormon and going to England as a Mormon missionary. [*Laughter*] We've become very close because of it, even though I don't like Mormons. We can talk about the scriptural things that she was never interested in before, and she has a fine husband. My family has gone in all different directions, but they're all good kids.

One thing I am curious about is if you are a politically oriented person.

No. I was brought up Republican. I saw Herbert Hoover get off the train in St. Paul when he was running for re-election. And I saw Eisenhower once when we went to Minneapolis and we all stood out on the street. I was very taken by Wendell Willkie when I was young. I was calling myself an Eisenhower Republican, because he was the first person I ever voted for that got elected. [*Laughter*] Gosh, for 20 years we were under Democratic rule. Twenty solid years, and then… But I sold a cartoon because of Dewey losing that morning. When I came back to Art Instruction that morning, of course Truman had won, and some woman came in who had voted for Wallace. She still was glad Dewey had lost. Somebody said, "How did you sleep last night?" I said, "Oh, I sleep well enough at night, it's living during the day I find so hard," and I sold it to the *Saturday Evening Post*. So, I figure I got $80 out of the election anyway. But I've never been involved in local politics or done anything. I've met President Carter and President Reagan. He called me on the phone when I was recovering from surgery, which was quite flattering.

Do you have any loosely defined political leanings?

No, no, I don't even want to get into that. It's the same as the religious thing. I'm not especially fond of all political cartooning. I think a lot of it is irresponsible. These guys write about things they really don't know anything about. They leap on the bandwagon the day after something happens and draw things that aren't even true. And some of them are terribly petty on both sides.

One of the remarkable things about the strip is that there are no perceivable ideologies.

Sort of a wishy-washiness…

No, no, not at all. It's really remarkable, because there are so many shrill ideologies.

Well, I do think about it. I really don't want to offend people, and I don't think it's necessary. I think it can be funny and remain kind of innocent, and yet I don't think you have to be sugary sweet or stupid.

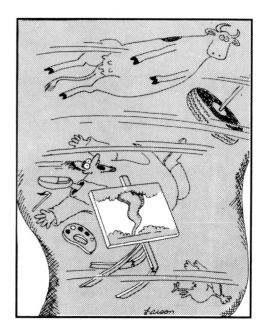

RIGHT *The Far Side*
by Gary Larson, n.d.

OPPOSITE *Action Comics*
#1, June 1938.

The Present and Future of Comics (in 1987)

Can you talk a little about the current state of the comic strip? Are there strips you like?

No. [*Laughter*]

I know you're not wild about the current propensity for one-panel strips...

Yeah. It was a strange direction. I think Bob Thaves with his feature *Frank and Ernest* is good. I suppose he was one of the first to do it, and that's perfectly all right. But now, I was looking at our own local comic page the other night—five features were one-panel comic strips. And several weeks before that, six of them were just one long panel. I don't know. It puzzles me. It could be due to the shrinkage of space, but it's a bad trend. I don't think that you really build up a group of characters that way. And that's what a cartoonist is going to achieve. Something should be done about it.

Are you fond of Gary Larson's The Far Side?

Oh, yeah, he's good. He has a unique approach and he draws funny. I like the way the eyeballs are always close together. He draws funny animals and funny people. But I do resent that he is being labeled as the "new far-out humor."

Do you find the current state of the strips despairing?

I think the profession is heading in a strange way.

Do you have any theories as to why?

Oh, I suppose the number one problem would be space, that we just don't have space on which to work anymore. A lot of the people don't know how to adapt to that space. And then, it's about following trends. One person does one thing, and pretty soon all syndicates are hiring people to do the same thing. I don't know if

I should take credit for it or not, but there seems to be a lot of what they call "sophisticated humor," with characters saying meaningful things. But in so many of them the character at the end does not say anything meaningful, it's just dumb. It just lays there. The person doesn't have the knack to do that kind of thing.

MARSCHALL: *Has the craft gone out of strips today? You have unique pen lines, thick and thin—I don't know what point you use, but it's like a fingerprint. A lot of cartoonists nowadays seem to think it's easier to use a rapidograph or a felt-tip pen or something like that. I don't think it necessarily reproduces better, and a lot of personality goes out of it.*

If you use that kind of pen, you have no thickness at all. If you use felt pens, the lines are just thicker, that's all. Of course, it's quicker—you don't have to dip in. I was a great student of pen techniques back when I worked at Art Instruction. My friend and I used to do what we called Bart pen demonstrations. The author of the original cartoon course was Charles Bartholomew, and he used to send out what he called "Bart pen demonstrations." This was a little card that had three sets of three pen lines: very thin, medium, and thick, all done with the same pen. And my friend and I used to practice making those when we had nothing else to do. We used to see if we could do three sets of perfect pen lines with the space between the pen lines narrower than the line itself. It was like the surgeon practicing with his scalpel. So, I became really pretty deft with the pen. Now, my hands shake and that spoils some of my pen techniques, but sometimes I can still do it.

That's characteristic, too.

No, what's funny is that when they try to get someone helping with the licensing or something else, they copy my work and they copy this shaky pen line and say, "Gee, that's nice. How do you do that?" I don't do it on purpose—my hands shake. [*Laughter*]

GROTH: *Did you read comic books when you were a kid?*

I not only read them, I bought every one that came out. I had the original first *Famous Funnies* that came out. Some stupid friends of mine tore the cover off it and it disappeared. But I had it for years. I used to buy *Tip Top Comics* and I can still remember the day when Superman came out in *Action Comics*. I took it over to a friend of mine and we thought, "Wow!" I knew this guy had something. The drawing was nice to look at. It wasn't as slick as the latest *Superman*. But it was fun to look at. I knew this guy really had something.

I used to buy the Big Little Books, I bought every Big Little Book that came out until I got overwhelmed by them. I was the librarian in my neighborhood, because the kids would come over and borrow my Big Little Books and my comics magazines. [*Laughter*] All my Big Little Books got lost in the fire in my dad's apartment.

Are you at all familiar with Carl Barks?

Oh, sure. But I never saw them when I was a kid, and I don't know why. I never read any Barks.

I was wondering what you thought of Walt Kelly's work.

I thought near the end, it became boring. I loved the older work, and I bought every *Pogo* book that came out. I bought the comic magazine and I read it and I was influenced by it. I would imitate his way of talking in it, the same way as when I was a kid I would imitate Al Capp's hillbilly way of talking. But near the end, it got so wordy that I would buy the books and read the first few pages of it and just couldn't get through it. It wasn't funny anymore. It's always a shame when people get so caught up with trying to give out their messages that they forget they have to be funny and entertaining. But he sure could draw. I only got to meet Walt once. I just said a few words to him one night at the Reuben Awards. I never really got to know him.

Were you familiar with Harvey Kurtzman's work?

Oh, sure, sure.

Did you like it?

I'm just familiar with it. A lot of them are wonderful. And the guys who used to draw for *Mad* magazine were sensational. Boy, some of them can draw.

I was wondering if you paid any attention to the underground comics of the late '60s.

I stopped reading comic magazines years ago. I got so totally bored with them, with the superheroes, all the muscles—the drawings all looked alike, and I just never read any of them. I never read any underground comics. What was strange about them was they pretended to be so different and they all turned out to be the same. They all used the same vulgar expressions and things. I got acquainted with a few of them from the Bay area and I said, "You guys pretend to do something so great and think what we're all doing is so bland, but actually, what I'm doing is infinitely more difficult than what you're doing. I'm drawing something that is good, but is clean and decent, and I'm not bothering anybody and I'm not hurting anybody." And I said, "I defy you to do that." They draw the same dirty pictures, with the same dirty expressions, and pretty soon they're all alike. What's so great about that? I admit that some of them are good—Crumb is good—but that has never interested me. Besides, you get back to spirituality. I've always been very grateful for what has happened to me, and I think it would be ungrateful of me

Pogo by Walt Kelly, May 5, 1953.

to use whatever sensibilities I have for wrong. So, I've always been very careful about that.

This is a sort of cliché question, but I'll ask it anyway: Can you tell us what you think the future or potential of comics is?

Depends on the editors. I don't think we have any choice. I think we're totally at the mercy of the editors and whatever they're going to do with these comic pages. And if it keeps up the way it's going now... I think there are good futures for a lot of people. I know they're buying all sorts of new things and all that. I don't think it's necessarily going to produce great new superstars. And I'm not just talking about just making a lot of money: I'm talking about somebody really great. Obviously, *Calvin and Hobbes* is one that seems to have the opportunity to do something really great, and I don't know if it will or not. It's difficult because of the space you have.

Do you think that the new formats coming out, such as book-length comic books, will have some...

Do you mean the reprints of comic strips?

No, I'm talking about the new formats that are being published.

I haven't seen them.

Have you heard of Art Spiegelman's Maus?

Oh, sure, sure.

That's the sort of thing I'm talking about, because you get away from the space restrictions and the editors.

Yeah, yeah. But I suppose, again, that they're at the mercy of the publishers and the distributors and it's a whole different profession; it's something that is totally foreign to me. What I think is a pity is something like that can't be transferred to the comics page. The newspapers won't even listen to this, but the potential is there and I think there's a lot of great children's book illustrators who should be in the comic pages, but are not.

Getting Older and Gaining Control

Have you resisted the temptation to take a vacation?

Quit for a year? So far I've resisted it.

But you've had the temptation?

I never thought I would, but the last few years all my friends are retiring and I'm beginning to wonder if I hadn't wasted my life. Yeah, wait till you're 65 or 64.

MARSCHALL: *You mean that literally?*

Mm-hmm. Not that I don't think I've done as best as I ever could with what abilities I have. I'm very happy and I've done more than I've ever dreamed I would do. Things have happened to me that I never dreamed of, and so I'll die content, as far as that goes. But there's still a big world out there that I don't know anything about and I'm married now to a woman who loves to travel and I'm thinking, "Gosh, maybe there is more." And, of course, I'm not very well educated, so maybe I should get back to school and learn how to speak French or something like that, or go to Cambridge. There are just so many things that I could be doing.

And after you've had heart surgery, too, and were on the brink of dying at 58, you begin to wonder, then, too. How do I know when the arteries are going to close up, and then—bang!—it's all over. Do I just want to sit here and just draw another daily strip?

Sparky, you did one of the tenderest—that's the only word I can find—continuities you've ever done after that. It was different than other things, but it wasn't out of step with the strip.

That was where Charlie Brown was in the hospital?

Yes, and it was like a composer shifting to a minor key for a while. You survived a quadruple bypass?

Yes. That's like what I was telling you about coming home from the army, and suddenly I'm a man, you know. I've done this and I'm feeling good about myself. I thought, "Boy, I don't want to go to the hospital, they're going to saw my chest open. I'm not that brave. I don't want to go anyplace. I don't want to do anything. I don't know if I can stand this." But I remember my kids saying, "But you'd better do this, dad, if you want to play tennis and hockey again. You'd

July 7, 1979.

better do it." And I went to the surgery and they explained what they did and they said, "It doesn't hurt when they saw your chest in half. It doesn't hurt at all." Well, [my wife] Jeannie and I thought about it for a couple of months. So, I did it and I thought, "Boy, if I do this, I'll really feel good about myself." But that first night in the hospital, when they take you in and they take away all your clothes and you've got to take a shower and they come in and give you a pill, I thought, "Do I want to do this?" I've gotten on airplanes, and I've gotten off before the plane has taken off because I didn't want to travel; I've backed out of things for years. I said, "I could get my clothes now and I could go home. I don't have to do this. I could go home and just take it easy and maybe survive, but I'll make a complete fool out of myself if I do it and my wife will be ashamed of me and my kids will be ashamed of me." So, I went to sleep and the next morning, it all happened. So, I thought, "Boy, if I survive this, I'll feel great." But I'm still the same person now that I always was. It didn't change me much. I still had the same fears I've always had. But if you don't have the surgery—I've talked to other guys—every time you go to sleep at night, you wonder if you're going to wake up in the morning. If you go away, if you go to New York and you're in a hotel room and maybe had too much to eat or something that night, your stomach is feeling kind of funny and you twist and you wonder, "Is this the night that last artery closes?" You can't live that way, which is why I decided to go ahead to do it. I've never put in my years that I promised that I would put in.

Promised to whom?

I was ready to quit, and we argued with the syndicate president for almost three years over what was going to happen. I said, "I want to own this thing. I'm tired of you selling Charlie Brown razor blades in Germany without telling me. I want to be able to do what I want to do and I don't want you doing anything but the strip. Either I get my way, or I'm going to quit." This guy, he couldn't understand it at all. "You make more money than everybody else. You want more?" I said, "Yeah, but I earn more, I've done more. You see, I don't want more money. I just want control so you guys don't ruin it." Well, fortunately, he retired. [His successor] came in and he and I sat down and within five minutes, he could see how sensitive it was. All I was asking is that they don't ruin it.

GROTH: *Do you impose a substantial amount of authority over how your work is licensed?*

October 12, 1985.

Well, I have control over everything. My contract gives control. They can't do anything without my OK and I can do anything I want, as long as it does not destroy the property.

MARSCHALL: *Have licensing and merchandising or reader reaction ever influenced you to do things with characters and storylines?*

No. There are a lot of temptations and that would be easy to do, but I've never drawn anything with the thought that it would be good for licensing. I've never even emphasized a certain character because I thought it would be important. Right now, it's very tempting. We're working on this movie starring Spike, and it's very tempting to push Spike in the strip just to give him more attention, so that people will be ready for him. I don't think I could do it if I wanted to, because I can't think of that many ideas for him. But I like drawing Spike in the desert, and I love drawing those rocks and the cactuses.

GROTH: *Are there certain ways that you would not want your property licensed, that you would veto?*

Yeah. They're always dropping it down to make it too childlike, and I don't like that. But I just can't get around it. Now they're coming out with the *Snoopy* quarterly magazine, which will be for very small children. But they promised it would be good quality. They're the same ones that put out *Muppets* magazine. It's a good outfit, I guess. They came out and visited us last week. Well, what do I care?

Do you ever feel like you're losing control?

No. But I'm getting old. I'll be 65 in November. And I wonder, "What's happening to me?" Someday, you're going to be old.

A Little Joy
and Enlightenment
Now and Then

Leonard Maltin, 1985

Peanuts, which sprang from the fertile mind of Charles M. Schulz when he was 27 years old, has generated 30 television specials, four movies, two Broadway plays, and countless merchandise. The collected strips have sold more than 300 million copies in book form. On the 35th anniversary of the strip, Leonard Maltin talked with Schulz about the evolution and longevity of *Peanuts*.

Destined for Comics

LEONARD MALTIN: *Well, your nickname is Sparky and I know this comes from the Barney Google character Sparkplug of years gone by—which is kind of fitting, that your lifelong name or nickname is based on a comic strip character. It kind of ties your whole life up with comic strips, doesn't it?*

CHARLES M. SCHULZ: Well, it seems to have been prophetic. I have been told that an uncle, whom I didn't meet till I was about 25, came to visit my mother the day after I was born and looked down at me and said, "By golly, we're gonna call him Sparkplug." Years later, I discovered that Sparkplug came into the *Barney Google* strip in June of 1922 and I was born in November, so obviously Sparkplug was an instant hit, in probably the most famous strip of its day. So, it was prophetic.

Do you feel that your whole life has been pretty much tied to this medium?

Yes. I sometimes say that I'm not sure it was a very great ambition, but my dad and I always enjoyed the funny papers. My mother used to say, "How can you sit there and laugh at something out loud? I don't understand that." I read all the comics that were available back in St. Paul in Minneapolis and Saturday nights were always a big thing for us, because then we could go up to the drugstore and get the Minneapolis papers that were to be printed and delivered the next day. So, I read all the funnies and loved them all and, as a delivery boy years later, I used to walk the streets of downtown St. Paul and I'd pass the *St. Paul Pioneer Press* and I'd see the Sunday comics coming off the press. Looking through the window, I'd think that, well, maybe someday I'll have a comic strip coming off those presses, too.

It's kind of like predestination. I think we create our destinies and if you have a direction in life when you're very young, I think that reinforces that. You seem to have had that direction. Did you ever have any wavering of thought about what it was you thought you were gonna do with your life?

I had a few doubts that I was going to be able to do it. Right after high school, I sent an application to Walt Disney and got turned down flatly, but that didn't discourage me. I used to see how good some of the cartoonists were, and I used to sit at home in my bedroom and draw comic strip after comic strip. I had my heroes, of course, and one Sunday afternoon my mother and dad took me to the library in downtown St. Paul and there was an exhibition of comic strip originals. I walked around this huge room and I saw the beautiful pen work of Roy Crane and some of these other people, and I went home and took all my drawings and tore 'em up and threw 'em away and started over again. I knew that I had a long way to go. Which I think is a good sign, because I receive drawings from people in the mail now and it's a pity that they don't know they've got a long way to go.

Yes, being self-critical is one of the key ingredients.

But, I think you can say I've always been obsessed by the medium. It's a strange medium because it isn't given much glory in our society. It's still regarded as maybe one notch below burlesque, I'm afraid. And so, you have to be very careful to judge the compliments that you get when people say how good something is that you're doing. It's better that you don't stick your head up, because somebody's gonna throw a rock at you—because there are others that just think comic strips are worthless, they're not even worth talking about. But, I was obsessed by it, and I think I have that strange combination of abilities of knowing how to draw pretty well and write pretty well and put it all together. I've said that if I could draw really well, maybe I'd be a painter, and if I could write really well, I'd do novels or write for the theatre or something like that. It takes a certain combination of abilities.

Now, just to go back half a turn. You're talking about the disrepute that the comic strip still enjoys in many circles, and yet I know you're not keen on the comic strip being lauded as art, either. Is that a contradiction?

I don't think you can label something art while it is being done. I think art is judged by how it affects future generations. And I just don't see many comic strips that have carried on their quality and that speak to future generations. I can think of only one or two that have had that ability, *Krazy Kat* being the obvious example. And for critics or anybody to say that this or that is art while it is being produced is insane. I think art is something like *Alice in Wonderland*, which was probably not art when it was being written, but is now art because it speaks to succeeding generations. So, it doesn't matter what people call something. What matters is, are you bringing any joy or any enlightenment to the viewer or to the reader? That's the only thing that counts.

You've now spoken to more than one generation, really. We're going on 35 years, that's a pretty long time.

Krazy Kat
by George Herriman,
April 4, 1931.

Well, if you want to call what I do art, that's fine with me, but I'm afraid to call it art. I'm afraid that I'll get shot down, so... I'm content just to be what I call a cartoonist or a comic strip artist.

Are you pleased, though, that there are museums that are recognizing the comic strip as something worthy of examination?

Yeah, until you see what other things go into them, and then you think, well maybe it's not art after all. [*Laughter*]

Do you ever have aspirations to do something that you feel is more consciously artistic?

Oh, yes. But, I still feel that what I do best is the comic strip. If somebody asked me for a drawing, they would like to have something to hang on their wall or something. Rather than give them a special drawing that I would make for them, I would rather that they have an original daily strip or an original Sunday page, because I feel that this is what I do best. Now, if I had the ability, I would love to be able to write a good novel or a stage play or something like that, but I'm afraid I don't have that obsession with words. I think that if I'm smart I'll stay right where I am.

If You Want to Get It Done Right,
You've Got to Do It Yourself

What do you think about comic strips that are inherited by other people than their creators?

I can think of offhand only one that is done quite well... the man who does *Snuffy Smith* picked up on Billy DeBeck's style and carried it off in his own direction. I think he's done quite well with it. And I suppose Dean Young and the other men have done quite well with *Blondie*. Beyond that, I think most of them are a total disaster and I think it's a pity to take a really good comic strip and have it destroyed by somebody else, simply because the syndicate wants to make some more money.

When you say destroy, do you mean artistically or from the heart?

Well, both. From the heart and artistically, they can't draw as well as the original creator. A good comic strip, like any form of creativity, whether it's a man sitting at a desk with a typewriter or a man at an easel or a composer sitting at a piano, a comic strip is done by one man sitting at a drawing board and it all comes out of him. Collaboration had worked only in rare instances and then only because the writer understands the medium. In most cases, writers of comic strips who do not draw them do not really understand the medium and if you are a writer of a comic strip, you are robbing yourself of visual humor. You're robbing yourself of the ability to create the pictures in your mind and transfer them immediately to the paper. You will keep yourself from 50 percent of your ideas. So, this is why collaboration doesn't always work, but it's still one person who is unique in all this world, taking his view of the world, his view of people and transferring it down to this funny little comic strip page.

As you well know, there are many comic strips that are produced by collaborations or teams, and in some cases, whole platoons of people. Some of them are good comic strips, but they don't have the depth. They don't have the signs that they are coming out of one person's mind and speaking with one voice, the way Peanuts *always does. But what I wonder is when and where and how did you determine that that was the only way you could work on a strip. You're one of the real bastions of individuality in this field that way.*

I've never really thought about it, but now that you force me to think about it [*Maltin laughs*] maybe I go back to my days when I worked at the Art Instruction school's correspondence course. I was surrounded by other young people who had ambitions to do different things. Some wanted to be painters, some illustrators, some fashion artists—we all had these different directions that we wanted to go. I think I would have sold out or had the feeling that I would have sold out in the eyes of these other friends of mine if I had simply turned into a factory. Because they knew what I wanted to do, they saw my ambitions, and I just wanted to do something that was good.

Now, I think I worked under many handicaps. My biggest handicap was the small size that the syndicate originally gave me for the *Peanuts* comic strip. I still maintain that they didn't have any confidence in it, otherwise they would have given me more room in which to work. The original *Peanuts* strip was about the size of four air mail stamps. [*Maltin chuckles*] And when cartoonists these days complain about not having enough room, I say, "Well look at what I did, I only had four little tiny squares to work in." And I had to compete against Al Capp, who had enormous panels to work in, and *Prince Valiant* and all of these other things, but I did it with what I think was quality. I was given a space in which to work, the same way as an actor is told, "You've only got 10 feet of stage, but do the best you can." And I did it. I think my whole approach would have been a little bit different if they had given me more room. Maybe it wouldn't have been any better, I just don't know.

What about the control, though, that you've insisted on in all of the outlying branches of Peanuts*? The merchandising, the other appearances of the characters in any kind of medium or different kind of print appearance. I know that you've always wanted to have control over the lettering, over everything like that. Talk a little about why you feel so insistent on those things.*

It started very small. I don't think we ever intended to have a licensing program. Everything that has ever happened, at least for a long while, was someone coming to us with an idea. The strip was the foundation of it all. And then someone said, "Well, maybe we should make some little plastic dolls out of these characters." OK. And I remember the sculptor coming all the way from New York with this little satchel of clay models, and we went over these things to make sure that they looked as good as we could make them look. And when Connie Bouchet came up from San Francisco with her ideas to do a date-book and other things, we went over everything to make sure it was proper. I just think it's absurd to do it any other way. I wanted things to be done as well as possible. This doesn't mean that everything was perfect and everything was wonderful, but it was the best that we could do under the circumstances. I just think that's the only way to do it. And I believe that I was the only one who had ever done it in this way before. But if you look back at some of the old licensed products that were put out about comic strips, some of them are pretty bad. Maybe they didn't care, I really don't know.

I have no way of knowing how the different cartoonists approach this thing and how the different
syndicates looked at it. But it was always a matter of
people coming to us with their ideas, and then we'd
either say yes or no and develop them. We never
searched out and said, "This should be done here or
there, and let's go find somebody to do it." Everybody came to us, and I think that's a better system.

*What about doing the strip itself, though? Obviously,
there are people who use assistants to do lettering or to do
certain tasks of that kind, and you don't and you never
have believed in that. I'm wondering, are you the kind
of person who, away from this job, believes that if you
want to get it done right, you've got to do it yourself?
Does that carry over to other parts of your life?*

No, and I'm not sure that I'm the person that can
even draw this strip the best. There are other people
that can draw much better than I can. But I think I
have a certain feel for this. I think I may not be the
best comic strip artist who has ever lived, but I'll
bet I know more about drawing comic strips than
anybody who's ever been in the business. I have a
feel for this rather insignificant business, but I know
what I'm doing.

When you're drawing, you are solving problems.
I very seldom draw for the fun of it. If I happen to
be on a rare vacation, I take along a sketchpad and
some felt pens and maybe I'll draw some trees or
mountains or buildings or something like that. And
I was saying to an artist friend of mine recently that
when you're drawing quickly from life this way, you
are solving a whole series of little tiny problems. As
you look at a window of a building, for instance,
you are trying to solve immediately how much of
that window you're going to draw; if you're gonna
draw every little element or if one thick line is gonna take care of it, and you instantly solve these little
problems all the time. When you're drawing a comic
strip, you are solving these little tiny problems.

And when I'm drawing, I know what expression
I'm going to put on those characters and I think it's
very important. And I don't believe in what you hear
in cartooning courses and books about inking in. I
don't ink in. I draw with a pen, I rough out a little
bit with the pencil, but what comes out—over those

ABOVE April 19, 1985.
OPPOSITE *Prince Valiant*
by Hal Foster, June 19, 1938.

pencil lines—may be totally different because I am drawing with the pen. When I'm drawing a wooden fence, I'm thinking wood; when I'm drawing grass—and I'm the only one that draws grass from the side view—I'm thinking grass; and I don't use the system that you see in these cheap how-to-draw cartoon books that if a character's happy, the smile goes this way, if a character is sad, the mouth goes this way. I feel it as I'm drawing and it just comes right out of the end of the pen, with the emotion that I have as I'm drawing this thing. And to turn this over to somebody else means that I'm going to look at it and say, "That isn't quite what I had in mind. When Charlie Brown is saying this, I want that little mouth to have the little twist that I think it should have when he says a certain phrase." And that's why I think I should do it myself. And when somebody comes up to me and says, "Gee, that was a funny strip you had last Thursday," I don't want to say, "Oh, I didn't think of that one, that was my assistant who thought of that one." It's my strip and I did it, for better or for worse.

What kind of feedback do you get from editors?

Almost no feedback from newspaper editors. Very seldom. Which is nice, I guess that means they like it. They're still paying for it and running it.

What about the syndicate that you work for? What kind of comments or suggestions have you gotten over the years?

Oh, dumb ones. [*Laughter*] Years ago, they tried a few points of direction, but the president of the syndicate had the philosophy that the cartoonist should live and die on his own ideas. Leave him alone and let him do it. If he can do it, fine; if he can't, he's never going to be able to do it anyway. And I suppose that's a good philosophy. I work with a good group of people now who do leave me alone. We have arguments over commas and things like that, but that's about it. Of course, since I first started, I now have total control over everything. It's nice to know nobody is allowed to touch anything that is done without my seeing it.

What about reader response? I know you get a ton of mail, and maybe that's not an exaggeration. [Laughter] What kind of mail is the most interesting and what kind gives you any guidance or direction, if any?

I don't pay much attention to what you would refer to as guidance or direction. I do what I think is funny. I received a letter from a young girl last year who said she thought it was time for Lucy to stop pulling away the football from Charlie Brown, that it really was rather cruel. Now, she may be right. As the years go on, you look at things a little bit differently. I've mellowed considerably. I'm not as sarcastic as I used to be, and the characters in the strip are not as sarcastic, so maybe I've changed as I've grown older. There are a lot of gratifying letters. If you know that you've drawn a strip that has encouraged someone who might have been ill or was having some kind of problem and has cheered him or her up, that's very gratifying. And I think knowing that you are pleasing a broad spectrum of readers is gratifying. To get letters

August 18, 1972.

from psychiatrists, ophthalmologists, athletes, school teachers, little kids—rather than just one segment of a reading public—is very gratifying.

It's certain you're not pleasing optometrists, though.

No, they don't like me. But, I have several ophthalmologist friends and I believe that the ophthalmologists are right. The optometrists don't care for it, they want me to replace the phrase and use the term eye doctor. But, I think a person should go to an ophthalmologist. [*Laughter*] I've done a lot of medical things, and they are all very carefully researched. When I did the series where the girls were going to have their ears pierced, I think I called up four different doctors to find out what should be done, where it should be done and if it was done in a doctor's office, what the pricing would be for all these different things, what the problems were of infection. And, of course, this also gives you a lot of extra ideas. Everything I do is quite carefully researched, and I rarely draw about anything unless I am fairly expert at it. I don't like surface humor on anything. The dumbest thing is to draw a bowling cartoon where somebody has not let go of the ball and is sliding down the alley. Sports cartoons like that are just ridiculous, anybody that would draw that shouldn't be allowed to. So, when I draw cartoons about something, I try to go beneath the surface of things.

You've brought us to the subject of content. How consciously do you put things into the strip that you feel are going to enlighten people about different subjects?

I'm not a teacher. I have no desire to teach people things, but it's flattering to be told that maybe I do enlighten now and then. I've done a lot of theological things and, again, I think I have gone way beyond what most of the comic strip artists have done with theological elements in cartoons. I never draw the little kids kneeling by their bed, talking to God in some cheap way. I can't stand that sort of humor. Linus really understands the Scriptures and he talks about them. Of course, Sally is very dumb about it, but I think I do things which have more depth along those lines. I've been doing a series the last couple of years where Linus—naturally, he still believes in the Great Pumpkin—has been going around like an evangelist knocking on the doors and saying, "Good morning, my name is Linus van Pelt, I'm here to tell you about the Great Pumpkin," and slam! [*Laughs*] I'm saying, "Let's be a little bit nicer to people who knock on your front door." You don't necessarily have to invite them in or something, but don't slam the door in their face.

So, maybe this is the extent of my teaching.

Do you feel that you are consciously trying to do a moralistic comic strip? Is that something you're very aware of?

It's pretty decent humor. I think everything that we've done has been pretty decent. Maybe you could say it'sh prudish, but I don't see anything wrong with being prudish and I don't see anything wrong with being nice. I think we have proved, with everything that we've done, that you can be successful and still do things that are nice. I've never done anything that's raunchy or had a double meaning or was nasty in any way like that. It's all been decent and upright stuff, and I'm proud of that.

I'm sure every cartoonist is tired of being asked this question, but it's an inevitable question to ask. How do you get your ideas day after day?

With me, I think it's a matter of obsession. I don't think I ever really stop thinking about it. There are ways which you can cold-blooded think of ideas. I've wanted to do this in front of a crowd though I'm afraid to do it, but I think that I could deliberately think of a cartoon idea at will. Give me a blank sheet of paper and give me five minutes, and I can draw something funny. But that's only for emergencies. I don't like to do that, but it's one way of doing it and there's nothing wrong with that. And it will provide you a certain percentage of ideas which are all right. But then there are the ideas that come because of some dis-

October 30, 1983.

tant memory or something that has happened to you recently, something which I like to do, something more emotional, something that really touches people...

My strip is filled with unrequited love. Everybody loves the wrong person in my strip and nothing ever quite works out, because people can identify with this. People can identify with unrequited love, people can identify with losing. But, it's all a caricature, of course. Almost all of us have lost at virtually everything we ever try to do, but Charlie Brown's the only one that loses at everything he tries to do. His actions are a caricature in the same way that his appearance is a caricature. Now, I can think of ideas just walking along the street, I can think of ideas riding along in the car. Looking through a magazine, a phrase will come to my mind that will prompt an idea. There are all these different ways, but it means thinking about it constantly, never having it totally leave your mind. And one thing will lead to another—you will think of one and, all of a sudden, it will open up a passageway that will lead to either a little story or a series of strips which may last for several years. I also keep little notes on my desk. Some of them have been there for over a year; there's a possibility of an idea there, but nothing quite comes. It just stays there and, all of a sudden, one day I'll find that I can use it, and it works. And it was worth waiting for.

Now, do you draw the strip principally to please yourself?

Oh, yes. Definitely. I don't see how you could possibly ever think of a certain audience and try to please them. To draw for children would be the most difficult

November 6, 1958.

thing of all. I'm always appalled at the amount of people who decide that they're gonna try some writing. "Oh, what kind of writing are you gonna do?" "Well, I think I'll try a children's book." I wouldn't try to write a children's book for anything, that's too hard. I don't know what pleases children, I don't know what makes children laugh. I just draw what I think is funny and hope that everybody else does. If they don't, there's nothing you can do about it. And I never test the ideas on anybody, I'm embarrassed to do that. I'm afraid they'll be committed to saying, "Yeah, that's kind of funny."

What about material itself that you incorporate into the strip? You often have stuff that's very sophisticated or in some cases, very arcane, really out of left field, things that certainly no young person would be expected to know. I know that when I was young and reading Peanuts, *I got a kick out of that. Even if I didn't know what it meant, I wanted to find out what it meant. From the Red Baron to references to* Citizen Kane *or whatever it may be, you certainly cover a pretty broad spectrum.*

Well, I discovered that you cannot please every reader every day. If you try, you please no one, no day. So, the thing to do is to reach out and try to please and flatter the reader with a real knowledge and a perception of his or her profession. If I do something medically, I know the doctors are going to be very pleased because I've handled it properly. If I draw a golf strip or a tennis strip or something, I do it authentically. Now, I mentioned Thomas Hardy in the strip recently. Nobody's ever mentioned Thomas Hardy in a comic strip before. But, if there's a Thomas Hardy fan out there, that person is gonna be with you the rest of their life, because you have flattered them into knowing that you love Thomas Hardy and so, now,

January 4, 1983.

we both love Thomas Hardy. It doesn't mean that you're gonna lose all the other readers who have never even heard of Thomas Hardy. Please a few people each day of the week and that's about all you can be expected to do, but it's very important. If you treat somebody's profession or hobby or something in a good manner, I think they'll be your friend forever.

It's wonderful to have a strip that will accommodate anything that I can think of. Somehow, I can work it out, and all the things that I've liked in my life, everything from *Citizen Kane* to *Beau Geste* to Thomas Hardy, I can use. And that's important. And it makes it fun, too.

There are some people who feel that a lot of the contemporary comic strips are feeding off each other or feeding off other forms of pop culture, and I think one of the things that's interesting about Peanuts *is that it really feeds off life. You might say that it's not about any one thing in particular, and it shows your broad range of interests. Have you ever thought about the state of comics in this way?*

Yeah, I think about it all the time. I think it's important for the cartoonist to realize that he has this little space in which he works, and he should be totally creative in that space and not draw from other mediums. I see a lot of cartoonists using expressions that they hear prominent television comedians or actors or something using. You should create your own expressions; your world should be your own world. And I'm afraid that a lot of comic strips begin and then level off very quickly, and you can see that that's as far as they're ever going to go. They never break any new ground, they never search for a new tunnel to go down. There are some risks in doing these things, but it's worth the risk. And I think it

April 16, 1966.

reflects upon your own interests. I don't think of myself as being a very interesting person or having broad interests, and I'm certainly not well-educated. Did you know that I played on the tennis team of the correspondence school? We used to hit balls against the mailbox. Yeah, I wanted to get that in there. [*Laughter*] If you don't use everything in your life in your strip, your strip is going to be a dull strip. And maybe you're a dull person, I don't know. I think you can almost tell by reading somebody's work what kind of a person that person is.

You're a celebrated person. Who are some people that you admire?

Well, starting at the very top of celebrated people, my all-time hero would be General Eisenhower. As I look back upon our attitude toward him in World War II, the G.I.s would have done anything for Ike, we held him in such esteem. If Ike would have said, "Race into that machine gun," they would have done it because everybody just felt such confidence in him. And there's a minister friend of mine, who now is retired and lives in Kansas someplace. A very gentle, kind, loving man who preached gentleness and love and kindness and not radical theology. He influenced all of us young people in his congregation and I've kept in contact with him. And then, of course, you never can leave out your own parents who tolerated this weird ambition. Neither my mother nor my father ever had any idea of what it was like to be a cartoonist or how to get started. My dad was a barber. Neither went beyond the third grade. But they didn't get in the way of my ambition. They didn't say that's foolishness and all that. They used to ask friends, "Well, what can we do? Where can Sparky get started?" and all of that, because they had no idea. But, I've always appreciated that they tolerated this strange ambition and didn't force me to go off to medical school or something like that, where I would have been an instant disaster.

Bringing *Peanuts* to the Screen

Now, let's talk a little about animation. It's rare that a comic strip has translated so effectively and so durably to another medium. There have been other examples, of course, but I don't think there's ever been an example where the creator was so intensely involved. I assume that came about the same way that everything else seems to come about for you: Somebody must have contacted you and said, "Can we make an animated film of Peanuts*?" Is that how it started?*

Yes, we were approached by several different people. It started with doing the Ford commercials. I was introduced by the people at J. Walter Thompson to Bill Melendez, which was a very fortunate thing, because Bill and I have become very close friends. He has so many great qualities, and what helps us work together is that we appreciate what each other does. I have heard Bill say many times, "I could never draw a comic strip," and I like to have somebody admit that he could not draw a comic strip, because a lot of animators probably think they could—there's nothing to it. I'm not sure I could be an animator. But I'm not quite as humble as Bill and I won't say I don't think I could be an animator. I can see things in my mind and know and see how they're going to work on the screen, which is why I think I've been able to make the transition from comic strips to animation. So I think I could be an animator, but I wouldn't want to be an animator. I like the creative part of it. I like being able to think of the funny things, and what I really like best is being able to think of something very complicatedly funny and then know that I don't have to draw it, that some poor animator's going to have to sit down with the terrible task of transferring some monstrous idea that I've thought of to little tiny bits of action. But it was a fortunate thing for Bill and I to get together. Like I say, we appreciate what each does.

What has made our animation efforts different from the others is the fact that our characters talk to each other. Our characters do not feed each other gag lines, they do not speak in tiny flashy expressions—they actually converse. Offhand, I can't think of any other animated series where the characters converse, where they actually say real live sentences. And it makes the character become very real. Of course, they're still cartoon characters. They're still drawn with the same style that they are in the comic strips, with a little expansion, which is nice, because it's a different medium. With animation, they are able to do some of the things with backgrounds and other things that I can't do, and sound effects and all of that. But, it's still basically the same group of *Peanuts* characters, and they are almost real because they talk to each other.

Now, what was the biggest challenge or hurdle in taking a two-dimensional, flat, mostly black-and-white—except on Sundays—comic strip, which runs four panels, and turning that into a half-hour animated color TV special?

One thing was learning how to write in episodes, which is very important. Each funny little episode must contribute to the story as a whole. If you think of the story first, you're liable to end up with weak episodes. So, I try to think of episodes and put them all together and fashion the story out of it. From the drawing point of view, the most difficult part was the fact that these were comic strip characters and they were not designed for animation, which means they don't have the rubber-like quality that animated characters have. On the other hand, I can't really think of a good animated character that has become a good comic strip character, because the rubber quality that goes into animation does not transfer to comic strips very well. For instance, Bill Melendez has had a terrible time drawing Charlie Brown's head and making it revolve, because I only draw it from the side view and from the three-quarter view, the same way Popeye used to be drawn. Popeye was always drawn from the three-quarter view. Suddenly, Charlie Brown had to revolve, so things had to change and this has been difficult. Fortunately, we're now working with limited animation, and I've told Bill that our characters don't have to have the old Walt Disney perfection. They're not human characters. If they were, we wouldn't need cartoons. We could use live actors, and they could do it better.

Popeye by E.C. Segar,
November 14, 1930.

So, there's nothing wrong with a character just turning from one position to another. You don't have to have it flow that smoothly. What's the difference? It's a cartoon.

Having tackled some half-hour TV specials, was it an ever bigger hurdle to do a feature-length film?

Yes. The biggest hurdle, of course, is that you have to please so many different people. You have to please not only the networks but the people who are going to distribute the film. And they give you a time limit, saying, "This film must run 75 minutes." Well, that's absurd to be able to set a time limit on something. You either have to stretch it out to make it go 75 minutes or you have to reduce it to some time limit, and that's always bad. We've learned how to handle that, but we've suffered because of it. I think our films have been better when we've gone back and trimmed them for running on television.

When the first Peanuts *special came along, I remember one of the things that was most exciting and most curious for me was listening to the voices. I had been reading* Peanuts *for so many years and, like every other reader, I had been speaking the lines silently to myself without ever having a clear picture of what those voices would sound like. What was it like when you had to face the actual problem of casting voices for those characters?*

Well, one of the qualities that makes comic strips good is that each reader hears a different voice and that's all right. When we started doing the Ford commercials, the biggest problem was what were we going to do with Snoopy. Snoopy can't think out loud anymore, and some of the advertising people wanted to give Snoopy a voice, which would have been a terrible mistake. And they brought in some tapes of character actors from Hollywood who tried to use a funny voice for Snoopy's thinking, but I just didn't like that and said, "Well, we'll lose a little something, but in animation and action we'll gain something else." They also tried adult voices for the characters, and we discovered that that didn't really work. So, we began using little kids' voices and we happened to get some real gems. I think in *A Charlie Brown Christmas*, the Linus voice was a marvel. As the years have gone on, we've learned that we have to keep down the Lucy voice, otherwise she shrieks too much. We have trouble now and then with the very young characters like Sally, because the children get so young that they can't pronounce the words. Frequently, Bill Melendez has to take a long word and chop it up on tape and paste it together to make it work. Some of the little kids can't read, so they have to take their cues from somebody reading their lines to them. All sorts of problems come up. Sometimes they don't emote as well as I would like. I remember working with one kid and we wanted him to scream, "Aaah!" He just couldn't do it hard enough, so I said, "Look. I'm going to whack you a good one on the leg now. When I hit you, scream," and I really swatted him a good one on the leg and made him scream, and that's the scream we wanted. [*Laughter*] When we did *The Big Stuffed Dog*, it was a pleasure for me to work with adult professional actors who took some of the lines I had written and really brought them to life. I'm afraid that most of the child actors don't bring your lines up to the level you would really like.

At that first audition you went to for children's voices, was it jarring for you to hear a child doing the voices you had heard in your head all the time?

Oh, yes, but I was pleased that some of the voices were really good. For instance, we discovered that there are a lot of Linus voices around. Charlie Brown was the hardest voice to get. We wanted a voice that is bland and dull and without character, and we've always had the most trouble finding voices for him. But I wasn't there for the initial recording sessions. I don't think I attended a recording session until we had done several different shows, and then I discovered how difficult they are. So, now I try to stay away from them if I can. It's just a lot of plain hard work

It must be, especially working with children and getting them to read the lines just the way you have in mind.

Oh, yeah.

When you talk about the Ford commercial, I have this indelible memory of tuning into the Tennessee Ernie Ford Show *every Thursday night at 9:30. I had to tune in every Thursday night just to see the opening little tease that they had with the* Peanuts *characters. That was the very first* Peanuts *animation, wasn't it?*

That's right. And we kept getting better and better. By the time the show was finished, we really knew what we were doing. The drawing was improving, and we really did some funny things. Those served as a wonderful background for our eventual stepping up to do *A Charlie Brown Christmas*. Bill Melendez was ready when he had the opportunity to do the first special.

That first TV special had one of the great credits in animation history. I think it was called "graphic blandishment?" I'd never seen a credit like that...

Yeah, that was a Melendez bit.

The idea was that he was actually just expanding on your artwork, is that right?

Yeah, yeah, yeah. I liked that.

Would you describe how your collaboration with Bill Melendez works?

One of the first things that happens is that our producer, Lee Mendelson, has to find out when the networks are willing to accept another show. For instance, we'll take the fall. We'll go back to Halloween and Lee Mendelson will say, "They want a Halloween show. OK, how do we write a Halloween show?" So, Bill Melendez comes up here to my studio and we sit down and we start talking about different things, and out of this first conversation comes a rough story. He goes back down to Hollywood and roughs out a storyboard, six panels on a sheet of paper. Then he brings it to me and I go through it, and we try to think of some more funny things. After about the third session, we're ready to polish the dialogue and get it just the way we want it. Now, that's one way of doing it. Another way is that suddenly I'm reading a magazine or I'm lying in my hospital bed three years ago, and I get a great idea and I call up Bill Melendez on the phone and I say, "Bill, I got a great idea. I'm gonna make you rich and famous!" [*Maltin laughs*] And out of this one little idea, a whole show will come about.

I'm thinking of two shows. The one where Snoopy was hijacked into a dog sled team, I got the idea from reading a *Sports Illustrated* magazine article about Alaskan sled dog teams, and it occurred to me that Snoopy would have a terrible time if somehow he were forced to become a sled dog. He runs on his hind feet, and he's just not in shape for that sort of thing. Bill has always said that was his favorite show of all, because it really had a little lesson to it, too. And then the other one I'm thinking about is *What Have We Learned, Charlie Brown?*, the one where the kids visit Normandy Beach. I wrote that in my head lying in bed in the hospital at 3:00 in the morning. I was searching for a certain key phrase and when that came to me, the whole sequence of *What Have We Learned, Charlie Brown?* fell into place. Three or four days later, when I got home, I called up Bill and he, in his usual enthusiastic manner, said, "Ooh, that's a great idea, we'll do it!" And so, we did it and we won a Peabody Award for it a few months ago. So, those are some different ways of doing it. I think being told that you must have a show done six months from now on a certain date—and because it's a certain time of year, it should be about this or that—that's the worst way to do it. It's too mechanical, and it will usually show up as being on the forced side. There's no one way to do it, and I think the spontaneous way is the best way.

What about some of the nuts-and-bolts of your collaboration? How involved were you, and are you, in the actual process of turning a script into the film?

When we first began, I think I made a couple of rough drawings to show them the way I think the characters should be drawn, but since then I just don't get that involved. I really should go down to Hollywood more often than I do and see what's going on. But drawing the daily comic strip is still the basis and the foundation of the whole thing, and I feel this is where I belong. Of all the things that we do—books, licensed products, television, etc.—I think the most important thing is drawing a good comic strip for your newspaper editor every day. The newspaper editor is still our number one client. He's the man who got us where we are, and he's the man that I think we have an obligation to please. So, if I have the time to go to Hollywood, that's fine, but drawing a comic strip every day is a burdensome task.

How do you keep your enthusiasm working on a strip day to day? You still regard it as a challenge, don't you?

Yeah, sometimes it's not that fascinating. Some Sunday pages, when you think of the idea, you know it's just going to be plain hard work. And others, you can hardly wait to draw it, because it's going to be so much fun—especially if there's a lot of action and a lot of wild expressions and things like that, then it's fun to do. But if it's going to be Schroeder playing the piano with Lucy leaning on it for twelve panels, you know it's going to be plain hard work. So, you draw around the page to keep from getting bored at it and to keep up the spontaneity. I draw in a couple panels and then I turn and read a magazine for a while, and then I go back and draw some more and anything to keep from this chore. And if there's a lot of lettering, you know it's just gonna be a couple of hours of hard work, of lettering this thing in and making it look nice.

Well, you work so hard and you're such a perfectionist and you're such a self-critic, too. What do you think about the way comics look in newspapers, when you see the finished product? Does it bother you that they've been shrinking over the years?

Oh, yes, it bothers all of us cartoonists, because so many of the quality of the pen lines are lost. This is always a pity, that you really can't see the fine work that is put into some of the comics. Some editors treat their comic page with great delicacy and arrange it so that they do look nice; others just don't seem to care, and this is always a pity. I'm flattered that I think my comic strip appears in certain special places in a lot of papers. This is nice to know that they regard it as being unique and special. But that's just part of the business, and maybe that's part of what keeps it from being art.

On Style

Let's talk about style. Because when the strip first appeared, it was almost radical in the departure from what was then the norm. What's happened since is that we have dozens of clones or imitators to some degree or another who've followed the style of simplicity that you really blazed the trail with.

I suppose it all depends on our background, where we came from, how we got started. The old-time cartoonists, the great ones like Clare Briggs and those men, came out of newspaper work. I think they swept the floor of the newspaper offices and they drew cartoons that were necessary for the daily paper about different things. Such jobs don't exist anymore. I was a product of the late '40s where you got your start by doing magazine cartooning, and my first cartoons were sold not only to our local paper in St. Paul, Minnesota, but to the *Saturday Evening Post*. So, when I finally broke through with the strip, I was a product of magazine cartooning, which is a very stylized cartooning, big heads and little tiny bodies. And I was not the only one doing that, there were other men who were doing it and doing it very well. So, when I sold the strip, then my style came out of that, but gradually matured to what it is now.

There are some people, though, who don't understand what goes into making something that looks simple. Can you talk a little about the "deceptive simplicity," I guess you'd say, of a strip like Peanuts?

It's hard to talk about the simplicity, but I think warmth is very important. I think my cartooning style has developed into a warm style, which is nice to look at. There are cheap styles of cartooning where things are done almost like advertising cartoons, so the character never has any warmth. There's a whole series of different types of cartooning. A cartoon figure advertising a brand new type of automobile tire, for instance, is a different type of cartoon character from the kind who has to function in a comic strip, and some men have never understood this. They don't know that the style of drawing has to be workable, so that the cartoon character can have emotion. If you don't draw properly, your cartoon character can never express any emotions that have depth. My characters talk more than just gag lines.

I know that it intimidates artists to talk about their art, or for cartoonists to talk about their style, because it's not something you're always conscious of. But, I wonder if you could talk a little about how conscious you are of the simplicity of, say, the backgrounds. There was a time when everything was very detailed in a comic strip, particularly the serious ones but even some of the funny ones. And when you came along with Peanuts, *you simplified all that and you put just kind of the bare essentials into the background, and yet it's always just what needs to be there. How did that evolve, or do you know how it evolved?*

Well, for one thing, I wanted to get the reader right down on the level of the characters. We never used camera angles so that we're looking down on the kids. We're right in there with them and I just don't see any sense in putting in a lot of extra things in the background to get across the point that you're talking about. But there has to be a consistency here, and I think there's a consistency in the style of caricature all the way through: The ears are caricatured to the same extent that the nose and the eyes and the fingers and everything else is; in other words, one element isn't drawn with more detail than the other elements. I've always had trouble with interiors, trying to decide just what I should put in and how much they should be cartoons or be drawn realistically. And even to this day it kind of baffles me, what I should do. The television sets are always drawn from the side

view, but in a way, I suppose it's like an abstract painter: You're taking these shapes and trying to make them fit into the four squares and make them pleasant, make them interesting, and make them contribute something to the design, because cartooning is still design. A well-drawn cartoon is a well-designed cartoon, all the elements work together so that they're pleasing to the eye.

Now, I think warmth is very, very important. Cartoon characters should have warmth, and if we're talking about simplicity, there is such a thing as drawing with a style that is too simple to have any depth. A cartoon character which is drawn with the same simplicity that an advertising cartoon might be drawn can never express any emotion. This character cannot say anything that has any depth of meaning, because he was drawn too simply. There are also corny styles of drawing where the cartoonist is trying for a little extra laugh, which is always a mistake. This is why I think you also should be careful with the names of the characters. If you get a laugh out of the name the first time it's used, then you should be content with that and not think that people are going to laugh at this name for the next 30 years, because they are not. So, all of these things work together, but I think we should always come back to the word warmth, because I think this is very important. And I think the comic strip should be fun to look at. It should be appealing to the eye. A poorly cartooned character has elements in it which just don't quite fit together. The reader, not being a cartoonist or an artist, may not be aware of exactly what it is that's wrong, but he'll be aware that there's something there that is offensive. There may be a squareness to the style which is bad, or like I said, a cheapness to the style. And all of this is very important, it's one of these things that takes years to learn.

And pen technique, again, is very important. To draw with the pen. I was speaking two or three years ago to a group of editorial cartoonists, and I admire the way so many of those men draw. Editorial cartooning has become elevated during the past 10 or 20 years to new heights. And I told them that you're not really a cartoonist, you don't have a pen technique, until you can reach over a portion of your drawing that's still wet and hold the pen in the middle and draw up there like that, holding the pen on the end the way a painter might do it. Then you have pen technique and you know what you're doing, you're really drawing with the pen because the pen point becomes like a like a brush. And you're really using it.

This is obviously something you develop over many years of working and through trial and error. Do you feel that you work any differently today than you did 35 years ago?

I work more slowly. My hands shake now. I don't know if it's caused by the heart surgery of three years ago, but my hands do shake, so I have to letter more carefully than I used to. I got my start lettering. I used to letter entire comic magazines. I was paid a dollar and a half an hour for lettering comic magazines. They would give me the finished drawings and then I would put in the bal-

March 24, 1979.

ABOVE August 23, 1952.
OPPOSITE April 6, 1996.

loons. I could letter very fast. And I could space out the lettering, I didn't even have to use guidelines, I could just letter it right in. I was real good at it. But now I have to letter more slowly. I wish I still had that dash of pen line that I used to have, but it doesn't quite work the way it used to. But I'm not ashamed of what I'm drawing, I still think it has some quality to it.

What about the actual style, though, or the format? Has any of that changed over the years?

It's difficult to tell, until I look at some of the reprint books. And when I see that, I think, "Gee, I could have drawn that better." You don't notice it when you're drawing day after day after day, but the characters change; they get smaller, they get taller, and they shrink, and then you find a reprint book coming out a year or two later and you think, "Gee, Charlie Brown's getting a little too tall. Or Snoopy's stomach isn't drawn quite that way now." What's interesting is that as you become better at something, you no longer can draw it. I think of Snoopy lying on the doghouse or some other things. I'd get away with drawing it at that time, but now that I've learned how to draw it better, I find that it doesn't work anymore. I can't fake it the way I used to. And cartooning has a lot to do with faking it. You're always faking things, because you're not drawing realistically, so you have to learn to work around it. For instance, my characters have heads that are so large because of the style that I have. And their arms are so short from the front view that they can't lock their hands above their head. So, if I want to have them do something where they hold something above their head, it has to be done from the side view where you can fake showing the arms stretch, the way animators are always faking things. So you learn what can be cartoon and what can't be cartoon, and you learn just how to fake it.

Well, when you do look back, and you have these many collections now that enable you to do that, what's the biggest change you've noticed? What has surprised you the most about the change in a particular character? What character do you think has changed the most, in your eyes?

Oh, Snoopy. Snoopy started off as simply a cute little dog, a cute little puppy. And then he grew to a very grossly caricatured dog with a long neck and I can't believe that I drew him that way in those days. If the syndicate had any sense, they would have called me up and said, "You're fired. We hate the way you're drawing." [*Maltin laughs*]

Now, Snoopy has become an international star in more than one medium, too. Do you have any explanation for why Snoopy in particular should be such a favorite around the world? I mean, as popular in Japan as he is here?

My theory would be that he's fun to look at, he's very original. And being a dog, it breaks the boundaries of language and race and all these other things, which is difficult with human characters. I guess that would be it. I think we've discovered, too, that people around the world laugh at pretty much the same things, which always surprises me. Because I never think about whether or not something will be understood in another country. There's no way in the world you could ever start worrying about things like that. But, I'm always surprised when young people from Italy or Sweden or Japan visit me and talk about different strips that they really appreciate it. That's very gratifying.

I should think. What do you feel like when you walk into a store and there's an enormous display of Peanuts *character merchandise? Maybe you'll see a hundred Snoopys on a wall in front of you. Do you connect to that very directly?*

Well, yeah, I look right away to see what they're displaying. But it's more gratifying to be driving to work in the morning in your car and see a child walk across to school carrying a Snoopy lunchbox. Then, it really hits home. And I think the time it hit home more to me than anything else was at the Ice Follies one night when we were filming a show. We had the Snoopy costume with a young man in it come walking down the stairs way up in the balcony, and as he did, all the children started yelling, "Snoopy! Snoopy!" And all of a sudden, it hit me that there was a time when there was no Snoopy. And I thought of that character and I drew him and there he is. And that made me feel good.

What about the evolution of Snoopy? Snoopy has become so much more than a dog, and so much more than just a conventional comic strip character. He's taken on larger–than–life proportions in so many different ways. I gather that you didn't set out to do this with the character. Do you have any notion of how it happened?

RIGHT October 18, 1980.
OPPOSITE *Li'l Abner* by Al Capp, March 29, 1952.

YOU SHOULD SIT ON TELEPHONE WIRES LIKE OTHER BIRDS...

10-18

The turning point was probably when he was lying on top of the doghouse and I don't remember how he got up there or why. I remember about the third day, I think, he rolled off and said something about life being full of rude awakenings. But one thing simply led to another, and once you know you're onto something, then you build on it. Snoopy's a good character because he's so flexible. You can do things with him that you can't with the others; you can put thoughts in his mouth which you don't dare give to the kids. And I think he has been really unique. He's a writer, and he's a pilot, and he's also a kind of a contradiction to himself. He's quite a hero and he thinks he's very self-sufficient and all that, but he really isn't. He depends totally on what he calls the little round-headed kid, and he says, "I can't even remember his name." which is just a little extra bit of funniness. And I think this is good, because we are a combination of all sorts of things, strengths and weaknesses and everything. Also, I think Snoopy is well-drawn—he's not overly cute. I hate to say Disney-cute, but I guess that's the best way. He's not scamp-cute, and he doesn't say cute things. But I just like getting back again to the word warmth—Snoopy is drawn in a nice, warm manner. I like Snoopy. I like his brother Spike, too. I really enjoy this poor dog that's living out in the desert all by himself and he has no friends, and that's opened up another whole range of ideas.

Just as the arrival of Woodstock certainly took the strip into a wonderful reservoir of ideas.

Woodstock is a perfect example of how important drawing is, because the development of Woodstock came with the development of drawing. A realistically drawn bird would never be able to do what Woodstock does, it just wouldn't work. As I began to learn to draw him in a funny way, I was able to use him more. We must never forget how important drawing is in this, much important than people ever think about.

In the evolution of the characters, physically and emotionally, have you ever caught yourself consciously changing something about the characters?

I suppose the most conscious thing would be trying to tone Lucy down so she's not as mean as she might have been before... I've eliminated characters because they just didn't work. I eliminated Frieda's cat because I discovered I really didn't draw a very good cat. I don't think anybody should draw a cat when Gus Arriola is around, because he draws such beautiful cats and other animals, so you should stay away from his ground. But also, the introduction of certain characters spoils the other characters. I introduced another brother for Snoopy a couple of years ago simply because I thought the name Marbles would be a great name for a spotted dog. But, I discovered that having another dog in the strip took the uniqueness away from Snoopy, it destroyed the little relationship between him and the kids. I

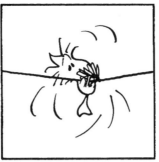

think that Linus now probably has the personality that Charlie Brown had when the strip first began. Things kind of shift. You start off giving something to one character and discover that it works better with another character. I think Charlie Brown had a blanket before Linus did, but it seemed to be funnier with Linus. It just worked better. I've always regretted that I gave Linus and Lucy the little brother, Rerun. I needed somebody to ride on the back of the mother's bicycle, so he works for that, but otherwise having him in with them just doesn't work at all. So, he never appears in that manner. But, in a comic strip, it doesn't matter.

In 35 years' time, have you ever thought about really shaking up some of the conventions that you have developed? For instance, have you thought about not having Charlie Brown be a loser at a certain juncture?

Yeah, it'd be the worst mistake you could make. It would be like Li'l Abner's getting married, which was the worst mistake that Al Capp ever made. *Li'l Abner* is one of the great comic strips of all time, but once Li'l Abner got married, the basic premise of the strip disappeared. And once Charlie Brown begins to win and you give into these little temptations, your whole structure will collapse. You have to watch yourself, because a lot of times you'll do it just for what we call a cheap laugh, or just to get some publicity. I could get a lot of publicity if I had Charlie Brown win a ball game or kick the football or something like that. But then, what happens after that? You've destroyed what you've built up and it's not worth it. But, it is tempting, and you have to watch yourself.

Here's something I'll bet you've never been asked before. Do you identify with Charlie Brown? [Schulz laughs]

I identify with all the characters. Probably more with Charlie Brown. I suppose I'm kind of wishy-washy like he is. I don't think you can draw any set of characters unless you identify with them to a greater or lesser percentage. You have to, because you put yourself into them.

Do you ever play favorites with the characters?

Yeah, there're some that I don't like as well as others. But, I think the eight or 10 that I use are the ones that I like the best and they are also the ones which provide me with ideas. This is very important, because the very nature of the characters that you have given them will provide you with ideas. We know that Marcie admires Peppermint Patty, but she's a little too smart to be a real hero-worshipper. And we know that Peppermint Patty has a terrible time in school, but she's not really dumb, it's just that she lives with blinders on. We know all these things and the longer the strip lasts, the more these personalities become developed, the more character they take on and then the more those characters give you ideas. This works the same way as, say, the old Jack Benny shows. You knew exactly where all those characters stood, and you can just play on those personalities all of the time. That's what people, I think, enjoy reading about. And they look forward to it, you can't let them down.

Now, there's always been some discussion about the idea that the Peanuts *comic strip features children but, of course, is not a childlike or childish comic strip. And yet it has an appeal to children as well as adults. Have you ever wrestled with that problem?*

No, because I think this is what made it unique from the very beginning and, again, it was the background that my cartooning career grew out of. Back in the late '40s, little tiny kids in gag cartoons in magazines were saying very pompous things and I think I just became part of this whole trend of writing smart-aleck things that were funny because they came out of the mouths of these little tiny kids. Now, this couldn't be done in any other medium; it can only work in cartoons, where everything is so greatly exaggerated. It wouldn't work with live actors. And then, as I began to do this, I looked back upon some of the old comic

May 10, 1953.

strips about children and found that they were a little too realistic and, many times, they were a little too cute. And I don't like drawing cute things. Although I will admit, when I look back upon some of the old *Skippy* strips, I often discover to my horror that he has done something 50 years ago which I just thought of today, so nothing is ever really that new. I was drawing a strip years ago where Lucy was mad at a balloon that had gotten away from her. The balloon was flying through the air and she was pleading with it to come back and then she was yelling at it, just furious because it wouldn't come back. And then she would plead with it again and then she would yell at it very angrily. And I happened to come across a J. R. Williams *Out Our Way* cartoon of a cowboy. He's out in the desert and he's going home at night, and his horse has run away. And he's doing the very same things to the horse that Lucy was saying to the balloon, except J. R. Williams thought of it 30 years before I did. And this is just the pattern of creativity. I see younger cartoonists these days doing things that I did 30 years ago. There's no answer to it, it's just part of the business.

Advice to Young Cartoonists

I wonder when people ask, as they often do, "How do I get started? What's your advice to a young cartoonist?"—it's not really advice about drawing and knowing how to set up a comic strip. It's really advice about living, isn't it?

Oh, definitely. I think the most important thing for any young person is to look to himself or herself and draw the things that he or she knows about. Forget about everybody else. You are unique, you're the only person like yourself that's ever been born and you are seeing things differently from anybody else. And when you get up in the morning, you face life differently. Well, put those things down on paper and add something to it. But don't be impatient. Too many young people want to be cartoonists when they're very young, and it's not a young person's profession. I think cartooning requires a good deal of maturity, because you are looking at life. Otherwise, you are cartooning what someone else has already cartooned.

Do you get a lot of young cartoonists asking you for advice?

Not as many as you would think. I don't ever get anyone that's any good, which is kind of depressing…

That's true. I was one of them. [Schulz laughs]

I get a lot of letters from uncles and grandparents whose nephews or nieces or grandchildren seem to like to draw, and they want me to write a letter of encouragement to this nine-year old child. Or else, they say, "What can we do to encourage the child?" And I always say that if the child wants to be a cartoonist, all you have to do is just stay out of the way. Maybe provide them with some nice drawing paper or some pens and pencils or something. But if you have to encourage the person to become a cartoonist, you might as well forget it. Why should you encourage somebody to be a cartoonist? A cartoonist is someone who wants to draw funny pictures. You don't have to encourage somebody to do it. Besides, they're much too young. Like I said before, cartooning is more for mature people.

Why do you feel that?

Because you have to cartoon by observation and young people don't have that much to observe, except maybe their family life or what's going on at school or the neighborhood. They aren't old enough to be able to observe and make really original comments on these things, which is what makes for cartooning. This doesn't mean that you can't draw for your high school paper or draw at a lower level of cartooning, but the secret is to be content then to draw and remain at this lower level until you grow up and maintain some maturity.

And yet, really, for most people, I guess it becomes a lifelong avocation if not career, doesn't it? I mean, it's not something you drift at and then reach your peak when you're mature, so many of them do try to attack it young. You tried to, and did.

Well, I got rejected continually. I didn't sell anything until I was, oh, about 26 years old. Sold my first cartoon to the *Saturday Evening Post*. I didn't even know they had sold it, I thought they had rejected it. I didn't understand the acceptance slip. *[Laughter]* There was a little note that said, "Check Tuesday for spot drawing of boy on lounge." And I thought the note meant that I should check on Tuesday, because they were mailing it back to me. And several hours later, I was talking to my dad, and I said, "That isn't what that meant. It means they're going to send me a check." And sure enough, on Tuesday I got a check for 40 dollars. My first big sale.

That must have been very exciting.

Oh, it was. But freelance gag cartooning is a tough business. Living and dying every week with opening the envelope, either getting a rejection slip or a "Sorry, nothing this week" note. That's why I like the comic strip,

Saturday Evening Post cartoon, May 29, 1948.

because the comic strip also gives you more flexibility. The comic strip will tolerate a few light left jabs and then a round-house right and a lot of variety. And you can toy with things and work them over, work around and kind of hassle them. But gag cartooning is a different business.

How would you sum up what you do?

When you're talking about people who make their living at this, I think you're simply discussing someone who just likes to draw funny pictures and that's what I like to do. I would be doing this if I had to do something else to make a living. I just enjoy drawing funny pictures. This doesn't mean that I'm having the time of my life every day. Sometimes it's plain hard work. I think cartooning has a certain quality and a certain charm unlike any other medium, whether it is somebody drawing for 2,000 newspapers or if it's somebody drawing a little cartoon on the outside of an envelope in a letter to a friend. There's a communication there, a bringing of joy, a bringing of happiness without being too pompous about it. I simply like to draw something that is fun.

The Wellspring
of Inspiration

Laurie Colwin, 1982

An admirer of Laurie Colwin's writing, Charles M. Schulz sent her a fan letter; the two struck up a correspondence and developed a mutual admiration for each other's work. In March 1982, Schulz invited Colwin to his studio to conduct an interview over the course of several days. Their ensuing conversation appears here for the first time.

The Renovation of Charles Schulz

LAURIE COLWIN: *You feel obviously strongly about this quality: What do you feel being adorable is?*

CHARLES M. SCHULZ: Well, I think adorable is the wrong word to use.

But somebody said it to you, and it just seems to have ignited your heart.

I *know.* I like to be adorable.

Then what is the quality that you're talking about? When you say, "adorable," what is it?

I think adorable intimates someone that you just like to be close to and hug and just love to be around.

Do you think your characters are that way?

Some of them, yeah.

Who do you think is the most adorable of them?

Snoopy.

He is pretty adorable.

But he's not to be trusted.

No. He's too critical, actually. He's not man's best friend.

Well, you can't blame it on him, because dogs are at the mercy of their owners. They can't vote and they have to admire their master even though their master may be the worst scoundrel in the world. You see guys walking down the street that you wouldn't want to have anything to do with... dog just trotting along, he's so happy he's with this guy and he doesn't know any better. I remember one strip where somebody says dogs are so trusting and Snoopy goes, "No. It's just that we're not very good judges of character." [*Laughter*] So, where were we?

If you renovate yourself completely—if you could be a completely different person—what sort of person would you choose?

I would like to have been better looking. I'd like to be somebody that would be instantly attractive to women.

Well, the fact about being adorable is that you just have no idea who would think you're adorable.

That's one of the things that keeps causing problems between men and women, because we look at things so totally different. And men simply do not understand women's minds and they're *always* misinterpreting things and going on completely wrong assumptions.

Well, that could be one reading of your strip—that the men and women in your strip do not speak the same language in any way. And the interesting thing about your strip, which is actually something that's been said about me, is that the women are terrible boys and the guys are just these poor romantic mushheads. All they want is to be loved and these girls are just being critical and bossing them around. The girls are very gutsy and the guys just hope that somebody will love them.

It's sad.

Well, I think it's more true than not. But the thing is, there is a lot about romance in

that strip. There's a tremendous amount of romance and, of course, Lucy and Schroeder are the high watermark of romantic mismatching.

And there's such lack of understanding between men and women. I'm still trying to formulate a lot of these thoughts in my mind, but they were stoutly denied by a woman recently. We were talking about this and I said that I don't think women are attracted to men's bodies the way men are attracted to women's bodies, and she said, "Baloney!" And that blew my whole theory. [*Laughs*] I think men are always searching for some kind of answer to this and never getting it.

Answer to what?

To being attractive to women.

Yeah, the thing that men and women suffer from is that both, until they're a certain age, think that there is something generally attractive, and it's usually not them.

Uh-huh. But you can sit in the coffee shop at the arena and look across and see someone and know right away that you would just like to go over and sit down and talk with that person. And yet dozens of other people will walk through there all day long and you wouldn't care if you ever saw them again. But suddenly one person comes in and you want to meet that person.

And do you go and meet them?

Oh, no. I don't. Sometimes, if the occasion…

Are they always women?

Oh, yeah. That's what I'm talking about.

Did you ever just see a man and think, "God, I want to meet that person." We're not talking now about romance, we're just talking about the way people connect with each other. I've met women that I think, "I have to know this person."

You usually want to meet men because of something that they have *done*.

You've never seen a man just walking around that makes you think, "Gee, that guy looks really interesting."

Never. But there are a lot of men that I would like to meet and talk with because of what they've done. Like Arnold Palmer or Sam Snead or a writer or something. But never just because of the way he looks.

What do you think about how that works—that you

are sitting in the coffee shop and 60 people walk by, and then there's just one *person that makes you think, "Gee, I just want to talk to that person." When that happens, what do you think is happening?*

Obviously, there's something about their physical appearance that attracts you. And it's more than just beauty. It has nothing to do with classical beauty or anything. There's just something about that person's face and whole structure that attracts you. Now, it doesn't always work out that way. You may go over and begin to talk and discover that there's really nothing much there for you. But sometimes there is. And then, maybe that's the way romances start.

Do you think that your characters are beautiful? Do you think they're attractive?

Yeah, yeah. I deliberately do not draw them ugly. But none of them are what you'd call beautiful or pretty.

No. They're all sort of homely and adorable.

Yeah. I can't draw pretty faces. And also, they don't caricature well and they don't express well.

You don't think they express well?

Not drawing pretty faces in cartoons.

Oh, I thought you meant your people, who are nothing if not pure expression.

Yeah. Like the little red-haired girl, I would never be able to draw her. We drew her in an animated feature because the animators could draw her better than I could. But she didn't have to do anything, she was just riding on a float. And I've never been able to draw what I would consider a real pretty little girl's face. I've wanted to several times, but it just doesn't come out right. I could draw the face, but it doesn't look real enough, and so I always go back to these kind of half funny faces—little button noses, big mouths, and funny eyes and things.

So now we're talking about the renovation of Charles Schulz. You wanted to look more like Louis Jourdan.

Yeah, but I've seen him lately and I think I'm aging better than he is. [*Laughs*]

So, who else would you have been?

I think we'd all like to be like Cary Grant. Wouldn't it be neat? But have a voice like Ronald Colman. Wouldn't that be great?

So now we have the aspect of Cary Grant, we look like Louis Jourdan, and we have the voice of Ronald Colman.

But I still would like to hit the golf ball like Sam Snead and play tennis like Arthur Ashe or Bjorn Borg or somebody. And then I'd like to be able to skate and play hockey like Bobby Hull. And draw like Picasso.

And you'd probably like to be as good a cartoonist as Charles Schulz, wouldn't you?

Yeah. Well, I'm satisfied with that. I wish I could draw better. I know my drawing abilities. I think I draw very well for what I do, but I don't draw well in the classical sense. I think I could have learned how to draw better than I do now if I'd studied more. But it's not important in what I do.

An Altered State of Consciousness

I want you to do what people in method acting call a sense memory exercise. I want you to...

...be a barber. [*Laughs*]

I want you to be alone in a restaurant having a wonderful lunch—everything that you would ever like to eat. But you're by yourself, and you're terribly content and happy. And the restaurant is filled with interesting people, none of whom you know, and you've never been there before. I want you to tell me what sort of things you see and think and what kind of thoughts would go through your head and what you would observe and notice. We'll say that every kind of scene was going on: there's two young lovers and there's two old lovers, there's a family, and there's a couple that have been married for 30 years.

If I didn't have anything to read...

No, no. You're sitting there and you don't *have anything to read. You're having one of those afternoons where you're just happy to be with yourself in a wonderful, nice, calm, happy frame of mind, and the people around are very—*

Sounds like I've died. [*Laughter*]

No.

In the first place, I would have gone to a newsstand and I would have gone through all the magazines trying desperately to find a magazine that I know that I could read while I was having lunch, because I would not go to have lunch without something to read. And I would have gone to a bookstore and literally would have paid $12 for a novel, just to have something to read while I was eating lunch. But, OK, you're saying that I would not have found anything to read.

Let's say you've got a magazine and a book and you've started reading them, but the people in the restaurant are actually more attractive than the novel. So, the novel's there, open, but you're not looking at it, you're looking around the room. I want to know what might be in your head.

If I were looking at the family and if they had small children, I would become terribly depressed, because I would miss my own kids so much. And I would wonder, if I were away from home now, what in the world I was doing here. I'd wish I were home at the ice arena watching Amy and Jill skate.

Well, suppose they were a family with teenage children.

It'd probably be the same thing. As long as it were a family like that, they would depress me terribly. When I had to make trips, I'd either be in railroad depots or airplanes, and if I heard a child cry I would immediately become so depressed that it would destroy my whole trip.

But there's never a part of you that would click off and just start observing?

Well, I'm telling you... I'm going from group to group. This is how a family would affect me. A married couple, I wouldn't pay much attention to them. It wouldn't mean anything to me. I think my marriage is very satisfactory. I might think of Jeannie and I sitting and having lunch together or something and maybe saying I should call her more often and we should have lunch together more often, rather than both of us off in different directions all the time. And that would probably be about all that I would think about that. I think that if I saw a very attractive woman there I would wish that I could be having lunch with her and talking with her. If I see somebody like that across the room I always think it's a pity that we can't just go over and introduce ourselves and just share lunch together and talk. We may never see each other again, but that would be all right. Why can't we do things like that? I did that once in an airport and I had a nice time. I was meeting somebody at the San Francisco airport and discovered that her plane was going to be two hours late—that it still hadn't even left Seattle, and yet it was supposed to be here in an hour. So, I knew I had a two-hour wait. And while I was inquiring about this, there was a younger woman standing at the counter and she found out the same thing. So, I walked away and I went over and I was looking through the magazines and everything. She was wandering around, too, and finally she came up right next to where I was standing. So, I introduced myself and I said, "Would you like to go have a cup of coffee while we're waiting?" And she says, "Yes. That would be very nice." And I introduced myself so that she would know that I was all right. [*Laughs*]

How did you do that? You said, "Hello. My name is Charles Schulz. I'm married. I have absolutely no..."

No. I said, "I'm Charles Schulz." I always say I'm the person that draws Snoopy. I never use the word "Peanuts," because I hate it so much. And she said, "Oh." She seemed very delighted to meet me. And I said, "Would you like to go and have a cup of coffee while we're waiting, because I see we have quite a wait?" And we did. And we had a nice talk and I asked her lots of questions about who she was, where she was from, and schooling and that sort of thing. And we left and I've never seen her again. And that was all right. I think that's what people should do. But there was a time when I certainly never would have done that, of course. And I admit I have a slight advantage now by being able to say that I'm the one who draws Snoopy. That usually gets me past the first barrier. [*Laughs*]

Have you ever have somebody look at you as if to say, "Oh really? Does he really... I don't believe this for a second. Who is this guy?"

No.

No. They think you're an honest fellow.

All right. So, we're back in the restaurant and now we have, oh, any other variety of person that might be sitting there. Well, let's just get down to what this question is really about. What makes your imagination work?

I do speculate sometimes on what the people do. If I'm looking at the men—whether this one's in advertising or that fellow's a banker, things like that. From that, ideas will come. And I think you're on the right track because my sitting there watching the other people could lead me then, in my thoughts, to Charlie Brown sitting alone at lunchtime and observing somebody. And that would start the chain of thinking, which may end up with Snoopy being out having lunch in Needles, California, with his brother. It could lead to Snoopy sitting at a table seeing a little French girl across the room or something like that. It's hard telling where it would lead. It could lead directly to an idea related exactly to what was happening, or it could lead to something totally different. But step by step it could—would almost inevitably—lead to something. Almost anything I do will lead to some kind of an idea. Rarely does it not happen. When I'm alone that way I'll *always* think of something funny—an idea for a Sunday page or something. Anytime I'm at a symphony, I'll always think of two or three funny ideas. The music, watching the man conduct. Suddenly it's just like it ignites your mind. It begins to work, and I'll always think of something.

Did you think of things when you were recuperating in the hospital?

Oh, yeah. I thought of a whole television show. I wrote the whole thing in my mind one night at 3:00 in the morning just lying there. The Omaha Beach one.

You thought of that in the hospital?

Well, I mean, I worked it out.

You did. So, how long were you in there before they did the surgery? You just went in and the next day they did it?

Yeah. I went in at noon and they conducted a few brief tests, and then the next morning was the surgery.

What did you think about the night before they did it?

I almost went home at 10:00 at night. I just had a last-minute panic, which I'm sure almost everyone has. I think people have last-minute panics in almost everything that they do—if they're going to get married, or if they're going to play in a tennis tournament or something. We all, at the last minute, want to run away. And suddenly at 10:00 at night everybody had left and I was lying there alone in the room knowing what I was going to face and thinking that I really didn't have to go through with this. This was still just my own idea. I could work this out and go home and just take the medication and live a very mild life, and not play hockey anymore or tennis or anything, and just do my work and probably survive quite well. I wondered what would happen if I just got in my clothes and ducked out. But, no. I thought I'd make a total fool out of myself, disgrace my family, and I just couldn't do it. So, I put it all out of my mind and settled back. And pretty soon a nurse came in and asked me if I wanted anything. And now I'm glad I didn't do anything, but I came close to it.

Then, what I wondered was, are you very disciplined in your imagination? What I mean is, sometimes I think that the real name of the game is conservation, and that people who work the way you do must be very steady and very firm in their minds, and they probably don't let their minds race unless it's absolutely right for their minds to race. I think after you do the kind of work you do for such a long time, you must be the real master of your imagination and your inspiration. Am I making sense?

Yeah, but I don't know what to say to that.

It's not a question you have to respond to. I just wonder if you think that's something that actually develops in a person who works the way you work. You seem on very intimate terms with your imagination.

I think that's right. I don't work in tremendous spurts where I do a whole bunch

February 5, 1979.

of things and then *not* do anything for several days. I prefer to work on a regular basis. I just think that I work best that way.

But you are confident that when you sit down something will come to you?

Oh, yes. I never worry about my work. I never worry about *not* being able to think of anything. The closest I come to worrying about not being able to think of anything is never again being able to come up with one of these grand themes on which I can play variations then for months or sometimes years to come—that I will never again think of a Linus blanket or a Red Baron or a Peppermint Patty falling asleep in school theme—that I'll just have to continue, for the rest of my career, rehashing the things that I've done, or doing daily gags, which I just hate to do. But I know deep down that as long as I remain alive as a person and as long as I continue to read a lot of different things and keep track of what's going on in the world and maintain contact with other people and, as I said, just continue to be alive, that these things will come. Those are the sorts of things that cannot be forced. You can force gags. You can deliberately sit down and write daily comic strip gags, but you cannot force these wonderful themes that will *last*. They have to come spontaneously just out of nowhere or else out of something else that you might happen to be doing. You might think of one simple little idea with Snoopy and the dog dish, and out of that might come one of the best themes that you've ever thought of. But I don't think you can force it. You just have to wait for it to come.

How do you feel when you work? When you're actually in the act of drawing or developing an idea for a strip, how do you feel?

When I have something that I know is good, I feel wonderful. I have a good time doing it, I enjoy the drawing, I enjoy making every little line as perfect as I possibly can, and I'm very proud of a lot of the ideas that I think of as I'm drawing them. I'm thinking what a great idea this is and I'm so proud of the fact that I thought of it and nobody else thought of it.

When you're in the actual act of creation, do you feel that you are in an altered state of consciousness?

I don't know anything about altered states of consciousness; that sort of thinking is foreign to me.

What I mean is, it's pleasure.

Oh, yeah, yeah.

Is it a certain kind of concentration that is specific only to your work?

I just don't know, Laurie. I just don't know. All I know is that these things come to me. I don't know where they come from most of the time. I just draw them, that's all.

This is the sort of thing that, sorry, I just don't buy. They don't just come to you. You've been doing it for a long enough time that you must have some idea of the wellspring of this...

I can do it mechanically.

Well, sure. But we're not talking about that. We're talking here about inspiration.

But you can't wait for inspiration.

I understand that and I understand about mechanics and craft and that you can probably do this in your sleep and you could probably come up with a fairly good idea if I said, "Go draw me a strip off the top of your head." But we know that the mind of an artist is like a databank—a specific databank—and he's drawing all the time off of what he's collected and what he's felt, thought, and experienced.

For the very best ones, when I'm doing them I'm like the tennis player who is what they call "in the zone." I have a very light feeling and I feel that my drawing hand is moving very quickly and lightly and my mind is working very quickly and lightly, and the words just come out just the way I want them. And, as the golfers say, "It was hit dead solid perfect," and that's the way the drawing and the ideas are on the goods days.

You have actually just described an altered state of consciousness.

Well, good. [*Laughs*]

What you're talking about is a peak experience.

Yeah. Somehow, I always relate these things to sports because I guess those are my interests.

That's a perfect parallel.

But, it doesn't happen all the time—just now and then.

This is not to make you think what a swell genius you are, but you must know that you're the only person doing what you, in fact, are doing.

I like to think so. In fact, I read the other comics often and I think, "Oh, why do they do that? Why don't they work harder? Why do they put down their first thought? Why don't they think about it a little bit longer and break beneath the surface a little more and try to make it better? Why do they settle for those first easy ideas?"

Do you reject a lot of first ideas that you have?

RIGHT May 11, 1953.
BELOW March 3, 1966.
OPPOSITE April 20, 1970.

Oh, yeah. Almost always.

Really. How many tries does it take you to get the thing—unless it just comes? We're not talking now about the times when it's just perfect.

Well, I have ideas on the desk here that have been laying there for sometimes a year before it comes out just the way I want it. And sometimes it never does and eventually I throw them away.

When Woodstock first appeared to you, for example, do you remember the development? Do you remember how he first appeared and what you thought of him and what you were after? Can you just give me a sort of sketch of the birth of that character?

Woodstock is a perfect example of how characters grow out of drawing. People tend to forget that cartooning is still drawing. It is not totally writing. And years ago, when the strip was first beginning and Snoopy was almost a real dog, I would draw now and then birds in the strip, and the birds were drawn quite realistically. You'd probably recognize them as being a robin or something like that. But after about 15 years, Snoopy became less and less of a dog.

One day, I started a series where he was lying on top of his doghouse and there was a nest on his stomach. And he was complaining that somebody had built this nest on his stomach and that these two little birds were about to be born. And when they were hatched, he was so anxious for them to leave. And they were poking their heads up, and they were kind of funny looking little birds. They were really the anticipation of Woodstock, but they still weren't quite what he is now. Their heads were a lot smaller. Eventually, they did start trying to fly and I had them fly off with the sounds of flitter flutter, flitter flutter. And then they would scramble back to the nest and he'd get so exasperated, because they wouldn't leave. Finally, they did grow up and leave. But then those two birds eventually became

one bird. Woodstock was not yet even Woodstock. He was Snoopy's secretary, because by then I had also started to have Snoopy do a little bit of writing. I did a whole series on National Secretaries Week. Snoopy would dictate things to Woodstock and Woodstock would do the things that secretaries do, making fun of them. And then I realized that I had a nice little friendship going there. But if Woodstock was Snoopy's secretary, it would most likely mean that this little bird was a girl. Well, having her be a girl spoiled the little relationship between Snoopy and the bird. So, after reading *Life* magazine and all about the Woodstock Festival, I decided that Woodstock would make a good name for the bird.

Then this secretary suddenly became a little male bird and instead of a secretary was simply Snoopy's friend, although he still takes dictation now and then. But that's how the whole thing over a period of years developed into one little character. And then, as the character developed, Woodstock took over a lot of the innocence that Snoopy had when he was a lot younger, the same way I think some of the other characters in the strip have taken over personalities of the others. There's this constant shifting, which is all right in a comic strip because it doesn't matter what happened yesterday. The only thing that matters is today's paper and you're not really required to be consistent. And that's how Woodstock grew into being.

After that, of course, the other birds came along. And I got the idea of having his beagle scout trips and they would go off on hikes, so I gave them funny names like Olivier and Bill and Conrad. And then, finally, another little girl bird came in named Harriet to bake angel food cakes with seven-minute frosting, and the only reason they allowed her into the troupe was because she brought along the angel food cakes. But I don't have her in very often because I get tired of drawing five little birds over and over. They're very tedious things to draw.

Why is that?

Because each line has to be perfect. If one little line gets wrong, then they're so small and it spoils the looks of them. So you have to concentrate very carefully when drawing them, although I can draw them without even penciling them in. But you still have to watch very carefully what you're doing.

Now, supposing somebody backed you up against the wall and said, "How does the mechanics of this work that a bunch of lines of a little bird who talks in chicken scratches— how does that thing deliver so much impact?" What would you say?

I think the drawing is *extremely* important. The drawing in my strip never is cute.

It certainly is never cute.

And it's never corny or trite in its drawing. I never draw to extreme. The drawing has a warm quality to it.

September 7, 1975.

Do you think your pictures are perfect for what they are?

Oh, absolutely. I think one of the secrets of good cartooning is that the drawing has to run parallel to the writing. You cannot express the emotions that I express in these characters, or give the emotions to these characters that I do, with a different type of drawing that would be extreme in its caricature. I don't think Donald Duck, for instance, could ever express the emotions that Snoopy does, because his drawing is an animated drawing. Animation doesn't work in comic strips. An animator's style of drawing does not work in comic strips because the drawing is too rounded, the brush strokes are too slick, and they are drawn to turn properly in their animated form. Comic strip characters don't have to do that. I think the drawing is really one of the secrets.

So, you'd consider your animated stuff something completely separate and apart?

I think we get away with our animated work very successfully and it's *much* more difficult than people realize. Bill Melendez and his animators don't get enough credit for bringing these characters to life. But if these characters had been designed specifically for animation they would not be drawn the way they are, because these heads do not turn the way they should. Snoopy's nose is drawn differently from the side than it is from the three-quarter view, and an animator would never do that. Plus, if he had been drawn for animation, Snoopy would not be as good as he is. He wouldn't have the warmth to suit what he is.

The Wellspring of Inspiration

Now, you have been able to generate a consistent stream of very high quality and high-level work without ever being trite or corny or sentimental or cute. This is one of the extraordinary things about the strip. It is never corny, it is never sentimental, and it is never adorable. The thing that I really want to know is why you, Charles M. Schulz, feel that you are the vessel or the conduit for these tremendous *and prodigious numbers of feelings.*

I think I have common sense.

No, we're talking now about the wellspring of your inspiration.

I'm talking about how to judge whether something is corny or overly sweet or overly sentimental—or overly intellectual, too. I have had intellectuals try to copy what I do, but they can't do it because they don't have the plain old Midwestern common sense to know when they've gone too far or not far enough.

Do you mean you've thrown out a million corny and overly sentimental strips that we will never see?

Not overly sentimental, because I think it would be difficult for me to do that, but I know I throw out a lot of things because they just don't work. My common sense tells me that they're just not right.

Yes, but common sense in this particular regard is the editorial or entrepreneurial impulse. What I'm talking about is that you're just one guy and this one specific person has been able for a very long time to sit down and do this extraordinary work. Maybe I'm asking questions that you can't answer and the reason that you can do this work is because your work answers these questions and there's no point thinking about it. But I am rather stupefied by the amount of real intensity in this daily strip, and I wonder what kind of person you think you are that it comes from you. That's what I mean.

I think the fact that it's so important to me is one of the answers. I realize that it's not Picasso and it's not Hemingway. But that doesn't matter. It's the best that I can do and it's very important in my life and I never allow it to be second fiddle in my life. I think about it continually; everything that I read, everything that I do can somehow be channeled into this strip. How it comes out, you're right—I doubt if I can explain it.

Let me ask you a simplified version of this question. Do you think you are more emotional than most people?

Yeah.

Do you think that you have more access to your emotions than most people?

Probably so. At least this is what friends tell me who get to know me after a while.

Do you feel that you are the possessor of very strong feelings?

Sure, definitely. And I think I'm lucky that I have an outlet in the strip and I know how to do it. I can use these emotions and translate them. I feel sorry for people that *have* no outlet for their emotions. They can't play the violin or write anything or sing.

ABOVE November 22, 1950.
OPPOSITE January 6, 1983.

Do you feel that you have spent most of your lifetime being very shy?

Oh, yeah. I always have been. But I'm getting over it, now that I'm almost 60. I think shyness can be a form of egotism, too. I think if we say, "I hate to go into a room full of people because I'm so shy," it's a form of egotism that thinks that everybody's looking at you—that you're so important that everybody's looking at you. And actually, once you get to understand us, you realize that we all have our own problems and we all have a certain amount of shyness and self-consciousness. And to think that everybody is looking at us is just egotism. I think I probably have been very egotistical in my life.

Everyone has been very egotistical in their life. But a lot of people feel that writers—this is mostly leveled at writers, though it's probably true of anyone who does any creative work—are people for whom the ordinary things of life stand in their path as monuments. For example, I was thinking the other day of a humiliation that I suffered when I was about 13, so crushing that I can barely think about it—and, believe me, it would never bother me anymore. Well, why? Now I know that that's probably common to all people, but the poignancy with which a lot of artists and writers feel these things is often the driving force that pushes their work forward. Do you feel that way about yourself?

Oh, yes. And it's interesting that the things that made school so miserable for me all those 12 years was simply my inability to react to what was going on. Now that I've gone back to night class and discovered that I've gained a lot of confidence and am no longer shy and fearful, I have become almost a smart aleck when I'm in class. [*Laughs*]

What class are you doing?

I've taken three semesters of German in night school and I took another class in the novel. And I have spoken my mind in those classes and have said smart aleck things, which I would *never* have done. I could *think* of them when I was a little kid, but I would never have *said* anything like that.

What sort of little kid were you?

I was a different little kid in school from what I was out of school.

Could you describe the in and out of school?

In school, I almost never said anything unless I was called upon. I started off very bright in the early days, but then when they promoted me a couple of times, I got in over my head. So, I was always the smallest if not the next to smallest child in class all the way through school, and this is always a handicap because you're pushed around by the bigger kids. There was never a lot of fighting or anything, but you just never had the chance when they chose up for the different games they had, even though I was good at them. I was a good baseball player, but I was always one of the last chosen. But once the game got going, I was all right.

Many are chosen but…

…few are called, yeah. [*Laughs*] So, my life really didn't begin until 3:00 came and I got out of school and could be with my friends around the neighborhood where we'd either play cops and robbers or cowboys or baseball or hockey or other games we were doing. And reading: I loved reading comic books, and what they called Big Little Books in those days, and sports stories. And I loved going to the Saturday afternoon matinees, seeing the cowboy serials and things like that. That was my life.

But the thing is, school is not school in your strip. School is life.

Oh, sure. I agree.

So, it seems like the things that happened to you in school provide a lot of material for you.

The emotions provide me material. The actual incidents, of course, are not there, because what my kids do in school is really not the same. It's almost abstract. For one thing, they're always drawn from the side view. I don't let anything interrupt the flow of the four panels. In the first place, I don't have much room. There's a mechanical problem there. I've got very tiny squares to work in, so I can't draw entire classrooms and things like that. But I wouldn't want to, because I discovered a long time ago that the reality of the drawing—the reality in the drawing—spoils the type of humor that I use. It makes the kids too real; and they can't be that real, the same way as Snoopy on the doghouse. Snoopy on the doghouse has to be drawn from the side view so that it does not

suddenly become a real doghouse. You cannot put a typewriter on the pointed roof of a doghouse without it sliding off. So, it has to be abstract. It becomes almost a design—just a simple little square. But it's a nice little design and it's pleasant to look at, which kind of pulls me away from what I was thinking about.

Your strip really is extremely *pleasant and beautiful to look at.*

And you know right away what the characters are thinking and how they're feeling.

When you ever look at your work do you ever say, "Why that is a perfect expression of what I'm like?"

No. I don't identify with the strip.

I don't mean each character in the strip, but when you see your work in front of you, do you say, "That's exactly apropos from it to me. I projected that, and it looks like what I am"?

I think the whole strip looks like what I am.

That's what I mean.

I think if you were to read the strip every day, you would know what I am. What amazes *me* is that people who look at it from the reverse who have known me for at least long enough so that they should understand this still want to know where the ideas come from. And yet, if they're around me long enough, they find that I say in normal conversation the very things that the characters say every day. These things just come to me, and so I put them down in the strip. And so, you read the strip, you know me.

If somebody asked you about a man who ran a strip for 30 years and never fell below a certain very high quality, what would you speculate about his mental energy, concentration, imagination—and, if you followed his strip from the beginning, could you actually write a biographical portrait of him?

I think so. You'd have to be pretty bright, I suppose.

Do you think that the career has followed your emotional life and changes?

Uh-huh. I think you'll find the fact there's no crudeness in the strip is one element, because I'm not a crude person. I never use crude words. I don't like crude words—not necessarily even words that we think of as being profane. I just don't like any words that are ugly. I don't like ugly sounds. I like funny sounds, so you see funny words in the strip, yet I'm also not especially fond of words. I'm not educated or intellectual enough to have a tremendous vocabulary. But, I like comic strip words and I like comic strip sounds. I like the appearance of a comic strip. I'm fascinated by the black-and-white tones of the comic strip. Anytime I see an original comic strip someplace, or anything about comics, I'm drawn to it immediately. Just the appearance of them fascinates me.

Who do you admire?

Not as many as I used to. [*Laughs*]

Fine, fine. What were the most important events in your life, and did any of them ever show up in the strip? I don't mean one to one—like somebody you knew died and somebody turned up in the strip in that way. But, were there things that happened to you that you found some way to express in the strip?

Losing a baseball game once 40 to nothing. That's been the foundation of the *whole* strip. [*Laughs*] Never anything political or economical…

You've actually made that a policy, haven't you?

I just don't think it's interesting. I think it's too easy. I think that most of the political things that are done in comic strips are too easy and I just ignore them.

I wanted to ask you, for example, if during the terrible years of the Vietnam War, when this country was really being torn apart, do you feel the strip had reflected that?

Well, I stopped doing the Red Baron things because *real* war is not funny. If you look back to the cartooning in World War II, you will discover that when the War first began, the cartoons and the stories were like *See Here, Private Hargrove*. There were jokes about doing KP and all those things. And then, as America suddenly got into it and discovered that war was *not* funny—there was more to war than doing KP—then Ernie Pyle and Bill Mauldin came out and, of course, cartooning was lifted to the highest level that it had ever been. And Bill Mauldin was able to recognize that in spite of all of the agony, men laughed—man always laughs in spite of what's going on. And Bill was able to tap this and discovered he was able to do it so well.

ABOVE February 6, 1979.
OPPOSITE July 8, 1999.

Now, it's all right in my strip to do takeoffs on World War I, because it is so distant we can laugh at it now. But Snoopy's Red Baron exploits are really more a parody of World War I movies than they were of World War I. So, that's what I'm getting at there. As the Vietnam War progressed, I realized that this was not funny, and if I had been in Vietnam *myself* and had been a combat soldier then perhaps I would have felt justified in doing something about it. But I don't think you can stand off to the side and be funny about something that you're not involved in that way. So, I stopped doing combat things with Snoopy, and I said that would be the end of it. But then, after the Vietnam War ended and the years went on, and suddenly there began to be books about World War I and World War II in all of the bookstores and there was kind of a revival of interest in this, I brought Snoopy back. But he very seldom fights in the strip anymore. Most of the strips about him being in World War II are where he's shot down behind enemy lines and is trying to meet a *Fräulein*, or else he's on leave in France and he's trying to talk to a little French maiden in his imagination with his guidebook. I think I worked out a real neat little system here whereby he is always thinking and talking, and even when he meets the other kids it almost looks like they know what's going on— but not really. A little girl comes walking along the street and Snoopy stops her, says something to her out of his phrase book, and she looks at him and walks on, and this all takes place in his imagination. But it works! I've worked out these little formulas. If he were to actually talk, then it wouldn't be as funny. I don't think talking animals are as funny.

No. Thinking animals are funny, but talking animals are not.

That's right.

You said in an interview that '68 was a very fruitful year for you and that a lot of ideas were generated. It's interesting that '68 was also a very intense year in political life, which is not to say that you follow politics. Did you feel that the ferment and the drama that was going on all around you in some way kicked you into a higher state of inspiration? For example, when Kennedy was assassinated—obviously you didn't do a strip about that, but did the way you felt about it go into your strip? Does life affect the strip, or does the strip have a life that is truly of its own?

I'm sure it does, but I'm sure it's so far hidden beneath the surface that I could never find it from events like that.

But, for example, if a person from Mars came with a history book and your strip and saw that in 1962 something happened, could he read the strips for '62 and see any sort of trend in the drawings? It wouldn't mean a literal equivalent, but something that was on your mind that translates into the strip in some way?

I really think it was more personal activities, Laurie. I think it was all the people that I was surrounded with, the fact that my children were now almost fully grown and I was involved with a lot of different people. It was the activities in my own life rather than the outside world, if you force me to examine it.

I did begin to meet a lot of our children's friends and hear the things that they were talking about, which is where Joe Cool came from, for instance. I love to listen to the younger people talk and be with them and hear the expressions that they use, and I drew a lot from them in those days. Now I've kind of drifted away from that again, because the kids are now in their late twenties and I'm missing some of that younger talk. I think that's what affects me more than events in the world.

In other words, these days the strip is an act of pure imagination because it's just you now, in a way.

I think so, yeah.

Do you think it's changed because of that?

I suppose it has. I don't think I make references to a lot of the things that I might have been making references to otherwise. I also think that the strip should live a life completely on its own. I don't think you should make references to other things too much like other mediums. A lot of cartoonists draw about things that are on television and use the expressions of things that TV people use. I think that you are creating something that is *your own*. You have your own medium and *you* should be doing the creating, you should be setting the standards. You should not be using expressions that some famous television comedian is using, because you should be creating the expressions that should be copied. I like to think that I'm setting my own standards, that I'm creating things that television people copy and are making references to. You've got a great medium yourself and you shouldn't have to look to other mediums for your inspiration.

So, I was asking you if the strip can be the objective correlative, as they say, for something that happened to you. Because during the time of your surgery, for the two months that you knew that you were going to have that, is there any taint in the strip, any idea of being scared—anything? What were those strips like when you had that on your mind? Did it have any outlet into the strip?

No. I had always wanted to do something where one of the children became seriously ill, but I've never been able to work it out satisfactorily because it touches people too closely and people become very sensitive about it and sometimes offended. The closest I came to it was when Charlie Brown said one day he felt woozy, and he left the pitcher's mound. And his mother and dad were not home, they were at the barber's picnic. So, he went directly to the emergency ward of the hospital.

July 13, 1979.

When was this? Was this before the surgery?

Yes, because I had always been wanting to do this. It was a perfect example of not knowing what direction this thing was going to go—it was led by the daily

episodes that I could think of. I did show him lying in the emergency ward saying, "Everybody's gone, I'm left here all alone. Maybe I'm going to die. Maybe I've already died and nobody's going to tell me." He's just lying there alone. But then I couldn't think of anything more, and it's very difficult in my format to draw things like hospital rooms and all of that without putting the adults in. So, I went off in a different direction then and I ended up dealing with the reaction of the other children in the neighborhood. His sister immediately moved into his room. It turned out that Marcie really likes Charlie Brown and she said to Peppermint Patty that one day she'd marry Chuck. She said, "When we grow up, if Chuck asked me I think I'd marry him. I love Chuck." And Peppermint Patty was stunned and said, "How could you love somebody like Chuck?" Patty likes Charlie Brown, but she is dismayed at the faults that he has. She can't stand that he's not as good a ballplayer as she is. And then, what turned out to be strange and, I think the neat part of the story, was that Lucy was the one that was the most upset of all—and she's the one that's given him the most trouble. She stood outside one day, and I had her talking to herself out in the yard, but she was talking out loud and she was angry. I didn't

show her praying, because that would have looked a little too trite. I had her just shouting in anger, "By golly, it's not right for somebody like Charlie Brown to be sick and he just better get well. And I promise that if he gets well, I'll never pull the football away again!" And she made the mistake of saying it out loud because Linus heard it and said, "Ah ha! I've got you, haven't I!" And that made a nice little story.

As soon as I got in the hospital, people were saying to me, "Oh, now you can do something about this in the strip. We're going to see this in the strip, huh? Somebody in surgery going to have a heart operation or something." So, I knew that I'd never be able to do anything like that. It would just be too self-conscious and too obvious, so maybe years from now something will come around. But, at least I learned what it's like to be in the hospital and I overcame some of my own personal fears of hospitals, which was a great help to me. Sometimes I lie in bed at night and I think, "Be kind of nice to be back in there one of these days. Everybody was waiting on you and you're so secure in your hospital bed." [*Laughs*]

An Intensity of Feeling

The world that you have invented is a world filled with insecurities—small insecurities within a very secure framework. There's a feel about the strip that it takes place in an ordered universe, so that people's jealousies and fears and anxieties can be visible because everything else is stable enough to contain. In other words, we know nothing bad is going to happen. Nothing terrible is going to happen. What's going to happen are the small terrible things.

Well, as adults we forget the tribulations of childhood.

You seem not to have forgotten the tribulations of childhood.

No. I haven't forgotten them, but most adults do. Once they get to be a certain age, they learn to avoid the things that children are trapped into. Like being out on the playground where there are kids that push you down and knock you over and won't let you swing on the swings that you want to swing on.

What do you feel is the quality that you have that makes your childhood close to you? I want you to give me a kind of

psychological portrait of yourself, because you say that your childhood is close to you. And, what is your temperament like?

I think that I'm reasonably mild in that I don't have great ups and downs. But, I have a very disturbing quality that seems to have come over me the last few years in that I seem to be living what you might call the feeling of impending doom. It may be something that could be attributed simply to the low blood sugar in the morning. I don't know. I hope that that's all it is. Maybe some electrical fault in my head, too. But, when I wake up in the morning, I wake up to a funeral-like atmosphere, as if today is the day I'm attending the funeral. But once I get up and start moving around—have our aerobics class in the morning—I generally feel better. I think activity is good for all of us when we have those kinds of feelings.

Do you feel yourself to be a melancholic type or person who has an access to some kind of real sadness?

I have had very little what you would call real sadness in my life, just the normal deaths and losses of parents and relatives. But, I live with these feelings of loss all the time. And yet, I think when crises have occurred in my life that I've handled them properly. I haven't let them totally disturb my life. But I do always feel very deeply even the little losses of people in life—people that come out and maybe spend just a day or two with us and then disappear. I always had the feeling that it would be wonderful if we could get all the people together that we know and we just all lived together. But I realize that wouldn't last but about a week.

But what is that desire really about? That's the thing.

I wish I knew. If I knew, perhaps I would be able to correct this melancholy feeling.

No one's saying that it's wrong to have a melancholy feeling.

I just don't understand it, and I've never had anyone explain it.

You are the only expert.

Well, I talked for a year once with a psychologist who never really got it totally explained.

What do you think? That's a very interesting and poignant desire.

I don't think I know enough about it to be able to explain it. I wonder if all these things go back to some kind of guilt, and yet I don't feel that I have much guilt in my life either.

Have you ever done a strip that you felt really spoke to this feeling? Have you ever done or developed an idea in the strip that you felt really got to the heart in some way of these feelings?

I can't think of any particular strip. Charlie Brown expressed what I was saying there a moment ago about goodbyes. He said he just hated goodbyes. He said, "What I need is more hellos." [*Colwin laughs*] and maybe that would be the closest. See, you have to make all these things funny in a comic strip. It's not like in a novel where you have page after page to be able to build up these emotions. The comic strip is inhibited in that you only have a reader for 16 seconds each day, and you have to say something funny at the end of each little strip. So, this kind of interrupts profound emotions like that.

Well, this is where you and I don't seem to agree about your work, because I think that these strips are *about very profound emotion. All the strips that I've read have in common the following elements: a certain purity of feeling, an intensity of feeling, and a clarity. It seems to me that* Peanuts *is about feeling. It's about very profound ways that people feel. It's about needing love and being frightened of fear and taking on everyone's rejections for your own, in the small way that people really do it. Because life is not made up of heroes and villains, it's made up of people getting a busy signal and the tremendous clang and resonance that sets off in a person's heart. It's just a busy signal, but it's not just a busy signal clearly to you.*

April 29, 1968.

But it's always rejection, isn't it? In a way, this is the foundation of what cartooning really is. Cartooning is always somebody slipping on the banana peel and falling or somebody getting hit on the head. I've had people write to me and complain that there should be more happy things in the strip—that Charlie Brown should be allowed to win a ballgame and kick the football. But there's nothing funny about kicking the football. What happens then? What happens after he wins the game? That's not funny. But loss is funny to all of us because we've all lost and we all know that the only way we can survive these losses is by laughing about them, even though these losses really hurt. When we get together and talk about loss, after the losses have disappeared for a few weeks or a few months, we can look back upon them and laugh at how depressed we were and kid each other about them. We've all experienced all those losses and using sports in the strip is just a vehicle for expressing the different kind of losses. We can't talk about business losses in the strip, because the kids are not involved in businesses. The whole thing is just a caricature of all these rejections and losses that we have in life. This is what cartooning really is. Cartooning is almost always the little guy getting beaten down in some way or the world being against him.

When did you feel that in your adult life?

In the army, I suppose. When you get into the army, you're suddenly tossed in with people from all over the country. Some of them are smarter than you, some are dumber, some are bigger and stronger, and there are all sorts of different kinds of personalities. If you don't want to really suffer, you have to learn to roll with these punches and avoid the situations that make life miserable.

Where has that happened after the War?

It really tapers off, of course, after you get older and established in your own life. I don't know where it would happen now.

But you still feel—or you did feel—in some way that you were in a playground and that an older bigger kid might knock you over?

Yeah. I've never been comfortable in country clubs and things like that. I don't like hanging around with a whole bunch of guys playing cards or things like that. I would never go off on a hunting trip with a whole bunch of guys and things like that. I don't like that kind of raucous behavior.

Do you feel you're a person who likes to be alone with a lot of people in the next room? Is that what you like best?

Yeah, definitely.

In other words, you don't want them to be very far away, you just don't want them to be with you.

That's right.

You actually want all those nice people around, but not in the same place.

That's right.

In other words, you feel secure but solitary.

That's why I like my studio. This is my ship and I have my own captain's quarters here and I have the people outside that I like and over at the arena and everything. And yet, it's all on my terms—I can go home anytime I want to and I can do anything I want to.

So, you could potentially be the boy in the playground who knocks the other kids over now.

Yeah, but I hope that I am not the psychological bully in the way I run my business. I'm very firm in everything that I do, but I don't think that I take advantage of people. I think about it often—that I have such authority in my business—and I hope that I'm not hard on people. I don't think that I am, but I *hope* I'm not.

Has anyone ever told you that you are?

No. I think that would be terrible because it would be so easy to do.

Do you think of yourself as a solitary person?

Oh, yeah. But I'm not as good at it as I was years ago. I've been alone *so much* of my life…

That's sort of an odd remark for a person who has five children.

Well, this was before I had five children.

I know, but you've had five children for longer than you didn't *have five children.*

That's right. I've been with my children longer than my mother was with me, which always astounds me. But I was alone *a lot* when I was small. I was alone a lot during the army days.

Then you are, in fact, Peppermint Patty, aren't you? You're the child that is lonesome a lot.

Yeah. I think you're right… even in the big nose. [*Laughs*]

Do you think that anything in adult life compensates for childhood loneliness?

Well, you have a little more freedom to be able to work your way out of it. Although I'm amazed at how little we do learn. I think it's almost sinful. I *do* think it's sinful to be bored. I did a film documentary recently where I talked about that. I think it's deplorable when you hear young people these days when they're asked, "How's school?" "Oh, it's boring." "Well, how was…" this or that that you did. "Oh, it was boring." I think it is sinful to be bored, because we're in such a *tremendous* world filled with so many great people and things to do and all you have to do is get out there and do them.

Do you think people aren't so much bored as they are depressed?

Well, maybe "bored" is just a catchphrase that's being used these days. I think people simply lack the maturity to handle all these things in their lives. I think maturity is the answer to all of life.

Oh, you do? And how would you characterize it?

The ability to face up to all the problems of life and not let them distort your life and get you into trouble. I think turning to such obvious things as smoking and drinking as a substitute for solving your problems is a lack of maturity. I admire people who go to a big city for a business trip and get there, say, on a Saturday night and their business meeting is not till Monday morning and they have to be in the city all by themselves on a Saturday night and all day Sunday, and they have the maturity to go out and find a good museum to visit.

And what would you do? You'd sit in your hotel room being scared of being lonely?

I used to, yeah. And there was no television in those days. I used to wander the streets. I used to wander the streets of Chicago and New York.

Wishing that someone would be nice to you.

Yeah. But nobody ever was. Wishing that I had the nerve to talk to somebody. I was in New York all by myself. I was beginning to work my way out of it when I came back from the army. I had to visit New York once to sign a syndicate contract, and I was there not knowing a soul in the city, and I walked down the street and I discovered that there was going to be a violin recital at Carnegie Hall, and I was just beginning to like classical music. So, I had dinner by myself and walked down the street on a nice spring evening in New York to Carnegie Hall, and I sat up in the balcony behind a mother and a daughter and listened to this young girl play Mendelssohn's Violin Concerto. And I really enjoyed it and I wanted so much to talk to the mother and the daughter who sat in front of me, but I didn't have the nerve. Now I would. Now I would talk to them.

What would you say?

I'd say, "Are you enjoying the concert? This has always been one of my favorite concertos. I'm from St. Paul, Minnesota," and this sort of thing. Well, I remember when I was trying to learn how to do this, I was on a train once riding from

St. Paul to Chicago, and I went up into the observation car and there was a girl sitting in front of me reading *Marjorie Morningstar*. I had just finished reading it, and so I thought to myself, "I'm going to talk to this girl." I would pursue the conversation and know more what to say. So, I leaned forward and I said, "Do you like the book?" And she said, "Yes." And then I didn't know what else to say and that ended the conversation. [*Laughter*] But we might have had a wonderful conversation up there in the observation car.

Expressing the Funny and the Profound

I obviously have a theory about how artists work, and I think one of the things about being an artist that makes artists in some ways happier than other people is that their energy keeps flowing. People who are constantly working out of their own heads are using what life gives them and bringing it forward, and then that energy of working sort of drives back into the person—they're like a wheel, in a way. So, my question is, are there things that your strip can't express? Are there times when you sat at your drawing board feeling terrible or sad or miserable or frightened? Did you ever sit at your desk and realize that there were things that were going on in your mind that were very pressing to you that your strip could not express?

I think there are things in life that are prohibited in comic strips. Death probably is the main one.

But you can do that by having a character pretend to move away.

I did that.

I know you did. That's really about somebody dying.

That's right, too.

And, of course, being resurrected as well.

The trouble is that we have to deal with editors and readers and you have to keep them happy. You'd have to bring the characters back, which is what I did at that time. And, disappointingly enough, a lot of the things that you do are simply dictated by the schedule that you have to keep. Days go by so fast. You don't have the luxury of being able to think about things for too long, unless you set one story aside and think about it and work on it while you're turning out some other strips, because the days just fly by and you have to get something done. Maybe you don't have it totally resolved in your mind, but you have to get it in anyway, and so you have to get something started. And then, also, a lot of the things that you do are dictated by whether or not it is funny on that particular day. I can't hold to a story line in an ironclad way if I can't think of anything funny for Monday, Tuesday, and Wednesday. What is more important to me is to be funny each day and let the story line go where it may. So, I may want to write a tragic story about Linus's family moving away; but when I get three or four days into the story, if I can't think of anything funny for Friday, I may have to change the whole story line to make something funny. It's very important that you be good every day.

Do you do these in blocks? You don't sit down every day and draw a strip. You draw in lots of how many?

Well, three or four strips in one day makes me feel satisfied. Two I will settle for, but I always go home with a feeling of unfulfillment.

Are you going to do a strip today?

No, because we're talking.

Did you do your quota beforehand?

Oh, more or less. If I didn't want to, I wouldn't have to draw anything for two months now—I could quit for two months.

Your medium requires scheduling editors and so on and so forth. But the thing about you is that you quite transcend that although that's part of the drill. You take off like an aerosol bomb. The art of it has nothing to do with the schedules, it's just the limitations on the art. But the art still exists. What I'm trying to say is that your entire personality is probably expressed in this strip.

I think so.

I'm sure that some things are not appropriate for a comic strip. But there are equivalents for those things. Could you speculate about certain things that you've done that relate to things like that?

Well, I have not yet really resolved it but I have hinted. We *know* now that Peppermint Patty does not have a mother, don't we? But we haven't really come out and said it more than a couple of times. We don't even know what happened to her. I've never said that she has died. I've never said where she is or anything, but I've hinted at it just enough to kind of make it a little bit poignant. And yet I've kept it in reserve, because I may do something with it someday.

Where is her mother?

We don't know.

Well, you know. Where is she?

I don't know. I haven't decided this.

Oh, I see. But it's right that that child doesn't have a mother.

That's right. And this is what causes some of her problems. I have doctors write to me who are very concerned about her falling asleep in class because they think it's a physical ailment, and they want me to do something about it. And I have a whole

January 17, 1975.

I THINK I FELL ASLEEP, MARCIE..DID I MISS ANYTHING?

YOU MISSED MATH, HISTORY AND SPELLING

10-23

I MEAN, DID I MISS ANYTHING?

ABOVE October 23, 1987.
OPPOSITE October 3, 1951.

stack of research here if I do do something about it.

Well, she's probably sad.

She is, because she's home alone a lot. I've said that in the strip that her dad goes off. He's a salesman apparently. I think I'm going to have him be a salesman of correspondence courses, and he has to be on the road. So, she's home alone a lot and she's frightened and she sits up late at night watching TV, and so she falls asleep in class the next day. But people don't want to accept that. They'd rather think that she has some ailment that can be cured so that I could use the strip in an educational manner.

I think all children feel abandoned or lonely. But with certain people it seems to have much more of a private life, as if it's an eternal flame in their consciousness. There are some people for whom anxiety is simply a childhood memory. And for you, it's a living creature. Is that true?

Yeah, yeah. I like to think that's one of the reasons that I can do what I can do. Maybe I'm wrong, but I like to think that.

Do you think that it requires having had to really suffer through a lot of things to do what you do?

No, but I think you have to be aware of the suffering and be able to identify in *some* way with that. You don't have to have gone through these things literally, but you should have had a touch of each of these things.

But you have gone through these things literally. Do you feel that your sufferings are very much like the sufferings of most people?

Probably. Probably average, wouldn't you think? Obviously, there are people who have had greater sufferings—indescribable sufferings—and then there are other people that nothing much has happened to at all.

Do you think that you are the sort of paradigmatic person of ordinary sufferings, and that you are so acutely aware of yours that you are able to express them for those who suffer them but don't express them?

I think so. And maybe it's just the *ability* to express them—that that would be the only difference.

Maybe other people know they're there, but can't even begin to express them. They simply don't know how. They feel these things, and so they react in certain ways. They take to drink or they take to not being able to go places, or they lose their jobs or they keep a certain job because they can't do something. It acts out in their life, but they don't express it to anybody. They never talk about it and they can't write about it or sing about it, so the results are there in their lives, but it's never mentioned. I have a feeling that my dad had it, but he never could talk about it. I just got a few hints near the end of his life that perhaps he had the same thing, but he did not have any way of talking about it.

Do you think that by having this strip as a way of expressing all this has taken or used to take some pressure off you to express it in your ordinary life? How expressive were you just as a guy, an ordinary fellow?

Not expressive at all. Oh, no, no. Had no one to talk to about these things and would probably be ashamed of them, too. It took me *years* to learn to talk about it—that it was nothing to be ashamed of and that people actually appreciated having these things brought out, because it enabled them to be able to admit to some of their fears and anxieties.

Did you know that the strip was expressing this for you?

I think it took a long time for the strip to express these things. I don't think these things were in the strip at the beginning.

Oh, I don't mean this feeling of emptiness specifically. But from the very beginnings of the strip that I saw, they're very emotional. They're about disappointment and rejection and fear and anticipatory fear.

But they're much more obvious in those days than they are now, don't you think? I don't think that the nuances were quite what they are now. But, of course, I was a beginner. The strip was just beginning, and it took a long while for the characters to develop to be able to work with them that way.

Do you ever look back and say, "All those years, that strip was my personal expression—it expressed everything for me"?

Probably so. Not as much as it does now. But I look back upon it and realize how important it was to me—that I needed it a lot—that life would have been very difficult for me if I had not had it, if I'd had another job of some kind. I wouldn't have given up though. I would have kept on trying.

Do you feel that you're different from other people?

We're all different from each other in many ways. We have to be. That's the remarkable thing about being human. We're all alike in many ways. We all are much more alike than we realize. I think it takes years to discover how much alike we all really are. We all have the same insecurities and desires for things.

But when you were a little boy, did you have the feeling that you were different in some way?

I had the feeling when I was a little boy that I was so plain and so ordinary that if I were walking down the street in downtown St. Paul and I came across one of my teachers or one of the kids that I knew in school, they would not recognize me because I was so ordinary.

What made you think that? I mean, was there a very handsome tall boy with beautiful red hair that was very extraordinary that you compared yourself to?

I just thought that there were a lot of kids that were much more distinct than I was in their appearance and in their personalities. They were much more outgoing and forward and they were more leaders. Other kids just seemed to be able to be the leaders in whatever they were doing, and I always just kind of followed along.

And what did you think was going to become of you?

I'd probably draw cartoons. [*Laughs*]

You knew that!

Oh, yeah. Maybe not when I was very small, because I didn't know such things existed. But once I knew they existed…

How old were you when you knew they existed?

I was probably very young.

So, in other words, you had a very early sense of vocation. But when you were young, despite the fact that you were a plain, completely ordinary person with no distinguishing features whatsoever, did you ever have the experience of walking into a room and saying, "These people are not like me."

I always felt middle class, even though I never knew what we were. My dad owned his own barbershop and we had a car. I knew that there were a lot of people outside of the community where we lived that had a lot more money. There were doctors or dentists and they lived in nicer homes. But I also knew that my mother and father had a certain amount of dignity and they were very well-liked people. I used to think that when I grew up I hoped that I would be as well liked as my dad was. In his community, he was very well respected and very well liked. Looking at it from this perspective, you don't think of a barber as being that important. But back then, we're talking about a generation of small businessmen, and I think it's quite admirable for a man to start his own business and to succeed at it and to be able to support his family through something like the Depression with dignity. And he did have dignity. He ran a very nice little barbershop and he made a fairly decent living, although he got terribly in debt on his rent.

Now you run a nice little barbershop here, don't you? I mean, you've done the same thing.

I'd like to think so. I've done the same thing.

You are a small businessman. It's not such a small business, but you started it yourself.

Uh-huh. Built it up step by step, and I think I run what would now be called a class operation.

What sort of guy was your father?

He was extremely honest.

Was he funny?

No.

Was he stern?

No, no, not stern. He never hit me once my whole life, and he very seldom became angry with me. I think the humor was on my mother's side of the family. There were a lot of funny people on that side. And my mother also was greatly respected in the neighborhood and by her own family. In a large family, there will invariably be one person to whom the others will turn when they're in trouble, and my mother was that one. They always looked to Dena when they needed help.

Did you want to be that sort of person?

That's right.

Did that happen to you?

Yes. But that's all right. I'm grateful that I'm the person that can help rather than needs help.

Do you feel that you've ever needed help?

Oh, yeah. That's hard to talk about, because I don't want to get into the divorce business and all that.

I'd just tell you from my experience that I've been edited a lot of times by some extremely excellent editors and I've found one editor who was a real nut, who I would say is the only person who ever really *got it. He just really understood what I was trying to do. A lot of people liked it and they got* parts *of it, and I know that there were people who were sympathetic to it, but this guy really just got it as if he had written it. It seems to me that sometimes in people's lives somebody else comes along who just* gets *you, or really understands what you're doing, or really knows something about you. That's the kind of help I'm talking about. Do you feel that you're an understood person or a misunderstood person?*

I have several friends who understand me.

Really well?

Yes.

And do you think there are people that truly understand what your strip is *really* about?

What bothers me more than that is the number of people who don't understand it. That really bothers me, especially when they've known me for a long time and when I find that they will quote something else and tell me how great they think

ABOVE July 15, 1965.
OPPOSITE August 7, 1971.

it is when I think it's just terrible—a real bad comic feature. And I discover that here all the time they've been telling me how wonderful my things are and then they will quote something else that is I think *terribly* inferior, and I wonder if they really understand.

We were talking in the car earlier about how the strip is about children and about you're a very positive, optimistic person, and I'm reading the strip thinking that this guy is not only a very weird person, but he is one of those people who is like a passionate, overemotional child.

I keep a lot of things hidden in interviews, Laurie, because I know that most of the time it's not going to come out right. So why get into it? I don't know what you have read, but you're talking about this positive business and all of that. In an interview, invariably they will ask, "Do you think you are Charlie Brown?" That has so many ramifications and you can talk about that at so many levels, and they don't want to hear it.

Well, you're obviously all of those people. [Laughs]

Yeah, that's the answer. But if you say, "Yeah, I'm a lot like Charlie Brown," that's what they want to hear. That makes the headline. And then they don't care anything about anything else. They've got their answer and that's all they care about for their article. So why go into it?

I think everybody who does what you do gets a lot of preconceived notions. For example, Snoopy gets to say all the dumb things that you'd like to say, but he's the only person who can say them. He can make all the really dumb puns that you're actually ashamed of, but when he says them they're fabulous.

And with Snoopy, we break the bounds of racism and sex and everything else. We start right at the beginning. Snoopy thinks the things that we put into the mouths of our own pets when we are talking baby talk to them. This is where it all started. And we all do that. We all have our favorite little kittens or puppies or things and we're feeding them.

We say very dumb things.

We say dumb things, yeah. But it's all right. We all do it. And we think the things that we want them to say to us.

You can say anything you want through him, because he's the perfect vehicle.

Oh, yeah. And he also gets very sarcastic. I carry it one, two, three, four steps beyond that. He is the perfect vehicle.

It's interesting that he's the writer.

Well, it's funnier that way.

It's also very interesting what he writes.

It's a great novel. [*Laughs*]

Well, he's a better writer than Joyce Carol Oates.

I've never talked to Joyce Carol Oates.

I don't think she'd get you.

She has no humor, does she?

No, no.

Now, you describe your strip as funny as opposed to it being, for example, tragic. But funny doesn't begin to describe the truly very complicated nature of the strip. Peanuts has emotional affect, as opposed to any other thing of its kind that I have ever seen. Now, paintings have emotional affect and music has emotional affect and so do books, while cartoon strips don't—but yours does. That must be something that you inchoately or intuitively went for, because it expresses what you obviously think is the most important thing. It seems to me that you think feeling is the most important thing.

Yeah. I was lucky that, whether I stumbled on it or not—I might have been able to do it with another vehicle—I think using the kids and the dog became the perfect vehicle. But I had to develop it over a long period of time to make the whole thing work. The panel wasn't just sitting there bright and shiny and beautiful at the start. I think I had to build the instrument little by little before

I could perform on it.

Do you think feeling is the most important thing, or do you think it's the most undeniable thing?

Feeling is very important. I do more than just think of gags. I really *feel* the humor in the strip.

But have you ever had the experience of drawing a strip and realized that whatever it was getting to, it got to something so profound that you felt yourself close to tears? Have you ever had that experience?

Oh, yeah. Sure, sure. I also laugh so hard at some of the things I'm drawing that I can't draw, my hand won't stay still.

So, you've reacted both ways. You've had strips that really have brought you close to tears.

Well, as close as I suppose you can get to them. Yeah.

It's Marcie who calls Peppermint Patty "Sir," right? When I first saw that, tears actually came into my eyes. I thought that was beyond charming. It is very moving. The first time I saw those characters, and when Marcie called Peppermint Patty "Sir," I knew exactly. That really hits, because you know the kind of awe and respect. She has a crush on her, but it's more than just a crush. It's a very specific kind of crush that is filled with respect.

Yeah. But she also knows the flaws that Peppermint Patty has. So, it's a good respect.

But it's very moving.

I'm glad you think so, because I really feel that relationship.

But how did it come into your head to call her "Sir"? It just [Colwin snaps fingers] clicked into your head and you thought, "What a great idea"?

It started with an episode where Peppermint Patty went to camp by herself and she was the tent monitor. And this little dark-haired girl came into her tent and said, "Sir, my stomach hurts. What should I do?" See, we're getting back to what we would call the hippie age, where I think there was kind of a mingling of the sexes. For a while you couldn't tell the boys from the girls. You'd be driving along in a car and you'd see some beautiful girl with long blonde hair driving a truck next to you, and then you'd look over and discover it's a guy. So, there was a little mixture of that, but that doesn't have too much to do with it. It just seemed like that would be an obvious mistake. What would she say if she were the sort of little girl that had respect for people in higher positions and she wanted to say something? "Ma'am" probably wouldn't be right, and she couldn't call her "Sergeant" or "Lieutenant" or anything, so "Sir" just seems to work.

It does work. And when you read it, you realize the tremendous reverence that these characters have for one another.

The *Peanuts* Family

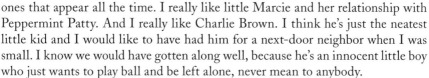

When you think of your characters, do they appear to you as people that you know terribly well?

Yeah. I know them very well, just like their line. And I like them. If I didn't like them, I wouldn't use them. These are the ones that appear all the time. I really like little Marcie and her relationship with Peppermint Patty. And I really like Charlie Brown. I think he's just the neatest little kid and I would like to have had him for a next-door neighbor when I was small. I know we would have gotten along well, because he's an innocent little boy who just wants to play ball and be left alone, never mean to anybody.

But he's more complicated than that.

Well, yeah. But I would like to have had him for a neighbor. Of course, I would have liked Linus, too.

Have other cartoonists ever asked you what it's like to work with the same people over and over for so many years? I'm asking you this because writers and painters and cartoonists are the only people who have to think about this. What is it like to be intimately involved day after day after day?

I think it's good. I think there are some cartoonists that couldn't stand it, that would feel inhibited by this. But I think others of us like having a set cast to work with. Some work with a *very small* cast. There are some cartoonists that have drawn strips literally for 30 years and haven't used more than two or three characters.

Like Blondie and Dagwood.

That's right. Although he probably has a dozen now, if you really start to examine it. But someone like Al Capp had a hundred characters, I'm sure. But that was the nature of his strip. Every new story that Al started invariably meant the creation of a new character—some startling new personality that he had come up with. But that was the nature of his humor. I don't need new characters to create new stories. If a new character comes in, it's generally because of the story itself. I never think it's about time I should have a new character and then just start off to try to create a funny little character. That isn't the humor that I have. But that was the kind of humor that Al had.

And if somebody were doing a Ph.D. thesis about…

And a lot of them have done it. [*Laughs*]

I bet. I was just thinking that if you take you and Al Capp—and who else in cartooning has created real families…

Milt Caniff was a good example. When Milt was drawing *Terry and the Pirates*, years ago, he had a marvelous list of characters.

Our paper had that one. But I never connected with it, because I like a more family setting. So, I'm trying to think of the sort of what you'd call the family creationists.

Beetle Bailey would be a good example.

There's a real form, just like there's a form for the novel, of how these things evolve and grow and how characters come in; but they also fade back, because only the most prominent characters stay.

Some characters are so good that they provide you with ideas. The very appearance and the nature of their personality means that you can get ideas from them all the time. Other characters just don't seem to work out that way.

So, in other words, the central group that you have are the ones who were constantly sparking off ideas.

Yeah. It's very similar to the old radio shows. Jack Benny had a certain group of characters—they were on all the time. Bob Hope had the same thing. And Red Skelton had the same thing. And some of our better situation comedies on television do the same thing. I don't think they do them as well.

This is clearly what people really love and admire, isn't it?

Oh, sure. Because they look forward to being with a certain person each day or each week. And they want something new all the time, but not too new. They want these same situations repeated, and they want these themes and variations. They look forward to Lucy's pulling away the football on Charlie Brown. If I don't do it one of these years, which I probably will *not* do, I'll get some letters saying, "What happened to the football theme? That was my favorite." And then others are very angry that I should allow her to do this to him every year: "Why is he so dumb, and why is she so mean?" And if I don't do the Great Pumpkin or if I don't mention Beethoven's birthday. Eventually, you get so many of these things that you can't do them all, and you're forced to drop a couple of them. And then people are disappointed. People want to see when Dagwood runs out in the morning and bumps into the mailman, but they want to see another variation of it.

It's very clear that readers feel that your characters are an alternate family, because they have a tremendous *family pull—you're pulled right into the strip. You long for them. When I was reading all the books that you*

RIGHT July 10, 1958.
ABOVE *Terry and the Pirates*
by Milton Caniff, October 9, 1937.

sent me, I read them one after another as if I were reading a novel. I got in the bed under the covers and I started reading strip after strip after strip. And finally, I thought that somebody should take every single strip that Charles Schulz ever did and put it into a gigantic collection. It should be like the Oxford Dictionary *in 75 volumes, so that people like me could just go day after day, year after year, and go through right from 1959 to 1982 and have every single strip he ever did.*

Well, we have them virtually all reprinted. [*Editor's note: In 2016, Fantagraphics Books released the 26th and final volume of the publisher's complete, chronological reprinting of* Peanuts *strips.*]

I know, but I meant in chronological order, so you could really do the thing. And I realized that I'm going to have to go out and buy every single one of these books—all 9,000 of them. Because what happens is, you create in the reader such a desire for these people.

Well, you could see the little changes as you were reading them, couldn't you?

Oh, yeah.

Sometimes I'll start with one character doing something, and it will shift over to another character and then become very prominent with that character the rest of the time. You know, Charlie Brown was the first one in the strip to have a blanket, but it really worked better with Linus. So, quickly I shifted it over to Linus and he was the one it really stuck with. And now, it's almost wrong for Linus to have a blanket. It doesn't seem right for him. He seems to be too secure in himself.

He's too old?

Yeah. So, I don't really do too many blanket things. Besides, I've thought of just about every one that I can think of.

Are you sad when certain things end, or are you relieved?

I'm relieved with a lot of things. But the "blanket" thing I used to enjoy so much, because I could do so many things with it. I used to like drawing the ones where Snoopy would sneak up and try and steal the blanket from Linus, and I liked drawing the wild fights that they would have about it. But that's all gone now, and I can't do that anymore.

Now that your children have grown and you are just living in a household of adults—besides your dogs, who behave in certain ways very much like some of your characters—have your themes changed? Has your point of view changed? Has your material changed? Do you have to rely more on your imagination and less on your observations?

The most obvious way it's changed is that I don't use toys in the strip anymore. When the strip was first running, the kids were very small and I did a lot of jokes about the kids playing. I even remember drawing Lucy in a crib falling out on her head once. And I used to draw tricycles and the kids out on the sidewalk doing things like that. I haven't drawn a toy in the strip in *years,* because I don't see them

May 25, 1952.

anymore. I have no connection with them. And also, I don't know whether because of that or not, the strip has gone into a direction where my kids are not like kids anymore. I don't even show them playing in sandboxes anymore. Now and then I'll show them at the beach, but it rarely involves them doing something with a toy or doing little kid things at the beach. I've done a few beach ball things with Sally, but it's always something that's beyond the realm of children. So, I think that would be the main change.

So, you think that your characters are now more abstractly expressionistic?

Definitely. And it's too late—*almost* too late—to back up. There are some things that cannot be done anymore because we can't back up.

Do you want to?

No, I don't want to back up. I like the direction I'm going, because no one can do what I'm doing. Sometimes they try to follow me, but they just can't. You have so many imitators. Whether consciously or unconsciously, they're doing what you are doing, and so you have to keep running off down new paths where they can't follow you. And it's very difficult for them to follow me now, because I'm doing things that they can't do.

Are you prouder of the strip in its condition now than you've ever been?

Oh yes. I think I've done things in the last few years that are the best I've ever done.

Are you more proud of the actual drawing now than you ever were?

Yes, I think I'm drawing better now than I've ever drawn. I think I've learned a lot. My only drawing problem is the shaking of my hands which I can't seem to conquer. When I first came home from surgery, I tried to draw around the third week I was back. I started drawing, but my hand shook so much I just couldn't draw. And I tried to sign some letters while I was home around the first or second week and had a terrible time just signing my name. When I wrote to Amy and Jill, I had to write very slowly—I just couldn't control the pen. I've had trouble with a shaky hand for years, but as the day goes on it will frequently go away and then I can draw a real good pen line. But now it seems to stay with me more than it used to. And for a while I really thought I was going to have to have help with the lettering in the strip, because I just could not hold the pen steadily enough to letter. But after a couple of weeks, I simply drew the strips and set them aside without any lettering until I decided what I was going to do. And then I, with very hard work and very much concentration, lettering quite slowly, I discovered I could do it and now I'm doing it. But it *is* an effort and it makes it a little harder work than it used to be.

Do you know what it is?

No. I haven't gone to a specialist to find out. I had one doctor prescribe some medicine, a very clear liquid. And he says, "Take this for about 10 days and see if it helps, and then give me a call." So, I didn't call him on the 10th day. But on the 11th day I was at home, it was in the evening. And he called me and he said, "Sparky, I've just been thinking about you, wanting to know if that medicine helped you any." And I said, "Well, I rubbed it on both of my hands and it didn't seem to do any good." And he was very quiet on the other end of the telephone. And then I said, "That was just a joke." [*Laughter*]

Have you ever tried acupuncture?

I would never try acupuncture. I just don't believe in it.

Well, it probably wouldn't work then.

I have a *lot* of doctor friends. They're very fine doctors whom I trust greatly, and I've had several of them who know I have this problem and have assured me that I don't have some serious progressive disease, which satisfies me temporarily. If it ever gets to the point where I can't draw anymore, I will probably go to someone to see if we can't lick it. If not, I'll just quit.

Supposing you just said tomorrow, "I quit." Would you not miss your characters terribly? Would you pine for them?

If I couldn't draw the strip anymore, I would hope that I could at least write animated shows, where I'd simply switch the medium. I would still be dealing with the same characters, because these are perfect characters for the ideas that I think of. I would still always be thinking of ideas, but I don't think I'd be thinking of ideas for other *types* of characters. I've got a whole repertory company here that I work with, and I need those people.

And you love them?

Oh, yeah. I like them. And the ones that appear the most are the ones that I like the most.

Do you like them or do you love them or do you do both?

Oh, I don't think it matters. I'm not neurotic about it. I could never say I love my characters. I find that a difficult sentence to speak.

Do you find them adorable?

I'm adorable, but they're not. [*Colwin laughs*]

So, what would you do if you were forced to give them up? What would happen to your imagination? How do you think your imagination would compensate for their loss?

I think I'd be in trouble for a while unless I found another outlet—unless I could try to write plays or movie scripts or something like that. I would definitely try to do it. And I think I could do it *adequately.* Whether or not I could do it really well,

I'm not sure. I have my doubts. Although I really like the screenplay that I wrote for *The Big Stuffed Dog*. I think it had some good qualities to it. It could have been better. But, after all, that was my first effort. Considering it was the first effort, I think it came off as a very pleasant show. So, maybe that would be the direction that I'd go. Then again, maybe I just wouldn't do anything like that at all. Maybe it would be fun just to forget the whole thing.

The Act of Drawing

What sort of things do you always hope people ask you in an interview?

I always hope that they will ask more about the drawing—that they will appreciate the balance of white areas and dark areas and things, because most of them ignore the drawing completely. Most of them do not appreciate the technique of just whipping in those lines that make up Linus's hair. That's very difficult to do. You really have to know what you're doing in making that line.

Are you ever sad that the beautiful richness is lost in newspaper production?

Oh, definitely. We're all sad about that. That's why comic strip artists enjoy having exhibitions of originals, because then you see the shiny blacks and the beautiful lines that are there that are lost completely.

Now, you sent me the panel about the novel, and it's so rich. It's like an Ingmar Bergman movie. [Schulz laughs] Remember those Bergman movies? The blacks are so velvety and delicious.

Oh, yeah.

And that's what that was like, it was very rich. I thought how sad to have this grayed out on a newspaper.

Oh, it's terrible. And just a simple thing like drawing the doghouse. I purposely tilt the pen in a certain way so that as the lines that make up the boards in the doghouse go across a little bit of the ink drops below the line, which simulates the feeling of wood on the doghouse. You have to know what you're doing with that. If you took a ruler and did it across, the doghouse would turn into a refrigerator. But that's lost in the newspaper reproduction. It just becomes a line. But I still have to appreciate it, for my own sake and for the sake of other craftsmen who will see it someday.

Is that why you like the books? Do you think the reproduction is significantly better?

In some cases, it's better; in some cases, it's no better at all.

Yes, but do you have control? On coated stock, you look great. Do you have that in your contract that you'd be on coated stock, or don't you care?

Yeah. But you know how publishers are, how they race out with things at the last minute and it doesn't come out.

The Peanuts Jubilee *had great paper.*

Boy, I had to fight for that though. And they ruined all the color in it. The syndicate had thrown away all the color proofs, and I didn't have time to go back and color all those things myself. So, they said, "Well, we've got somebody here who can do it, and they'll do a good job." And they miscolored the whole book. I was so aggravated. They used nice colors, but they put them in the wrong places.

Have you ever thought of some book that you would like to do, over which you would have complete artistic control?

Yeah. I would like to do another thing. The *Peanuts Jubilee* you saw was just the paperback edition. That was a big $32 book—a beautiful thing. I wanted to put out the *best* comic strip book quality that had ever been done, and we came very close to it. I don't know of any one that was ever any better. But publishers don't like to put out coffee table books of comic strips, and I really had to fight to get that. At that time, $32 was quite a price to pay. But it sold well. I'm not sure if anybody would want to do it, but I'd like to put out another nice big collection on my 35th anniversary. I could always say, "OK, then that's it—no more books of any kind." Maybe then they'd do it. That's the only thing they'll listen to: "OK, I'll quit."

I wonder if you've ever had a story fly into your mind that made you think, "This is not a story for the strip, it's a story for a book. And I'm going to do this book and they're going to do it on colored stock and I'm going to do the coloring—everything is going to be perfect."

Yeah. I've thought of that. But, in a way, I'd feel like I was wasting it. I'd hate to not use it in the strip, too. It's nice to be able to get double action from things. There are things I've thought of that we have done in animated cartoons that I *can* do in the strip, which is always a delight. It's nice not to have to waste those things. We did that marvelous film, which Bill and I were so proud of, where Snoopy has a dream. I don't like doing dream things, but we couldn't avoid it. In the dream, he becomes hijacked to become a sled dog in an Alaskan sled dog team. And he's civilized, of course, and he runs on his hind legs and has a terrible time. Did you ever see that? It was so funny. He's hijacked and he's lashed into this sled dog team with all these ferocious Alaskan sled dogs and he's running along, trying to keep up, and it's just exhausting. And when they camp out at night, the other dogs won't let them curl up with him, and he can't eat with the others because they're too ferocious.

February 7, 1992.

Does he talk in the animations?

No. But the moral of the whole thing was that he was just getting beaten down and he couldn't do anything, and all of a sudden he couldn't take it any longer and he reverted back to become a *real dog*. He fought for his own rights. He snarled and he fought the lead dog off, and he got the meat and he got water and everything and he became the head dog. And some people didn't like that. They said that it was too violent. But we thought the lesson there was that he—like some people—

might have to revert back to his original traits to survive. He was simply overly civilized. And it was a great story. We had a lot of fun with that. And it was the only one that we ever did where he was in the whole thing—it was just all Snoopy.

What other questions do you always hope vainly that people will ask you?

I think the sustaining ability has always fascinated me—the knack of keeping yourself at a high pitch. I relate a lot of things to sports. The ability for a championship golfer to sustain his concentration over four days is really something. And for a tennis player to win Wimbledon—to be able to concentrate day after day after day, playing five set matches all week long—is something that few people can do, and I think that's what makes a champion. To become a champion comic strip artist, I think you have to have the ability to sustain this effort.

What is your concentration like? You've had lots of kids around and lots of other things to do. Is there a corner or a portion of your brain in which that strip lives in kind of pure air, and you can always turn to it and you can apply concentration to it, just the way a stove has a pilot light? Like the pilot light's on, and then you turn the burner on.

Yeah. Years ago, I had a man who played the viola say to me that playing the viola was his religion, and at the time I didn't know what he was talking about. I would never say that drawing the comic strip was my religion. But I think it's comparable to a lot of people's view of religion in that it is the thing to which I retreat and which keeps me going. And I think the man's viola playing was the thing in life that kept him going.

Do you ever feel that when you're working you're sort of meditating?

I don't know much about meditation.

I don't either. But I know that when I'm working there are times when my mind becomes incredibly blank and pure and channeled and clear at the same time. So that instead of doing 95 things at once, I'm only doing one.

Yeah. And then there are other times when your mind just doesn't work. You try to think of something and—bang!—it just gets shut off, and you wonder, "Am I ever going to get back to this kind of light feeling that I had?" It's just *heavy*. It's ponderous—nothing happens.

Oh, you feel that your mind is like a fish tank with a lot of warring fish in it? [Schulz laughs] Just flippering and fluttering. Do you ever feel that way?

Never thought about it like that.

I don't want you to think that I think you're a misunderstood genius. I mean, Yeats said, "If it does not look like the product of a moment's thought, our stitching and unstitching has been for naught."

Uh-huh. Good.

It is good, because most people who do this sort of work work like mad, and it's terribly hard—like drawing Linus's hair. There are probably 5,000 people in the country who have drawn something, who say, "Boy, look at that hair—that is really hard to do." But the rest of the people just see that it's Linus.

Oh, they think it's easy to do.

Or they think, "Why, that guy scratches that stuff out in four seconds."

Uh-huh. But it took a long time to learn how to do that in four seconds. You know what? You mentioned something from the poet there that reminded me of something marvelous that S. J. Pearlman said, which gave me a great deal of comfort. I read someplace where he said that in this country we worship the huge things. We worship the big novel and we worship a mural on the wall. He said, "People are continually asking me when I'm going to write the great novel." He said, "I am content to stitch away on my own embroidery." [*Laughter*] And I think that's the attitude that I should have. People might say, "Do you ever do any real drawing? Any real art?" No, I'm content to stitch away at my embroidery.

Has anyone ever come up here and filmed you working?

Yeah. But I hate that.

Why do you hate people to film your drawing?

That gets us back to the old hand shaking business. I don't like to have the camera focus in on my quivering fingers, that's all.

So, this is just vanity?

Yeah. That's reasonable, I think. And also, it can't be that spontaneous. You're drawing on two different levels: When you're first drawing the comic strip in pencil, you're just roughly spacing things out, and then when you're drawing in the pen and ink you really have to concentrate—and that's a different sort of thing. I'd rather somebody doesn't watch that.

March 23, 1999.

But it certainly would make everyone aware of the tremendous difficulty and complexity.

Yeah. We've done it. But again, the camera can't get right in there down on top of your fingers very well, so we end up drawing a larger drawing with a felt pen or something like that. And the thing just kind of magically appears, and we have to settle for that. But the actual pen-and-ink drawing is difficult to do, and it's probably a little bit slower, too, than the camera can tolerate. And, of course, television doesn't want to concentrate on anything more than a few seconds before moving on to something else.

Do you have anything to say about the invention of the felt tip pen?

I'd love felt tip pens if they didn't dry out so much. You get one that you really like and then it only lasts for a little while.

How long does it take you to break in a nib?

That's another problem. Both the bottle of ink and the pen nibs cause problems. It's a good idea to keep your bottle of ink at a comfortable level. So, you have two bottles—you have your working bottle and then you have a large bottle that you use to refill the small one so that you have just the right level. If it gets too low then the pen won't carry the line through; if it gets too full, then it makes a big blob on the paper. And a brand new pen point is difficult to work with. It has a period of maybe a week or two where it's just right, and then it begins to fade on you. But you keep holding out—you're unwilling to change and go to a new one until it just gets intolerable and it spoils different lines, so you finally give up. You're always fighting the battle of equipment.

Have you ever used a Rapidograph?

Yeah. But I like a line with variety. I have a marvelous pen point. I'm the only person drawing that uses this particular pen point, and it was a sheer accident. When I worked at Art Instruction, we used to sign the diplomas when the students graduated. Maybe once a week they'd bring up some diplomas, and they gave us these pen points that were the kind you might find in a bank. They were dip pens. I started drawing with mine, and I discovered that it was a very strong point that could make a nice fine line when held in one direction, but it could also hold and stand the pressure of making a very broad line without the pen point being too flexible. And I've been drawing with that same pen point now for 35 years.

Are you terrified that the maker is going to stop making them?

He already has.

So, what'd you do?

I bought everything they have. I now have about two-dozen boxes of these pen points. When I run out, then I'm going to quit.

Two dozen. How long do they last?

Quite a while. I don't think I'm in any trouble. [*Laughs*] I would hate to have to start drawing with another pen point. I don't know what kind I would use.

Oh, I see. You own two-dozen boxes and each box contains 144. I think you will have stuff for several thousand years. [Laughs] And what kind of ink do you use?

Black India Ink.

Just any kind? Do you have an ink preference?

Mostly Higgins ink.

Do you have any other requirements? Do you care what kind of drawing board you use?

Oh, yes.

Are you fussy about light?

No. I'm not fussy about light, as long as it's not too bright. I used to have my drawing board in another area here, but it was a little too far from the ceiling light. For years, I worked with one of those lights that attached to the top of the drawing board, but I discovered that wasn't necessary—just kind of a nuisance. I have one at home on that drawing board but it's not necessary here. You don't need the traditional north light for drawing something like this. I do like to be totally alone, of course, and I like to be in a place where I can't be surprised when someone comes into the room. I always make sure that my drawing board is facing the door so that no one can sneak up behind me. And I've had to train several secretaries not to come in and say, "Here's something I wanted to show you," lay it on top of the drawing table, and have it slide down right into the wet ink. [*Laughs*] I've had that happen many times. Those are the little quirks that are necessary.

Do you have paper that you especially adore?

Yes, I work on only either two- or three-ply smooth surface Strathmore. To me, that's the best kind.

Do you love that feeling of the pen gliding over the paper?

Oh, yes. When I was in my late teens trying to draw comic strips, I used to go down to a certain art supply store in St. Paul and I would buy maybe two sheets of drawing paper. At the time, it cost maybe 50 cents a sheet and that's all I could afford. And then I would come home and cut it into strips of three, and I'd get six comic strips out of it. I've always loved the feeling of art equipment like that, but I've never been a fanatic about it.

Do you love the sound that the ink and the pen make on the paper?

I never think about that. I like the sound of a pencil sharpener grinding. I don't sharpen the pencil very often either. Some people have automatic pencil sharpeners or electric pencil sharpeners, but I've never felt that need.

You don't like a real sharp pencil?

I don't need one. No, not too sharp.

What number would you use?

I like the #2 pencil. That's all I ever use. My equipment is very simple, really.

Are there certain characters that are just so pleasant to draw that you just love to draw them?

I like drawing Linus. I like drawing Marcie, Peppermint Patty, and Snoopy. Woodstock is a little of a problem, because you have to concentrate to make sure that every line falls in just the right place and it has to be very spontaneous. Charlie Brown is hard work to draw, because his head is so difficult to get just right. And I love doing the Schroeder/Lucy things, but they're a chore to draw, because you have to turn the paper around and around to make sure that you get Schroeder leaning over the piano just right and to fit everything in. And you have to fake a lot of things in cartooning, because these characters cannot be drawn doing things that real children do. So, you have to fake the depth of what is happening a lot of times, and you have to concentrate very hard in order to get that to come out right so that the perspective is reasonable. Schroeder *really* could not sit and play the

piano the way he does—a real child just wouldn't work out that way. We are always faking in cartooning to make things come out right.

Well, you're always faking in everything to come out right because, in real life, characters don't behave the way they behave in fiction.

Yeah. Well, for example, if I want one of the kids to be holding something over his head, it has to be drawn from the side view, because from the front view or three-quarter view their arms are too short to reach over the tops of their heads. So, you have to fake it from the side, and sometimes the far arm can't be doing what the nearer arm does. You always have to work out these little compromises, and I think that's one of the secrets of being a good cartoonist.

Being a Force for Good

Do you feel that you are fulfilling a purpose in what you do?

Oh, yeah. Sure.

And do you ever think it was ordained that Charles M. Schulz would do this?

I think it, but then I'm horrified that I would be so egotistical as to think that God would ordain me to do something. Maybe it would be better if I just shook my head and nodded so it doesn't come off on tape. [*Laughs*]

Well, your talent singles you out, doesn't it? Don't you ever meditate on that fact?

Oh, I think about it, yes. But I think it's a very dangerous way to think.

It doesn't mean that you're a great guy or a swell guy or that you're better than other people. But your talent singles you out. Of all the millions of people in the world, most of them aren't talented, and certainly the only one who is as talented as you are in this regard is you. So, you are special, and you are a specialist.

And therefore, I think that if it is true, I've done the best I could to carry this out. That's why I *do* feel deeply about it, and I feel responsible. And I try to do things that are good and have something good to say that is decent.

Speaking about you as an artist and your work, do you ever feel that you are actually the agent of good?

Yes, and I think I've proved it. I think that I have proved that you can take something which is basically innocent and good, totally void of vulgarity or anything, and make into one of the most popular entertainment items that has ever existed —not only in the comic strip itself, but in all the products that we do and in the television shows and in the four movies that we've done. The book *Happiness Is a Warm Puppy* was the number one best seller in 1963. A totally innocent little book, and yet it sold more copies than any other book in 1963. And in an era when they said that it couldn't be done—in an era where vulgarity and things were beginning to creep into publications where it didn't used to, they said it just couldn't be done.

Do you ever think of yourself as a strong force for good?

Yeah, I do. I try not to think about it too much, because I think it's dangerous thinking. But I do think so. I don't draw cartoons to be good or to teach or to instruct or to serve any purpose. I draw cartoons because I like to draw cartoons. I do them for myself. But if I *have* to think about being a force for something, I do think it's a force for good.

So, in other words, you think that you are a good man and what issues forth from you is, in fact, good?

Uh-huh. Is that all right?

Yeah. Do you feel that the good you do comes back toward you?

Oh, sure. But I don't think that it is a theological truth that you are rewarded for the good that you do. That's Old Testament thinking, which I don't think is true at all.

That's very dangerous thinking. It can be proved to be false very easily.

So, you feel that worshiping of God is an offense to the Almighty, and the true nature of the Almighty is that he wishes that we would be kind and loving to one another?

I think that's worshiping God in spirit and in truth.

April 25, 1960.

Do you have scriptural backup for this belief, or did you come to it just because you believe it?

Both. I don't look for scriptural backup for it, but it says, "Pure religion undefiled before God is this—to visit the widows and orphans in their affliction and to keep oneself unstained from the world." That's a pretty good description of any religion, I think. And, of course, the fourth chapter of Matthew, where Jesus describes the people that visited those in prison and those that were hungry—that was a marvelous description of what pure religion is. And these people didn't do it for God, they did it for the people. And afterwards they were told that they had done it for God and they said, "When did we do anything like that?" They were so pure in heart that they did these things out of the goodness of their heart, while the others who wanted to do something for God were doing it by bringing their gifts to the altar, which is a lot easier. It's a lot easier to drop five dollars in the collection plate than it is to visit somebody in the hospital, and that's where the deception comes in. It's a lot easier to attend Sunday morning or Saturday evening services than it is to help other people. And the worst thing to do—the worst thing of *all*—is to pay others to do it for you, to have a paid priesthood and a paid ministry, who are your intermediates for God. That's just ridiculous.

You don't believe that there are people who are specialists in this regard?

I believe there are people that are better than others at working with people, like Mother Teresa and the others—that are just good at that. And some of us are not good at that.

And you don't believe in symbolic gestures such as the celebration of the Mass, for example?

No. I think that grew out of paganism. *Real* Christianity never celebrated a Mass.

Well, he said, "Do this in memory of me."

Yeah, so they had dinner and they passed the wine around. That's not Mass, "Do it in memory of me." Catholicism does it as a sacrament, and by doing it you receive grace from God. He never said you'll receive anything. You see, they...

...thought he said you'd receive eternal life. "I am the resurrection and the life."

Yeah. But it's a nice symbolic way of people getting together. And doing it in remembrance of Him, if that's what they want to do, and the gathering together is fine. He said, "When two or three are gathered together in my name, then I am in the midst of them." I think that's wonderful. But to think that you receive an actual segment of *grace* for doing this... It's always dangerous, of course, to talk about what other people believe, because you may not be interpreting them properly.

When you went to visit the chateau and you thanked God for sparing you and sending you back and for giving you such good things, does that constitute for you a religious experience?

Uh-huh.

Have you had several or many such experiences?

No, not really.

Did you have any religious feelings before your surgery, or did it make you turn in any way?

My only feelings there were praying for the protection of my family.

Do you ever have a real sense that God is with you?

I don't know. Yeah, I guess so. But not with me any more than anybody else or because of anything that I've done or anything like that.

No, just a sense of you and it?

Yeah. I think so.

I wonder if you ever get a sense of… I don't like to use the word "power," because you'll misinterpret it, but a sense of benign power when you're working—when your arm is working right and your hand is working right and this energy is going through you and your mind has that light quality you describe. If you ever feel a sense of presence that is almost like a religious experience.

I'm afraid not. I'm afraid that I have what you could almost describe as a superstition of taking myself too seriously. It's almost as if the minute that I do that, it will all be taken away from me. It's a childish superstition, but you can't help some of these things.

Actually, I was thinking of something a little more mechanical. Well, last week I had to write this grant proposal, and I was just getting back to work. I hadn't really done any writing for a while, and when I sat down to the typewriter and started writing this grant proposal, I couldn't type right. It felt like the action on the keys was all funny and strange. I realized that when I sat down to do my own work, my hands were on the keys like a person playing the piano. But when I sat down to do this other stuff, it was as though I were using a different typewriter. And then I realized that there were times when I was working when I was filled with the power of doing the work—that everything suddenly starts to flow in some wonderfully correct way, and I get filled with this sense of exultation.

I like the pure drawing of the comic strip where I can do exactly what I want. I hate it when I am asked to do a special drawing of a sort for a particular purpose—for a cover to something, or to advertise something—and invariably the characters will be forced to do something that they normally might not do, and then it's just like drawing through mud. I remember once for a Ford advertisement I had to draw all the characters riding in the top of a long bicycle where they had several seats on it. I would *never* draw anything like that normally, because the characters just don't fit into that, and it was a real chore. I'm always asked to draw several of the characters together doing something, and they're not made to do that. It's just a plain effort to do it, and I'm always so glad when it's done. That's why drawing the comic strip itself is such an open thing, and I'm free to do with it what I want.

Do you still get a sense of absolute wonderment and mystification when you sit down at your drawing board that you not only do this, but that you do it so well and that it's yours to have?

Yeah. I've never really thought about it that way, but I think you're right that maybe one percent of the time something like this comes true. When

October 25, 1961.

I'm doing something, I'm really amazed that I'm able to think of these things and that they come out the way they do. When I make a really neat little drawing and the drawing itself is clever or funny or whatever you want to call it—it just fits right—I suppose I am kind of amazed. Very pleased.

Do you wonder where this all comes from?

Well, gee. Can that have any kind of an answer? Comes from where? What do you mean?

I was thinking about where talent comes from, because in New York City people really believe they create their own talent. And they honestly feel that if they can do something well, they're better than other people. You seem not to feel this way. And it seemed to me when I was writing one of my books that talent was something that you were either lucky enough to be given or you were lucky enough to inherit or you were lucky enough that your genes connected in a funny way, and that it was a sin not to use it. But just because you had it didn't necessarily mean that you were better than the next fellow. It just meant that you were lucky enough, or God had given you this particular gift. That's what I mean when I say, "Do you wonder where it comes from?"

Oh, I think it's hereditary. I think you just inherit certain combinations of ability. And one of the areas where luck comes in is being born at a time where there's an outlet for these abilities. I was lucky in that I was born when comic strips existed. Seventy years ago, there wouldn't have been an outlet for this ability and I would have had to do something else, or maybe I wouldn't have been quite as good as it. I'm sure I would have found some place to use this unique combination of abilities, but it wouldn't have been as "just right" as it is now.

You think of yourself as a Christian, don't you?

That, I can't answer.

Well, let me put it a different way. You think of yourself as a person of religious feelings of some sort. Not codified or organized, but…

Yeah, yeah. I think of myself as a member of the Kingdom of God.

OK. And so, as a member of the Kingdom of God, do you ever feel, not singled out in that way that makes you better than other people, but do you ever feel that you were given a gift?

Oh, yes. I feel I was given a gift and I feel an obligation to use it *well*, which is why

I have never drawn anything that was vulgar or smutty or whatever word we want to use these days, because I feel that would be a misuse of my abilities. And I try never to draw anything that degrades anyone else or mocks anyone else. I could never be a caricaturist and I'd make a terrible political cartoonist, because I could never draw a cartoon about anyone who took me out to lunch. [*Laughs*] I just can't do that kind of thing. People say, "Where did you get the idea for…" such and such a character. "Is it somebody that you knew?" I could never even base the characters upon friends of mine or people I knew, unless they were nice qualities. The closest I come to that is borrowing the names of friends, but I do that mainly for copyright purposes, so that strangers won't think that I've stolen their names.

But your characters are not necessarily nice. They're not terribly nice.

I know, but they're not patterned after anyone else either. They're patterned after not only my own observations, but my own bad qualities, because I think I am in every one of the characters to greater or lesser degrees.

What do you think your worst qualities are?

I think I've toned it down considerably. I used to be quite sarcastic, but I learned that that simply was a bad thing to be and didn't pay, and I was lucky I didn't get slugged on several occasions. [*Laughs*] But this, of course, comes from among what you might call witty people, too. Witty people are frequently sarcastic and put other people down. But it's a terrible trait to get a laugh at other people's expense, so I've tried to learn to control that.

But your characters are quite sarcastic, and they are constantly getting laughs at other people's expense.

Yeah, but that's all right because we're all involved in that together, and that's what cartoon characters are for. We're supposed to laugh at them and get laughs at their expense. That's why they exist. It's still funny to see a cartoon character get hit on the head with something, because there's nothing funnier than seeing somebody get hit on the head.

Why do you think that is? Because we're so happy that it wasn't us?

I don't know. People talk about that all the time, and that's usually the answer. But it is funny as long as you know the person isn't hurt. And a cartoon character cannot really be hurt. He gets bonked on the head and he flips over backwards and he's lying there and the stars are there, but in the next panel he's all right.

April 3, 1970.

On the other hand, do you remember Tom and Jerry *cartoons? They were* incredibly *violent. I mean, the characters were always being squashed or hit. I remember as a child I found those cartoons very unpleasant, because I couldn't believe that the character was going to survive all that.*

Well, they carried it to its *absolute extreme,* and the fact that they were *so* extreme I think is what made it funny. If they had only done the things to each other half-way, it wouldn't have been as funny.

But your characters wreak a kind of tremendous *psychological carnage on one another in a very mild, subtle way. They're constantly sniping and fighting and doing what most of human life is like. It's a constant small, rather tender battle, don't you think?*

Well, I think this goes on all the time. It goes on in families continually among the children. It goes on in offices. It goes on in schoolrooms all over. And the cartoon is supposed to caricature these things, some more broadly than others. I like to think that mine caricatures these things; subtly some days, sometimes it's very broad.

I think the reason Peanuts *really rings very true to me is because everybody in the strip is a tough guy, except for the ones who are very tenderhearted. And they have their own protective device, which is to be filled with bafflement and puzzlement like Charlie Brown. That's really his kind of defensive armor in a way. Because he's the sweetest. And it seems to me that these people are always being surprised by their own sweetness, or they're surprised by their own love—and, actually, they're always surprised by good things. You always see characters begrudgingly expressing love and affection for each other, which is actually a very New York kind of character trait. But it's much more poignant than somebody who just goes around loving everybody. These characters transcend their own personalities to be better.*

Yeah. That pleases me for you to be able to say that.

Do you work on that actively or do you think that's true?

No. It just comes out naturally.

But it is true, isn't it?

Yeah, sure. There's one other thing, of course: There is some hitting in the strip. Sometimes some of the problems are solved by someone hitting somebody else, which is just comic strip humor and is necessary, where if you're working in another medium you wouldn't do it. Charlie Brown is picked upon, for instance, by a tough bully when he's out of town at a baseball game. He goes to get a baseball autographed and he gives it to this kid who is the equipment manager for the ball team. And the kid says, "What if I don't give it back to you?" And

April 15, 1953.

Charlie Brown's totally defenseless—nothing he can do about it. The other kid is bigger. He's got the ball and he can't get it away from him. What's he going to do? At the last minute, Snoopy comes racing up pretending he's the World War I Flying Ace and grabs the ball out of the kid's hand and gives him a good kick, which Charlie Brown can't do. That's a comic strip way of solving the problem, and people accept it and think that's great. Or else Peppermint Patty will come along and she'll whoop the kid one because she's tough and she can do it. But Charlie Brown is not tough, he can't do it. He knows he'd end up getting beaten up. But that's just a comic strip way of solving these problems—like we want a superman to come along and do it.

The fact is, the superman in this case is a dog or a girl, and so you've actually changed all the terms. The little boys are not the heroes. The little girls are the heroes, and the little boys are the little girls.

This again is comic strip land, and it goes back to what I call the Maggie and Jiggs syndrome. It is not funny for a little boy to be mean to a little girl. We don't accept this in our society. But it is funny for a little girl to be mean to a little boy. We can get away with that. It's funny for Maggie to hit Jiggs with the rolling pin. It's just disgusting, repulsive, if Jiggs hits Maggie with the rolling pin. It's because men are supposed to be stronger than women even if they might not be. So, it's the time-honored thing in comic strips.

But it's also the charm of role reversal. I mean, it is charming to reverse the roles. You get so much more mileage, don't you think? [Schulz laughs]

Sure, yeah. But it works in comic strips in a unique way that can't work in other mediums. In television, somebody can't throw a rolling pin at anybody because it would really hurt them. Maggie could bonk a rolling pin off of Jiggs's head, and he'd be all right in the next panel. Or she could throw smashed dishes all over, which might not work in another medium.

This is a little side trip, but it is interesting, if we remember Dr. Fredric Wertham or whatever he was called.

I have his book right up there.

You do? My theory is that television really has made people more violent.

Oh, yeah.

But the fact is that in the old comic strips, Maggie was constantly smashing that poor thing over the head. And the Katzenjammer kids were doing horrible *things. Those strips were truly filled with a kind of hilarious violence and mayhem. Do you think they affected people that way? Or do you think it's because they weren't real people?*

I doubt it. I really doubt it. I think one of the most deplorable things in *modern* television stories is what we do with automobiles. We have replaced the cowboy "horse galloping across the prairie chase" with car chases that appear to be very innocent. People roll over in their cars. The police are made to look like fools by

Bringing Up Father by George McManus, May 22, 1939.

the hero, who zigzags through the streets. And you see the police car suddenly sail over a cliff, roll end over end, the police crawl out and they shake their fists or are made to look very stupid. You roll over end over end in a car, and you've had it. And I think young people are made to believe that they can get away with these things in a car. But you hit a tree going 20 miles an hour and you'd probably get killed. But they make it look like these things can happen, because of their stunt preparations and everything. And I think that's very deceptive and I think it's irresponsible of the television people. But I think Hollywood is filled with irresponsible people.

Do you ever feel that you're a voice crying in the wilderness?

Sure. But I don't care. I'm proud of it. I'm proud of the fact that we put on nice TV shows. And yet they're not boring and they're not cute, but they're good television shows. We've done a lot of wonderful things and I'm proud of that. I don't think we're irresponsible—we're *very* responsible in everything that we do. I think Bill Melendez, Lee Mendelson, and myself think about these things in a very responsible way.

The Weight of Celebrity

Now, when we were at lunch yesterday, two people came up to you, one of whom knew somebody that you knew and one of whom just knew you, although you didn't know him. And I wonder, what do you feel about being a celebrity or being identified? The awful thing is that people think you're terribly nice so they feel that you will be nice to them.

I think autographing is a *real* problem, and I wish there were some way of explaining it so that people could understand. There's one part of me, of course, that is delighted that someone should want one of my drawings, because this is really what it's all about, being able to draw something that makes somebody else happy. That's all right if it's done in a minimum and not under any pressure, and on a nice piece of paper with a good felt pen or a nice book or something like that. I do not like being surrounded by 50 people, all wanting some kind of drawing and all poking the paper in my face. I do not like book autographing unless it is *very* controlled. I want to know exactly where I'm going to sit and have people come by one at a time and tell me what they want in the book, and I can pace myself so that at exactly two o'clock we'll be done and that will be it—*totally*—and then I can get up from the table and leave and go off someplace by myself or with one or two other people and have a quiet cup of coffee and a piece of apple pie and relax and just get away from the whole thing. But autograph parties, if they're not controlled, tend never to quit and go on and on. And then when you're all done, you get upstairs in the department store and they've got 400 more books there waiting for you from people who have telephone ordered them or something, or the employees themselves have 50 books that they want signed. That sort of thing just drives me crazy. And I *cannot* keep up anymore with the mail requests for autographs that come in and for special drawings for people for their pastor who is leaving after serving the church for 40 years, and could I make a special drawing for him because he's used your cartoon characters in his sermon so much. I would like very much to please this man, and I try to keep up with those things. But, after the heart problem I discovered that I couldn't. I had to cut back on those things. So, we just don't do it anymore. I regret not being able to do it, but some of the requests are so unreasonable—people sending in eight books to be auto-graphed with different names in them to give as Christmas presents. During the holiday season, books like that coming in every day really become a burden. And if you're feeling great and if you've got nothing else to do, it's not that it takes that long, but it's just another intrusion that comes in the day and really begins to get to you after a while. I don't like people to come up and grab me. I don't like people to come up and throw their arm around me and say, "Hi, Charlie. It's good to see you!" I don't like that.

February 4, 1955.

I can certainly understand why you wouldn't. But you can certainly understand what people probably think of you who don't know you.

But why can't someone be satisfied? As Bill Cosby once said to me, "Why can't they be satisfied with coming up and saying, 'My name is such and such' and be willing simply to shake hands with you and say a few words? Why do you have to *sign* something?"

Because they want something that you made.

Yeah. I realize that. One thing I do *not* do is write the inscription for people in a book that they want in it, which to me seems totally absurd. Someone will send a book to be autographed and they say, "Please put in it: 'For Aunt Jenny, thanks for all the wonderful times you gave us at Christmas.'" Well, I'm willing to sign my name and draw a Snoopy, but I think they should put their own personal message. Why should I put their personal inscription in it? So, I don't do that kind of thing. The whole business of answering mail really is a problem, too, in that people don't understand the forwarding processes and we get so many things that come in too late. We get letters from school children who have to do a school project and will write. They'll write to their local newspaper, who will send it maybe to United Features, who then forwards it a month later, and by then the kid's got an "F" in his school report because he didn't get the thing in. Well, he didn't realize that he had to write it well ahead of time to give us time to respond.

Do you respond to most things the children send you?

We respond to *everything* that we get. But I don't do it personally, because I can't. Everybody who writes to us gets a response.

Does it annoy you or perplex you or do you ever find it unpleasant? Do you ever wake up in the middle of the night and say, "These people think I'm theirs!"

No, no.

But they do think that you're theirs.

No. I think of that during the day but not in the middle of the night. [*Laughs*]

You know what I mean. Do you think that?

Yeah. I suppose it's the guilt in the final analysis that bothers you. You feel guilty because you cannot really respond and do the things for the people that you would like to do, because there is a lot of gratitude to this—that you're allowed to do what you want to do and to make a living at it. And it's wonderful that people like what you draw, but you feel guilty for being annoyed about these things.

But I think they do think that you are theirs.

Well, a lot of people don't understand the scope of the whole thing. I'm sure a lot of people think that because the strip is so small—it's a very tiny little thing—that you can draw the thing in five minutes and this is all you do, and *maybe* you only draw for your local paper. They don't realize that it runs all over the world and that you've got a lot of other things to do and that it's a full-time job. They have no comprehension of this, and probably think that they're the only person that writes to you. And then there are other people who say, "I realize that you must get thousands of requests. However..." and *they* are the "however." Why do they think that they are the "however" and that out of the thousands of people you turn down that you are going to answer their request?

The interesting thing, of course, is how often they write. I think one of the problems that you have is that your characters become so close to the reader, or the reader becomes so close to them, or they become so much a part of the reader's daily life, that you are invading their consciousness. Whether you like it or not, you are in the minds of every person that reads the San Francisco Chronicle. *Every morning, people who are habitual newspaper readers, like me, sit down and probably, of all the people who read the* Chronicle, *82 percent of them read you first. They probably pluck out that green section and think, "I'll just see what the Snoopys are doing." The fact is that you, Charles Schulz, are with those people even if you just dart across their consciousness like a fish in the water. And so, it makes sense that they would feel that you'd be available to them.*

Yeah, sure. I have felt that way with others in other fields. The mere fact that I should have made contact with you and asked if I could meet you and that we could have lunch together was something. I called Margaret Drabble when I was in London.

You did!?

Yeah. And she came in and had tea with me.

She did? What was she like?

Yeah. Wonderful, wonderful lady.

You just called her up on the telephone. What did you say?

Well, a little boy's voice answered and, of course, I had no idea if she would know who I was and if she was receptive to this kind of thing at all. But I said, "This is Charles Schulz. I'm from the United States, and I'm the man that draws Snoopy; if your mother's home, could I talk to her?" And I heard the boy run through the house yelling, "Mom, Charles Schulz is on the phone!" and I knew I was all right. [*Laughs*] And she came and she was very pleasant.

*What did she say once she picked up the phone? [*In British accent] "Oh, hello."*

"Oh, hello. Yes." Uh-huh. And she said, "Well, you would never be able to find your way out to where we live, and I have to be in London tomorrow for a television appearance. So, I could come to the hotel and we could meet, say at 11 o'clock, and talk for a while, and then I have to be at the station." And so, she did. I was a little bit paralyzed in that I couldn't think of the things to say to her that I wanted to say, and I couldn't remember what I wanted to ask her anymore. Well, Laurie, I couldn't remember what I wanted to ask you when we met. I just knew that I liked her books and I wanted to meet her.

Who else have you done this to?

Several times I tried to call Joyce Carol Oates, years ago, but I never was able to get hold of her. I had always wanted to talk to Sam Snead. All my life I had wanted to talk to Sam Snead. It took me literally 40 years before I finally met him and that was that. We said a few words.

Were you happy to meet him? Or were you disappointed?

Yeah. No. He sent me a big photograph of himself with a very kind remark on it saying, "You can hang this in the outhouse to keep the rats away." [*Laughter*] Typical Sam Snead humor. I can't remember any others. Well, when I was young, I wrote to several cartoonists and to this day I resent a couple of the non-responses that I got, because I know from my own experience now that they could not have been that busy. But the man who drew *Prince Valiant*, Harold Foster, wrote me a very long handwritten nice response. I've always thought, "See, he did it. Why couldn't the others have done it?"

Is that part of your feeling that you must answer your mail?

Oh, yes. And I answer everything that I possibly can. It just is a matter of not being able to answer all of it. If we get a package of 300 letters from kids in one day, I can't answer all those letters. Besides, they all really want virtually the same thing, so they do get a response and we just do the best we can. I know some people that never answer their fan mail—never even *see* it. The syndicate does the whole thing or else just throws them all away, and I think that's deplorable.

Well, I always answer everything I get, although I obviously don't get anything like the quantity that you do. That's why I buy postcards in the hundreds. I find a postcard I like and I write to the museum and say, "Please send me a hundred." It usually costs $36 or something like that. Then, if people write to me, I write them a little note—a postcard— unless they write something that requires a letter. I've actually made some friends—actual, real friends—in that way. But I realize that I never wrote to anybody, so I never expected a response. But since I love the mail so much, I would be very hurt if I wrote to someone and they didn't answer me.

Also, answering mail is very expensive. It's *very* expensive to do all this.

But you have very strong feelings about the sort of person you ought to be or are.

I would like to be a nice person. I want to be known as a nice person.

You want to be loved, too, obviously.

Oh, yes. Sure.

And you want to be thought adorable.

That's right.

Do you want to be admired?

I don't know about admired as much as I would like to be thought of as—you used the word Christian some time ago in the interview. I would like to be known as someone who had Christian attributes.

Could you say what they would be?

Kindness, forgiveness, understanding. Tolerance is a difficult word to use because

I suppose it indicates superiority to some people. Willing to go the second mile, the third mile. Generosity. I think I'm a reasonably generous person.

Do you feel that in this way you are simply being rigorous about your good qualities, or staving off your bad qualities?

I think I'm trying to be what the Scriptures teach us to be: to fulfill God's will for us, to be the sort of person that we're supposed to be.

Do you think you're a good person? Do you think it's easy for you to be good?

Probably, because I like goodness. I like gentleness and kindness and goodness. It doesn't bother me that I can't pull a fast deal on someone. I just have no desire to pull a fast deal on someone. I'm always very generous in business dealings and very honest.

Do you hate anybody?

Yeah.

Are you a good hater?

I carry grudges for a long time hoping that someday I'll get revenge. [*Laughs*]

Have you ever gotten revenge? Or has life done it for you?

I wouldn't *get* revenge, because at the last minute I would realize you're not supposed to get revenge. It is not good. There is a truth to it that revenge does you no good, nor are you really getting even. But there are people I would like to get revenge on.

Do you feel that you are a vigorous and strong hater?

Yeah, yeah. I translate this in the strip, too, I think.

Do you think that you cultivate your hates as you cultivate your loves?

No, no. I try not to have them. But I have been wronged a few times and I keep saying that someday I'll get revenge on those people. But I never will and I don't really want revenge on them.

Is there anyone whose opinion [of your work] you would love to know?

Yeah. I would like to know what Andrew Wyeth thinks of my work. [*Laughs*]

Didn't he send you a picture?

He was forced to, to be nice.

Why was he forced to do that?

By a friend. His wife had asked this young man who knew me if she could have a strip where I mentioned Andrew Wyeth's name to give to Andrew for his birthday. And I feel terrible that it was one of the most poorly drawn strips I've ever drawn. I wish he had a strip that was beautifully drawn, but she gave it to him. So, I said to that young man, "When you give it to him, would you tell him that I admire his work, and does he have anything that he could give me in return—just some kind of a drawing that's around the studio." And so, he brought back that little drawing that I have.

That's a beautiful drawing, isn't it?

Yeah. I'm very pleased with it. I'm sure I'm the only person in Santa Rosa with an Andrew Wyeth. And I know I'm the only person in Santa Rosa who is *owned* by Andrew Wyeth, which is even better, isn't it? [*Laughter*]

Who else?

Who else? Gosh, I was so pleased when I found out that Billie Jean King read my strip and liked it and was a real fan, and actually had named her dog after Lucy. That really pleased me. I know you won't like it, but I was very pleased to discover that Ronald Reagan liked my strip and especially was pleased with the Lucy football gag. He said he always looked forward to that every fall. And I don't know if Ike ever liked my strip. Probably not. Some of the cartoonists, of course. But I never like to get into the cartoonists' names. I would hope that Eudora Welty likes my things. I met her once…

Did you tell her that you named that character after her?

No. That was later, so I don't know if she's ever known that.

Why don't you tell her?

Oh, I don't know. I don't think you'd tell things like that. You hope that she knows. If she doesn't know, then why should I tell her? I had hoped, of course, when I first read your books that you knew who I was. I was afraid that you would have no idea who I was.

I don't think there's a citizen of this country who has the use of their faculties who doesn't know who you are, don't you think? [Schulz laughs]

Probably not very many.

I think even people in a Trappist monastery would know who you are.

In fact, I got a letter from one priest who said that when he was going to this certain seminary, the only things they were allowed to read were the *New Testament*, their prayer book, and *The Gospel According to Peanuts*. [*Laughs*]

So, there you are. Do you get letters from foreign places?

Oh, yes. We get a lot of mail from Japan, quite a few letters from England. The Italians are very fond of comic strips. It really covers almost the whole world.

This comes back to my original question. And it is the question that I think is the most interesting and it's the most perplexing. It's the one probably that nobody has an answer to, which is that you have created something that is universally admired and loved and is universally connected with. And that people all over the world feel a true and pure connection with these very true and pure creatures. And that is a truly astonishing thing, because it's a remarkable and unique achievement. The question of things being universally understood or anticipated or beloved is extraordinary, because in human history millions of things have been scribbled, but few have been remembered. For example, if you've ever listened to the music that was written around the time of Haydn and Mozart, have you ever heard people like Ditters von Dittersdorf?

No.

You don't want to, because they're really awful. But millions of people were writing music around that time—or not millions, but lots were—and what we hear is only the best. And of all the people writing plays, we only really know the best. And when you go in the bookstores in little towns, you find thousands *of books written by people like Joseph Hergesheimer. He wrote many books. You've never read one.*

Have you ever gone into a furniture store and looked at a little bookcase that was for sale made to look nice? They've got a little setup of a dining room or something like that, and they've put some books in the bookcase. And in the bookcase is a book that was a Book-of-the-Month Club selection back in 1949 and it looks so lonely and totally lost there, and nobody's ever going to read that book again. But at that time the potential was there—it was selected by the Book-of-the-Month Club, and the author was so happy. And now the book is just gone. It's sitting in that little display. I think that's a great observation. [*Laughs*]

It is, because they are *lonely. But you look at them and the other thing you say to yourself is the same thing you say when you read the list of Nobel Prize winners for literature. Some of these people, not only did you never hear of, but when you* have *heard of them it's shocking because they're such terrible writers.*

You're right.

So, to have people respond to what you do everywhere, to have made a bunch of characters that people...

You're talking as if it *really* is something important, aren't you?

But it is!

OK. Why then has book after book come out recounting all the great things that have happened, say, since the '50s—in those years and all of that—and I am never mentioned? Someone will write a book about the great humorists in our country. I am never mentioned. Again, it's that thing that I insist that these people just *don't* think that comic strips are that important. They just don't understand it. We're left out continually. *Charlie Brown Christmas* has been on television more than any other film except

June 10, 1979.

for perhaps the *Wizard of Oz*. We are the longest continuing run on the history of television, and yet when they write the history of television, we are lucky if we get one half inch of mention or something. For some reason, there's something about cartoon characters or comic strips that just are not regarded as worth anything.

The Value of a Comic Strip Artist

We were talking about your universal appeal, which is a subject that you seem shy about. And you seem shy about it because you feel that cartooning is considered a lower form. But you don't feel it's a lower form.

No.

You feel that it's a very high form.

Yeah. That's why I maintain that it's risky to talk about it—stick your head up because of the way we are continually ignored. How can I maintain that cartooning is as high an art form as anything else when cartoonists are denied the Pulitzer Prize simply because these people just don't think comic strips are worth that much?

Are you afraid if you say it's art it will look like you're beating your own drum?

Yeah. And it doesn't do any good either. Milt Caniff has been fighting for the Pulitzer Prize for comic strip artists for 40 years, and they won't listen to him. That's aggravating. And then there are those comic artists in the National Cartoonists Society who insist that comic strip drawing *is* an art and that we belong hanging in galleries. And they try to prove it by hanging their comic strips in galleries, but their comic strips are not that good. And that's a waste of time, too, because there are a lot of comic strips that do not belong hanging in galleries. Just because something is drawn does not make it art. Drawing is not art.

Do you think George Herriman is art? Do you think Rube Goldberg is art?

I think Herriman was but not Goldberg.

Who else of the great past do you feel is art?

Very few of them, among cartoonists. I think Clare Briggs was. He did a panel called "When a Feller Needs a Friend" and things like that—a good old time, scratchy, wonderful drawing. J. R. Williams—some of the things he did. This doesn't mean that *everything* they did was art, but there are selected things that were art that will last forever.

The reason I asked this is because the person who does the thing is his own artist in a way. Frankly, I don't care if you think you're an artist or not. Your strip seems to me more like, in its condensation, modern poetry than anything else. Modern poetry is

very intense. *It tends to be short; it has a direct impact; and it has to be absolutely at its minimum—less has to be more. I'm speaking now about modern poetry as written by W. B. Yeats and Wallace Stevens as opposed to whoever is writing now. That stuff is short and it's very direct and it has to be. It's an arrow pointed directly at your heart and mind. And there's no comic strip that I can think of about which you can say that but yours.*

Well, I'm proud of it. I think I've thrown myself into it.

If I asked you to give me an honest estimation of your talents, what would you say?

I think that I really am one of the best comic strip artists that has ever been in the business, but that's the extent of it.

That's all you'll say?

Yeah. That's the extent of it. I don't regard myself as an artist. I think I know what real art is. I think that my comic strips will live in *comic strip* history. But I know how quickly pop art dies, and it could very well be that I'm just a successful pop artist, that's all. And pop art does not speak very well to future generations. There are things that are pop art that become classics as future generations begin to like them and then they stay with us. Very few things. I think *Alice in Wonderland* is a perfect example. It was just pop art when he wrote the thing, but now we regard it as a classic, because our kids like it as well as kids did a century ago. But very few comic strips can say that. Even the great ones. Very few of them hold up.

Let's go one step further. What do you think is your specific talent in what you have to present—not in what you actually do?

I think I'm speaking to people about things that really affect them. I think I'm doing what poetry does in a grander manner, but I am doing it for the layman. I'm identifying things that the average person only feels vaguely. I am defining emotions. And a perfect example of this is if somebody says to you, "Today, I feel just like Charlie Brown." He doesn't have to say anything more. You know how he feels, don't you? And I think poetry does that for us. Poetry defines emotions that most of us cannot express, or it should. Good poetry does.

Or it says the thing that you feel.

Yeah. And I think that cartoons do that, too—a cartoon character can do that. I think Charlie Brown does that. Or if somebody says to you, "Boy, you're a real Lucy, aren't you!" They've hit you right between the eyes.

Well, of course.

We were talking in the car yesterday about the levels on which the strip works, which I don't think you like to talk about, because it makes you think that somebody might be accusing you of being an artist. But the fact is that on one level these people are not caricatures, they are character types.

July 1, 1959.

You know why I don't like to be accused of being an artist? Because I'm setting myself up to be put down.

In other words, you're afraid that someone will have artistic expectations that you'll…

No. I *know* for sure that as we turn the page I will be totally ignored in other circles. We cannot deny that Picasso was an artist. Nobody denies that.

No. But we can certainly say that a good deal of what Picasso did was a lot of crap.

Yeah, I suppose. But, generally, he is still regarded as an artist. You see, I'm trapped in a medium which is not regarded as art.

I don't care what they say. I care what we say.

Well, that's why I don't want to stick my head up too high.

Let me ask you something. If you stood on the top of one of these hills and just had a moment with yourself, you do think you're an artist of some kind. Don't you, honestly?

I'm proud that I've done the very *best* that I could have done with what abilities that I have, my whole life.

But look at the way you think about that strip. There's white space and there's black space. There's design…

I think that I am a better artist than a lot of people who are regarded as artists. There are people who hang in galleries and they'll say there's an art exhibition and they are called artists—they call *themselves* artists. Their paintings will be reviewed and all of that. And yet, I think what I am doing is better than what they are doing.

Do you think that you are not taken seriously enough? Do you think that the appellation "comic strip" is limiting to what you think you're capable of?

Yeah, I do. I think that I have achieved more than any other cartoonist has ever done as far as accolades and being recognized.

Does it ever frighten you to think that you have actually achieved your heart's desire?

No, it doesn't frighten me.

Does it ever baffle you?

It pleases me. It pleases me to think that this nonentity kid from St. Paul, who nobody ever thought was going to be anything and had failed all those subjects, turned out to be probably, if not *the* most famous, then maybe at least the top three famous kids that ever graduated from Central High School.

Who were the other two?

I don't know who the other two were. [*Laughter*] But that's really something when you stop to think about it: that a kid who was an absolute *nothing* in high school and nobody paid any attention to should grow up to be the most famous one who ever graduated. Isn't that astounding? It makes me laugh and it makes me think what a triumph that is.

But how early on did you know that you were going to do something that would go in a straight line?

Oh, I suppose when I was 16, 17. What is interesting is to look back at a couple of letters that a friend of mine sent to me after the War. He and I corresponded. He became a school teacher in New York City, and I called him recently. We finally found out where each other lived, and I called him and we talked. He was in my squad in the army. I was 23 at the time we began to write these letters, and he saved three or four of them. And Jeannie and I were both so impressed at the amount of ambition that I had that showed up in those letters.

What did they say?

About what I was doing and how I was going to go about it, and it seemed to be all I was thinking about. In fact, in one of the letters, I mentioned, "Oh, surprise! Guess what? I'm getting married!" But that was almost an aside. Then, I went back and was talking again about what I was going to be doing and about what I had sold and that kind of thing. I was really a very driven person. This didn't mean that I just went home and drew pictures every night, but I certainly had my heart set on one goal. And, one time at Art Instruction, the man who was the head of the department called me into his office and told me that one of the officers had said that he should talk to me—that they wanted to assure me that if I wanted to make this a career of working for their company that I could be quite assured that I would have a permanent job. They liked my work there and said that I had a future with the company. And I said, "Well, I appreciate that, but you know what I really want, don't you?" And he said, "Sure." He was an animal painter himself and an illustrator. I said, "My ambition is to have this comic strip, and that's what I want to do. I appreciate this offer, but I still hope eventually to have my own feature." He said, "Yeah, I understand." Then, he said, "I feel the same way, so I know just what you mean." So again, that shows how directed I was.

It never occurred to you that you weren't going to do it?

It didn't matter. No. I would never have quit. It wouldn't have mattered if I didn't do it. If I had had to do other work for the next 50 years, I don't think I ever would have quit.

Supposing no one had ever bought the strip. In that case, you'd still be working at Art Instruction doing a little strip for your own entertainment and pleasure?

That's right. Or selling to very small markets, and thinking that I don't care if nobody else likes it. This is the best that I can do.

How old were you when you realized that you were a great success?

I was about 50.

Really, that late?

Yeah. Success is an odd thing to measure.

Well, in what year was it clear to you that Peanuts *was a gigantic hit?*

Not more than a few years ago.

But it's been a big hit for at least...

December 3, 1952.

We have to measure this, Laurie. Are we going to measure it by who's got the most papers, who makes the most money, who gets the most fan mail, who's the most popular? Does being the most popular mean that you're the biggest success? Well, I've got all those.

OK, fine. But when did it dawn on you that the strip—not you doing it, but it itself—had a life of its own?

Only within the last few years has it really been proved to be true. Because there were other guys that were more successful than I at a certain point. Walt Kelly was much more successful than I until I caught up with him. So was Hank Ketcham and Mort Walker. I was not an instant success overnight like they were.

Do you think you're a competitive fellow?

Oh, very competitive.

Do you hate to lose?

Yeah, sure. And I want my comic strip to be the best one on that comic page every day. And yet, when I look at the comic page I see a lot of the others, and I wonder why mine is any different. I don't understand that. "This is a funny one and that was a funny one, and why didn't I think of that, and how come mine is more successful than theirs?" And then I think, "Well, I shouldn't think about that." I should go back and shut out the world and hunch over the drawing board and try to make a neat little picture.

Do you think life has gotten easier for you or more mysterious for you?

More mysterious all the time. I don't understand it. I don't understand how human beings are able to struggle through all the things that we do and laugh as much as we do, laugh and form the friendships that we do, and have the faith in each other that we do, and the love for each other that we have. We talk about mother-love so much. Not being a mother, I don't understand that, but I know it exists. But we don't talk about father-love very much, and yet all the men that I know just think the world of their children. I learned that quite a while ago with fathers that would stop by and visit the studio—businessmen that had to be here for one reason or another—and they would all talk about their kids and they were all so proud of their children. And yet, mother-love is the thing that we worship so much, which is understandable. But fathers—most of the fathers that I know—really love their kids.

Do you find that there are things that you thought you knew that you don't know anymore, or answers that you once had that you've lost or now know aren't the whole truth?

Yeah. Absolutely. That's a good point. I have noticed among novelists—you wouldn't deny this, of course, because you're a novelist yourself—that as they progress, the books get longer and longer and longer and fatter. I think it's because as the men get older, whoever they are, they discover that everything is *not* as crystal clear and black and white and they begin to write in circles and see more sides to the stories, and it takes more to tell the stories. A perfect example is James Cousins, whose first few novels were very short, and they kept getting longer and longer and longer.

How would you like to be remembered?

I'd like to be remembered as the best comic strip artist that there ever was.

And what else?

That he was a very good person. A very good person. I would like to be a good person. As I said before, my ambition was to be as well liked as my father.

Do you think you have succeeded?

I think I'm pretty well liked by a lot of people, yeah.

 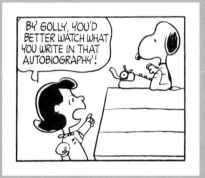

Gary Groth is the publisher and co-founder of Fantagraphics Books. He has edited *The Comics Journal* from 1976 to the present, written comics criticism, and conducted interviews with the world's greatest cartoonists.

Rick Marschall is a newspaper strip historian. He edited *Nemo: The Classic Comics Library* from 1983 to 1989; packaged many collections of classic strips, such as *Popeye*, *Little Nemo in Slumberland*, and *Polly & Her Pals*; and has written extensively about comic strips.

Leonard Maltin is a film critic and historian. He is best known for his reference work *Leonard Maltin's Movie Guide*, his 30-year run on *Entertainment Tonight*, and his regular appearances on TCM. He teaches at the USC School of Cinematic Arts and holds court at leonardmaltin.com.

Laurie Colwin was, according to the *New York Times*, "an author, self-described 'refined slob' and passionate, idiosyncratic home cook." Perhaps best known today for her highly personal food writing, she wrote five novels, three collections of short stories, and two collections of essays. She died in 1992.